恋练有句

16天搞定考研英语
语法和长难句

（第2版）

谭剑波 编著

群言出版社
QUNYAN PRESS

·北京·

读研之后，会有一万种可能！

你为什么考研？读研之后，到底会给自己的未来带来什么可能？
各位亲爱的考研同学，不妨听听我的经历。

❦ 决定考研

18年前，我本科毕业后，有幸成了一名大学老师。我当时之所以本科毕业还能教本科，很大程度上是因为我是男生，而且毕业于武大，要知道当时高校招老师几乎不要本科生，只要硕士博士。在高校工作的那两年，我十分努力和敬业，在教学之余给学生教歌、讲故事，因负责全校第二课堂而经常举办千人讲座，讲台上的我激情四射，很受学生欢迎。我那时沾沾自喜，觉得自己能力很强，感觉这辈子待在高校就满足了。

我的终身大学老师梦被某个下午题为"热烈欢迎××博士加入我们"的大会粉碎了。那个下午，全体教师热烈欢迎新来的博士，领导提出"两年内实现教学队伍100%硕士化，40%博士化"的短期目标。会后，领导还专门召见我，他严肃而又不失调侃地说："小谭啊，你一个本科生教本科，不觉得害臊吗？"我当时的回答现在想起来都很可爱，我说："还好啊！"

从那个下午开始，我决定考研。我当时带四个班的课，负责第二课堂，还经常和男同学打成一片，留给考研的时间真的很少。我报考了一个比武大排名更加靠前的学校，成绩出来后，明显高出了往届的分数线，我非常开心。但我的开心被一个月后公布的校线击溃了——分数悬在线上，很危险。当时有人牵线让我找某个领导"活动活动"，在某个中午和领导"意思意思"的过程中，该领导剪着指甲，斜眼看我，举止傲慢，我很生气，说了一句"我的分数完全够，不需要您操心"，然后起身，甩了一下我黑风衣上的"五四青年"白围巾直接走了。

一波三折的调剂

离开领导办公室后，考虑再三，我决定提前调剂。调剂很顺利，有将近十所大学电话邀请我去复试，且暗示我胜算很高。我最终选择了三所，分别是广西大学、华南师大、福建师大。

在一个下着大雨的周五，疲惫不堪的我乘坐二十个小时的绿皮无座火车（我把座位让给了一位孕妇姐姐）到达了广西。第二天赶去广西大学报道，外语学院的一位副教授接见了我们五位候选人，看了看我"武大毕业、高校任教"的资历，频频点头，意思基本就是"欢迎你，别担心复试"。我在回酒店的路上，居然被一位彪形大汉尾随，回头一看，发现是和我一起报道的大叔。聊天中得知他年过四旬，是一位高中英语老师，考了八次研。他在得知我毕业于武大后对我进行了真诚而强烈的批评："小谭，你这么好的本科，怎么可以选择广西大学这种烂学校！你这完全是自毁前程！"又得知我在高校任教后，他更加富有责任感地指责道："谭剑波，你疯了吗？我比你大十几岁，我用我的良心和阅历告诉你，你一定要放弃这个烂学校，对自己的未来负责。你不像我啊，我老了没办法，只能将就啊！"我被他说得有点眩晕。很少有一个陌生人如此担心我的前途，我非常感动。他看我面色沉重，继续追问道："你没有别的调剂选择了吗？"我说还有福建师大（没提到华南师大），他一听福建师大，忽然提高嗓门大呼："好学校啊，东南富饶之地啊，名校啊，你应该去福建啊！你怎么对自己这么不负责任啊！"

在这位大叔殷切、严厉的教导下，我认识到了自己的幼稚和错误，果断决定放弃接下来的复试。在决定之余，我对大叔充满了感激。

离开广西后没几天，华南师大就通知我去复试。我买好了票，正要出发，这时福建师大也联系我了，是外语学院的院长亲自打来的电话。这通电话长达50分钟。我们谈起南北差异，聊到教育、语言学，还说了苏格拉底。最后院长对我说："我们这里已经有了武大都暂时没有的英语博士点，欢迎你来我院读硕读博。"挂了电话我很激动，立刻就告知华南师大外语学院我不去复试了。我很难忘记华南师大那位女老师恳切的语气："剑波同学啊，你真的要放弃华南，去福建吗？你要考虑好啊！真的很可惜啊！"我回应道："谢谢您，不过您多虑了，福建师大蛮好的呢！"

就这样我去了福建，上午复试，中午出结果，我被录取了，且三年不用交学费，每年额外补贴1000元资料费和500元交通费，也就是公费读研。我很荣幸，在福建师大师从知名海归学者刘亚猛教授学习西方修辞学。亚猛老师曾在美国当了16年博导，后来谢绝国内顶级985学校邀请，回到母校福建师大任教，他学术底蕴深厚，温良谦恭，和蔼可亲，感染着身边每一个人。

与此同时，我也得知了广西大学的复试结果，另外那四位候选人，当然也包括那个大叔，都被录取了。此时我才知道，原来我们五人候选，却只有四个录取名额。我这才明白了大叔对我的"关心"，才明白了一些道理。

到了研二，有一次和同学谈起曾经的调剂，我无意间提到了华南师大，我同学万分惊讶："谭剑波，华南师大是211啊！！！"你猜我说啥？我说："啥是211？"他说："你不知道211、985吗？"我问："啥是985？"你可能非常诧异，也无法想象，我读研二了，却一直不知道啥是211，啥是985。可能，这就是所谓的知识"盲点"吧。我问他："福建师大是985吧？"他很嫌弃地对我说："你说是，它就是！"

失去广西大学，又失去华南师大，后来我才得知二者都是211。

你或许会问："你后悔吗？"

我暂时不回答你。

❀ 走进新东方

在研一的下学期时，我参加了一个"老乡聚会"。那天晚上，我弹琴唱歌，谈吐不羁，众人被我逗得哈哈大笑，好几个男生女生对我"眉目传情"。聚会结束后，一个学地理、名叫水晶的小姐姐走过来亲切地对我说："剑波，你这么才华横溢，这么可爱有趣，你应该去新东方英语培训学校啊！里面的很多老师月入两万呢！"我一听"两万"这个天文数字，想起以前在高校任教的四位数，马上决定要试一试。

水晶本来就已经在福建新东方少儿部任教，在她的"撮合"下，我见到了福建新东方校长、北大高材生刘军老师。我和刘校长聊得很投机，约定了下周一来试讲考研完形。可几天后的试讲却给我泼了一盆凉水。我的试讲相当失败，我讲了不到五分钟，校长就打断我说："我给你提以下15点建议！"我一边听着建议一边使劲喝水。校长说："你别喝水！你紧张啥！"我说："我哪里紧张了！"我特别嘴硬。

中间的磨课充满了坎坷，我被骂了三个月，试讲了几十次，流着泪，捶胸顿足，但，我一直没有放弃。在刘军校长的亲自教导和培训下，我在第四个月迎来了讲课打分的首个第一。后来我有幸被送到北京总部接受全国新东方名师的培训，并聆听俞敏洪老师的当面教诲。进入新东方的第五个月，我成了福建新东方国内部主管。而后的四年，我除了拿到硕士学历学位证书以外，还几乎走遍了福建省每一所重点高中、每一所大学做讲座。每一场讲座几乎都是全校师生出动，座无虚席，讲座一小时，签名两小时。我在二十出头的年纪实现了月薪两三万，解决了温饱，奔向了小康，也打下了扎实的教学基本功，成了一位名副其实的新东方名师。

🎯 听从心的召唤

2011年，我与刘校长挥泪告别。之所以离开，放弃高薪和虚名，是因为我深刻感觉到自己学习的时间太少，讲课的时间太多，我越来越感觉到自己的无知，知识不断输出，觉得自己逐渐沦为浅薄的灵魂裸体。一如苏格拉底很触动我的一句话："为什么我知道的越多，越发现自己无知，我什么都不知道，我只知道自己无知。"我决定投简历，再次竞聘高校工作，接受学术的洗礼。

也许是命运的眷顾，我得到了六所大学的面试通知，有贵阳的，广州的，武汉的，还有大连的。后来，我选择了远在西北的兰州大学。我的人生经历过两次传奇的电话面试。其中一次是跟福建师大外院的院长，另一次就是和兰州大学的领导。记得那天晚上七点，我正在福州鼓楼一家咖啡厅和朋友闲聊时，突然接到兰大一位领导的电话，对方一开口就是："Good evening, Sir!"我深知这个电话的重要性，赶紧找了一个安静的角落和领导开始畅聊。这位领导对佛学很感兴趣，而我那一段时间正在接触《金刚经》，且自以为"感触颇深"，凭着无知者无畏的精神，深情讲述了我对"着相"，对"悲智双运"，对"空"的理解，领导用英语说"也不要太执着于佛学，佛学的目的是为大众服务，为社会谋福利，我们一方面要学习这些文化，一方面更要坚持四项基本原则"，我回答："您所言极是，不可太执着空，因为，空也是空。"领导听完沉默了十秒，然后便赞口不绝。之后，他又安排了另一位领导给我打了电话，这一次是汉语交流，最后这位领导对我说了一句："Mr Tan, welcome to Lanzhou University!"

此后在兰大英语系的五年任教生涯，对我的人生至关重要。我有了更多的时间读书，有了机会面对985学校的学生。这个五年，我第一次感觉自己在学术上得到了淬炼。我曾经多次参加全校授课比赛，并拿到过语言组第一名。在这期间我还写了一本20万字的小说，只是它至今还藏在我的文件夹里——我担心自己一跃成为著名作家而耽误了考研教学，所以不敢出版，哈哈哈~

❀ 两次"诱惑"后的回归

可能是我骨子里有一种探险的基因，在宁静的校园中生活太久，而家又在千里之外，我也面临成家立业的昂贵现实。于是当两次诱惑来临时，我心动了。

2015年我正式辞职，成了某考研机构的英语主讲老师之一。2020年，我迎来了再一次"诱惑"，也因为疫情，我把课程转移到了线上，加入了另一家在线教育机构。这家机构对我有知遇之恩，我对它充满感激。但每天在直播间的表演式教学、追求营业额的生活又让我感觉背离了一个教师的良心，无法适应。当然，其中也可能有我个人的问题。

于是当2021年11月，在老东家新东方在线的再次真诚邀请之下，我选择了回归，重新回到了新东方的讲台。

于是，有了今天我在新东方在线的考研长难句和考研阅读课程。

于是，有了今天我的这本书的问世。

于是，有了今天这一大段文字，有了我对你们的坦白和倾诉。

其实，到此，我还没有讲出最最重要的话语和信息。

你还在吗？亲爱的读者。

如果当年那次"活动"成功，我就不会去广西、福建；如果不被那位大叔"关心"，我就不会转战华南师大；如果不是对"211、985"一无所知，我就不会误打误撞放弃华南师大而选择福建师大；如果不进入福建师大，我就不会遇到影响我一生、曾在美国当了16年博导的学者刘亚猛教授；如果不就读于福建师大，我就不会受到北大高材生刘军校长的亲自栽培，迅速成长为福建新东方首席名师（我去任何一个别的省会城市，都很难有这样的机会，因为那些地方的新东方学校已建校多年，不会有太多的机会很快给到我）；如果没有在新东方四年的锤炼，我就不具备以硕士研究生身份进入985高校兰大工作的资历前提，也就不会得到进一步历练，成为包括《恋练有句：16天搞定考研英语语法和长难句》在内的十多本考研英语辅导书籍的作者。

所以我要感谢当年我失去第一志愿读研的机会，感谢大叔的"关心"，感谢我放弃华南师大的懵懂，感谢曾经的失落、辗转和曲折。

同学们，当你经历苦难和失意的时候，你也许会怨恨命运，感叹造化弄人，但如果你坚持下去，努力前行，跌倒后再爬起来，保持善良，保持纯真，相信"相信的力量"，那么在多年后，当你回忆起往事，你会感谢曾经。你会发现过去的那些陷阱和坎坷，在多年后点连成线，线汇成面，无意间勾画出了人生的美好蓝图。

最后我还要说，如果我不考研，我就无法进入新东方教考研，如果我不读研，就无法具备进入兰大任教的基本资历，就无法具备担当考研英语教师的基本身份。

所以，读研或许不是万能的，但读研之后，会有一万种可能。

今天，我已经成为国外某所大学的博士生。在考研教学之余，我全力以赴，继续努力，生命不止，奋斗不息。我希望我成为我喜欢的自己，也希望成为我的学生——你——愿意相信的人。

所以，请你在面对挫折和苦痛的时候，要相信命运正在磨练你；请你在经受磨难的时候，要坚信"欲戴王冠，必承其重"！让我们一起加油，一起努力，一起从考研开始，考验人生，从《恋练有句：16天搞定考研英语语法和长难句》开始，恋上英语，恋上学习，一起拼搏，一"研"为定！

2022年11月于北京

使用指南

扫码看使用指南

长难句始终贯穿于考研英语的各大题型之中，令不少同学头大。于是市面上不少图书应运而生，挑选真题里的一些长难句逐句讲解如何拆解。但长难句之难，真的只是拆分一个又一个句子就可以解决的吗？所谓看病最忌讳"头痛医头，脚痛医脚"，解决长难句也是如此。想要真正搞定长难句，就一定要明白它的底层逻辑是什么。不应是局限于能听得懂别人的拆解，而应是不仅自己会拆解能理解，而且更会自己造句和翻译，所以必须是讲和练紧密结合。

而长难句的底层逻辑其实关键点只有两个：词汇和语法。词汇自不用多说，类似咱们的汉字，如果没有一定的词汇量做基石，阅读以及理解就根本无从谈起。咱们的"恋练有词"和"恋练不忘"就是分别通过加强大家对考研核心词汇和词组的积累，在帮助大家解决这个问题。另一个关键点则是语法。因为语法讲的就是如何连词成句。语法作为语言的骨架，知识点繁杂却至关重要。虽然考研英语重点考查的是考生的综合阅读能力、写作能力、翻译能力等，但语法和长难句始终贯穿于各个题型之中。若没有良好的语法基础，考生便很难理解动辄几行的阅读长句，拆分复杂的翻译难句，更无法写出结构漂亮的作文美句。

此外，学长难句还必须清楚：学它是为了什么？就考研而言，就是为了帮助解题！所以讲也好，练也好，都必须紧扣真题，特别是如何用学到的这些语法知识去解题。因此，本书高度结合了近年考研英语真题，同时为便于考生理解，对书中选用的部分真题例句或练习进行了改编，通过最简洁明了的语言、最生动形象的讲解、最直击考点的例句，帮考生迅速搭建一套扎实的考研语法知识体系，了解这些语法知识如何从考研长难句而来，又如何回归考试中帮助解题，稳扎稳打提升实战能力。

◆→ 构成及特点

本书分为三个部分，最大的亮点是细致全面、循序渐进、讲练结合、贴近真题。

Part 01 为基础阶段。

在这一阶段，作者甄选英语一和英语二真题例句，系统剖析相关语法知识点，通过16天的讲解，帮助大家快速搭建自己的考研语法体系。并在每个语法点后设置相关练习题，用于巩固检测，提升学习效果。为了帮助考研同学更好地学习这一关键部分，还配套视频课程进行点拨讲解，并将书上的讲解和配套视频课都按Day进行了规划，便于同学们安排学习。

Part 02 为强化阶段。

该阶段主要进行核心长难句的复盘与总结。本部分精选考研英语阅读真题中的21个经典长难句，全面覆盖Part 01基础阶段所讲的语法知识点，以练固学。并且每个长难句都直接对应考研阅读真题的解题句，讲解结合解题进行，通过还原考场，帮助考研同学在学会分析语法结构的同时，了解阅读命题中常见语法出题重点和干扰信息的设置，通过搞定长难句搞定解题。

Part 03 为复习检测阶段。

该阶段主要侧重考生自己的检测练习。学长难句拆解，如果只看书听课只看老师拆解而自己不动手练，就和站在岸上学游泳一样，是永远也学不会的，所以必须自己动手练习。而且前面两部分都是老师讲，实际到真题里你会不会用也需要检测，所以本部分精选100个真题例句和经典语法句子，并采用分两步训练的形式来进行。先通过选择题来检测你对知识点的掌握和了解，经过这一步的巩固和强化，再进入句子拆分和翻译环节。另外还提供了考点提示、核心词汇注解，并在附赠解析中给出答案详解和图解分析。这就如同学习游泳时教练必定要在旁边密切关注，提供教具或是跟随指导一样。并且这100道题的任务进一步切分为20关闯关活动，确保检测练习数量和质量并重！

此外，本书还附赠了《翻译写作加分宝》，配合Part 03的100道闯关题，专门针对每道题的语法考点设置了各种对应的翻译写作填空小练习，难度适中，既是对前面讲过的语法知识点的一个加强复习，亦可助力考生实际提升自己的翻译和写作能力，实现考研英语翻译和写作的加分。

至此，全书从语法的框架搭建，到长难句的带练，到这二者在真题阅读、翻译、写作各题型里的实际应用，真正做到了从真题中来，又回归真题解题！

 学习规划建议

本书最核心的部分如果只是看书听课学习，16天就可以完成，但若想学得更为扎实，学完更会灵活运用，必须投入时间，自己实操拆解，学练结合。如下综合考虑考研同学英语水平不同、复习可投入时间精力不同、目标分数也不同的特点，以及本书的资源配置，按三个阶段做了相应的复习建议，供同学们参考使用。

第一阶段

对应Part 01，建议用时16天

图书内容	Day 01	Day 02	Day 03	Day 04	Day 05	Day 06	Day 07	Day 08
听课建议	Day 01	Day 02	Day 03	Day 04	Day 05	Day 06	Day 07	Day 08
完成日期								
图书内容	Day 09	Day 10	Day 11	Day 12	Day 13	Day 14	Day 15	Day 16
听课建议	Day 09	Day 10	Day 11	Day 12	Day 13	Day 14	Day 15	Day 16
完成日期								

第二阶段

对应Part 02，建议用时7天

图书内容	核心句 01-03	核心句 04-06	核心句 07-09	核心句 10-12	核心句 13-15	核心句 16-18	核心句 19-21
完成日期							

第三阶段

对应Part 03，建议用时10～40天

图书内容	Round 01	Round 02	Round 03	Round 04	Round 05
完成日期					
图书内容	Round 06	Round 07	Round 08	Round 09	Round 10
完成日期					
图书内容	Round 11	Round 12	Round 13	Round 14	Round 15
完成日期					
图书内容	Round 16	Round 17	Round 18	Round 19	Round 20
完成日期					

PS：第三阶段建议搭配《翻译写作加分宝》进行，具体建议如下：

适用人群	学习建议	预计用时
基础非常薄弱 如四级未过	第1天：Part 03的Round 01 第2天：加分宝的Practice 01 第3天：Part 03的Round 02 第4天：加分宝的Practice 02 以此类推	40天
基础中等 如四级通过六级未过	第1天：Round 01 + Practice 01 第2天：Round 02 + Practice 02 以此类推	20天
基础较好 如六级通过	第1天：Round 01-02 + Practice 01-02 第2天：Round 03-04 + Practice 03-04 以此类推	10天

图例说明

为了能让大家对句子结构和成分一目了然，加深理解，我们用不同的符号标识对书中讲解的部分例句或练习的成分做了区分，下面为本书所用图例说明，供大家学习参考。

句子成分	符号标识	举例说明
主语	双下划直线 ＿＿＿	**【2016年英语一阅读 Text 1】**
谓语/系动词	单下划直线 ＿＿＿	France, (which prides itself as the global
表语(从句)		主语　　　　定语从句
宾语(从句)	单下划曲线 ～～～	innovator of fashion), has decided
定语(从句)	圆括号 ( )	谓语
状语(从句)	中括号 [ ]	its fashion industry has lost an absolute right to
补语	尖括号 < >	宾语从句
同位语(从句)	大括号 { }	define physical beauty for women.
连词	▲	

最后，本书的顺利出版并非我一人之功，而是我们教研团队集体智慧的结晶。同时，特别感谢考研英语程思斐老师和新东方大愚文化的聂伟纯老师、刘洋老师、孙岩老师等各位老师的鼎力协助，他们在书稿审查校对以及编写思路方面给予了关键性的指导意见。由于编者水平有限，疏漏在所难免，还望各位读者不吝赐教。最后，预祝大家在考研中取得理想的成绩！

2022年11月于北京

Contents 目录

Part 01 搞定 语法

Part 02 搞定 核心长难句

Part 03　语法 与 长难句 大闯关

恳恳恳地努力，
牢牢地坚持，
加油，考上！

恋练有句

16天搞定考研英语语法和长难句

Part 01

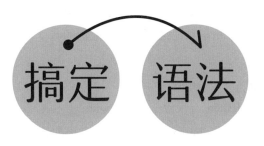

　　在本部分，我们将分16天系统讲解考研英语的核心语法理论，并结合大量真题实例，阐述语法理论在考研英语各个题型中的实际应用，帮助大家搞定语法。

考研英语语法总论

在本节课中，我们将解决以下问题：

① 什么是语法？ ② 为什么要学习考研英语语法？
③ 学习考研英语语法对我们有何具体帮助？

一、什么是语法？

语法是语言的结构规则，具有一定的民族特点和相对的稳定性。如果说词汇是语言的原料，那么语法则是使用原料来构成词组/短语、从句和句子的规则，赋予语言以意义。总的来说，英语语法体系包括词法和句法两部分。

1 词法

词法即词的构成、组合和词形的变化，在考研英语完形填空、写作等题型中较为常用。词法的学习更侧重于积累和记忆，不仅要记词的音、形、义，还要特别注意词性及搭配。

例 1 Women are exposed _____ stress.

[A] in [B] on [C] with [D] to

解析 本题考查介词to的用法。be exposed to是固定搭配，意为"暴露于；遭受，面临"，符合句意，故选D。此处介词to的基本含义是"于"，类似的搭配还有：belong to（属于）；due to（由于）；commit to（致力于）；be subject to（从属于）；be addicted to（沉溺于）等。

参考译文 女性面临着压力。

我们再来看一个例子稍作巩固：

例 2 The correlation between happiness and investment was particularly strong for younger firms, which the authors attribute _____ "less codified decision making process".

(2016年英语二完形)

[A] with [B] on [C] to [D] at

解析 本题同样考查介词to的用法。attribute...to...是固定搭配，意为"把……归因于……"，符合句意，故选C。同上题，介词to的基本含义是"于"。

参考译文 幸福感与投资之间的关联性在较年轻的公司中表现得尤为明显，作者把这归因于"不那么墨守成规的决策过程"。

2 句法

句法是句子的各个组成部分和它们的排列顺序，在考研英语的所有题型中都有应用。句法的学习重点是掌握句子成分、基本句型和各类从句。我们看下面这个例子：

例 1 I second you.

解析 second是多义词，常用作数词，表示"第二"，作名词时表示"秒；片刻"等，但若忽视句法，将此句中的second错误理解成数词或名词，译成"我二你"或"我秒你"，句意显然不通。原因在于句子缺少必要的谓语动词，句法结构上不成立，因此我们需采用second作动词的含义来理解此句。人称代词I是动作的发起者，作主语，second作谓语动词，表示"支持，赞成"，人称代词you是动作的承受者，作宾语。三个单词构成一个完整的主谓宾结构的句子。

参考译文 我赞成你。

再看另一个例子：

例 2 I find you a dog. = I find a dog for you.

解析 人称代词I是动作的发起者，作主语，动词find是谓语，表示具体动作，人称代词you和名词短语a dog分别作谓语动词find的间接宾语和直接宾语，是动词的行为所指向的人和动作的直接承受者，构成一个主谓双宾结构的句子。若不了解主谓双宾结构，直接按单词顺序理解句子，易误解此句为"我发现了你和狗"，那就闹笑话了。

参考译文 我给你找了条狗。

二、为什么需要学习考研英语语法？

英语不是我们的母语，在没有大量源语输入和输出的前提下，即便不是为了参加英语考试，仅为了正确地使用英语，我们就需要学习英语语法。在考研英语中这一问题尤甚，长难句出现的频率很高，贯穿于完形填空、阅读理解、翻译等各个题型之中。一篇完整的考研英语阅读文章长度在400词左右，由约20个句子组成，也就意味着平均每个句子长达20词。以下列句子为例，我们来初步体会一下考研英语句子的难度：

1 In fact, those who thought that the images higher up the attractiveness scale were real directly corresponded with those who showed other markers for having higher self-esteem.

(2014年英语二阅读，共27词)

2 Writing in *The New Republic*, Alice Lee notes that increasing the number of opportunities for board membership without increasing the pool of qualified women to serve on such boards has led to a "golden skirt" phenomenon, where the same elite women scoop up multiple seats on a variety of boards.

(2020年英语一阅读，共50词)

3 Many Americans regard the jury system as a concrete expression of crucial democratic values, including the principles that all citizens who meet minimal qualifications of age and literacy are equally competent to serve on juries; that jurors should be selected randomly from a representative cross section of the community; that no citizen should be denied the right to serve on a jury on account of race, religion, sex, or national origin; that defendants are entitled to trial by their peers; and that verdicts should represent the conscience of the community and not just the letter of the law.

(2010年英语二阅读，共98词)

　　面对这种动辄数行、成分复杂的长难句，我们常常很难分清句子层次，无法辨别主要信息和次要信息，感到无所适从。究其原因，在于我们语法知识的匮乏和长难句分析方法的欠缺，没有搭建起一个完整的语法体系。只有先掌握语言构成的一系列规则，学会理清复杂的句子结构，才能保证我们阅读理解的正确性，而阅读理解能力的提升又有益于翻译和写作水平的提升。

三、学习考研英语语法对我们有何具体帮助？

　　学习考研英语语法能够帮助我们"秒长句、译难句、造美句"。首先，我们要学习基本的语法知识，快速定位长难句中的主干部分和关键信息；然后，我们在所学语法知识的帮助下，准确地翻译长难句；最后，我们将所学的语法知识融会贯通，写出层次分明、逻辑清晰、表现力强的句子。下面我们逐一阐明。

1 秒长句

　　要在长难句中迅速定位句子的主干部分，找到关键信息，最简便的方法是从该句的语法结构入手，删繁就简，突出核心。具体而言，我们要使用"主干公式"找出句子的谓语，把复杂的句子结构简单化，厘清句子最基本的含义。"主干公式"分为以下几个步骤：

a. 找出所有动词

　　由于谓语要由动词来充当，所以我们首先将句子中所有的动词都标记出来，这些动词通常分为以下四类：

动词
- 实义动词 (Notional Verb)
  - 及物动词 (Transitive Verb, *vt.*)　ask、love、say等
  - 不及物动词 (Intransitive Verb, *vi.*)　go、walk、work等

  ⇓

  表示动作、意思完全、能独立用作谓语的动词，包括及物动词和不及物动词
- 系动词 (Linking Verb)　be、become、turn、get、look、appear等
- 助动词 (Auxiliary Verb)　be、do、have、will等
- 情态动词 (Modal Verb)　can、could、may、might、shall、should、must、will等

b. 去掉非谓语动词

步骤a中的动词还包含了非谓语动词，所以我们要把它们排除。非谓语动词即不充当谓语的动词，有动名词（V-ing）、分词（V-ing/V-ed）、不定式（(to) do）三种形式。

c. 去掉从句的谓语动词

若句子为复合句（即含有一个主句和一个或一个以上从句的句子），我们还需要将从句的谓语动词排除，以帮助找到主句主干。从句的标志是从句引导词，包括that、what、which、where、why、when、who等，以及其他从属连词，包括while、after、before、since、until、if、as、because、unless、than、whether、so that、now that、as if等，某些情况下从句引导词可以省略。我们将在后续章节学习各类从句，此处仅作简要说明。

去掉非谓语动词和从句的谓语动词后，最后剩下的动词即主句的谓语动词。

我们来看以下两个改编过的真题例句来加深理解：

例1 A study by Sarah Brosnan and Frans de Waal of Emory University in Atlanta, Georgia, which has been published in *Nature*, suggests that it is all too monkey, as well. (2005年阅读)

解析 按照"主干公式"的步骤，我们首先可以找到三个动词：has been published、suggests和is，然后去掉非谓语动词和从句的谓语动词，可以排除has been published和is，因为它们前面分别有从句引导词which和that，由此判断出主句的谓语动词是suggests。提炼主干成分，句子可简化为A study suggests...（一项研究表明……）。

参考译文 由佐治亚州亚特兰大市埃默里大学的莎拉·布鲁斯南和弗兰斯·德·瓦尔进行的一项研究表明，它也是"猴之常情"，这项研究成果发表在《自然》杂志上。

接着我们以一道阅读理解题为例，看看"主干公式"如何帮我们抓住句子核心，迅速找到答案。

例2 Davidson's article is one of a number of pieces that have recently appeared making the point: the reason why we have such stubbornly high unemployment and declining middle-class incomes today is also because of the advances in both globalization and the information technology revolution, which are more rapidly than ever replacing labor with machines or foreign workers.

(2013年英语二阅读)

The article is used to illustrate _____.

[A] the impact of technological advances [B] the alleviation of job pressure

[C] the shrinkage of textile mills   [D] the decline of middle-class incomes

解析 题目问文章被用来说明什么，答案在冒号后对于point的具体解释中，因此我们直接来分析冒号后的这个长句。运用"主干公式"，首先找出句中所有动词，即have、is、are和replacing；然后去掉非谓语动词replacing；最后去掉从句的谓语动词(why)...have，(which) are，最后剩下is，因此is为主句的谓语动词。去掉其他动词所在的从句和定语、状语等修饰性成分，只保留谓语动词is所在的主干，句子可以简化为the reason is because of the advances...（原因是因为……的进步）。四个选项中，只有A选项提及了核心关键词advances，故A选项正确。D选项中虽然有很多词在原文中出现，但不属于句子的主干部分，是干扰选项。我们通过"主干公式"提炼出该句的主干部分，找到了解题的关键。

参考译文 戴维森的这篇文章只是近来发表的众多此类文章之一，这些文章都阐明了这一观点：如今我们失业率居高不下以及中产阶级收入持续下降，也是因为全球化的发展和信息技术革命的进步，这两个领域比以往任何时候都更快地使用机器或外国劳工取代（本国）劳动力。

2 译难句

利用"主干公式"秒懂长句只是考研英语语法的入门级别，因为考研英语文章中句子的特点除了"长"之外，还有"难"。我们理清句子结构之后，还要学会将它的意思准确地翻译出来，并利用长难句对英汉语言的理解和表达进行字斟句酌、求同存异，以达成透彻理解、准确表达和综合应用，这样才能破解考研英语的难点。我们如何翻译下列两个句子呢？

1 I don't love you because you are beautiful.

2 I don't teach because it earns good money.

大家是否翻译成了"我不爱你因为你很美"和"我不教书因为能赚大钱"呢？这样的翻译只会贻笑大方。这里使用到了语法中的否定转移，我们要把否定还原到后面来理解句子，正解应为：

1　I don't love you because you are beautiful.

　　= I love you not because you are beautiful. 我爱你并非因为你很美。

2　I don't teach because it earns good money.

　　= I teach not because it earns good money. 我教书并不是为了赚大钱。

　　类似的句子还有：

3　Humans do not cry because they are sad.　　(2011年英语一完形)

　　= Humans cry not because they are sad. 人们哭并不是因为他们伤心。

4　It's not harder for me just because my memory is clearer.　　(2013年英语二翻译)

　　= It's harder for me not just because my memory is clearer.

　　并非因为我的记忆更清晰，我就更痛苦。

　　再来看下面这个包含了"A...no more...than B"结构的句子，该如何理解呢？

I am no more beautiful than you.

　　是"我不比你更美"还是"我和你都不美？"no否定的到底是句中哪个成分呢？在实际应用中，有很多同学将"A...no more...than B"错误翻译成了"A不比B更……"，实际上这个结构的意思是"A和B都不……"。这句话正确理解应为"我和你一样都不美。"在考研阅读中，如果没掌握这个特殊结构，理解文章就可能会有困难，再看下列两个句子来巩固一下吧：

1　It is no more regrettable than the loss of the case-endings of Old English.　　(2005年阅读)

　　参考译文 它和古英语中变格词尾的消失一样，都不值得惋惜。

　　注：case-ending是专业术语，意为"变格词尾"，case指"格"，如主格、宾格等。变格词尾就是指一个词在作不同的格时，需要加不同的词尾。如whom就是who作宾语时的变形。

2　Sandberg would be no more newsworthy than any other person.　　(2013年英语二阅读)

　　参考译文 桑德伯格和其他任何人一样，都没有新闻价值。

3 造美句

　　秒长句让我们看懂阅读，译难句让我们掌握翻译，这些大量的输入最终成为高效输出的参考，帮助我们造出漂亮复杂的写作长难句。把长难句当作简明丰富的学习资源，对长难句的词语搭配、表达方式、句型结构和连贯衔接等进行分析和学习，从中选取具有鲜明书面语特色的句型作为句子写作的参考和样板，无疑可以有效增强英语写作能力。我们试着将以下五个部分组合成一个句子：

- With people's living pace quickening,（随着人们生活节奏加快，）
- it is universally acknowledged that,（人们普遍认为，）
- information technology can, directly or indirectly, change our life,
  （信息技术能直接或间接地改变我们的生活，）
- due to the fact that information technology improves the efficiency,
  （由于信息技术提高了效率这一事实，）
- ..., which is very thought-provoking and deserves a further analysis.
  （这发人深省，值得进一步分析。）

以上五个部分分别用到了以下语法点：独立主格结构（With people's living pace quickening）；主语从句（it is universally acknowledged that...）；插入语（directly or indirectly）；同位语从句（the fact that...）；非限制性定语从句（, which...）。这些语法点的融会贯通，造就了一个长达40词的高分长句：

With people's living pace quickening, it is universally acknowledged that information technology can, directly or indirectly, change our life due to the fact that information technology improves the efficiency, which is very thought-provoking and deserves a further analysis.

参考译文 随着人们生活节奏加快，人们普遍认为，信息技术能直接或间接地改变我们的生活，因为信息技术提高了效率，这一点发人深省，值得进一步分析。

通过上述讲解，相信同学们已经对搞定语法的必要性有了一定的认识，接下来本书将按照下图所示逻辑串讲所有考研英语核心语法知识点，从秒长句懂阅读、译难句促翻译到造美句提作文，逐一击破考研英语的核心板块，帮助同学们全面增强英语语言的学习和运用能力。

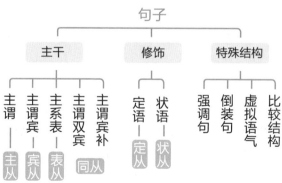

一、找出句子主干，并翻译该句子

1. As perhaps Kelsey will discover after her much-publicized resignation from the editorship of *She* after a build-up of stress, abandoning the doctrine of "juggling your life," and making the alternative move into "downshifting" brings far greater rewards than financial success and social status with it.

(2001年阅读)

2. Declaring that he was opposed to using this unusual animal husbandry technique to clone humans, he ordered that federal funds not be used for such an experiment—although no one had proposed to do so—and asked an independent panel of experts chaired by Princeton President Harold Shapiro to report back to the White House in 90 days with recommendations for a national policy on human cloning.

(1999年阅读)

二、阅读理解

Whether such a sense of fairness evolved independently in capuchins and humans, or whether it stems from the common ancestor that the species had 35 million years ago, is, as yet, an unanswered question.

(2005年阅读)

What can we infer about such a sense of fairness from the paragraph?

[A] It evolved from an uncertain source.

[B] It can be only found in humans.

[C] It was developed by the common ancestor.

[D] It might be found in other animals.

一、找出句子主干，并翻译该句子

1. 解析 该句中的动词有will discover、abandoning、juggling、making和brings，其中will discover在从句引导词as之后，作从句的谓语动词，故排除；abandoning、juggling和making是非谓语动词，故排除。因此主句的谓语动词是brings，主语由and连接的两个并列的动名词短语充当，句子结构可简化为abandoning the doctrine...and making the move...brings...rewards...。

参考译文 放弃那种"为生活忙碌"的人生信条并转而追求比较悠闲的生活所带给你的回报远远大于经济上的成功和社会地位，或许凯尔西因不堪压力重负而公开地辞去她在《She》杂志社的编辑一职之后也会有这样的发现。

2. 解析 该句中的动词有declaring、was opposed、using、to clone、ordered、be used、had proposed、to do、asked、chaired和to report，其中was opposed和be used在从句引导词that之后，had proposed在从句引导词although之后，均作从句的谓语动词，故排除；declaring、using、to clone、to do、chaired和to report是非谓语动词，故排除。因此主句的谓语动词是由连词and连接的两个动词ordered和asked，句子结构可简化为he ordered...and asked...to report...。

参考译文 他宣称反对利用这种不同寻常的畜牧业技术去克隆人类，下令禁止使用联邦基金做这样的实验——尽管还没有人提议要这么做——并要求由普林斯顿大学校长哈罗德·夏普罗主持的独立专家小组在90天内对有关克隆人的国家政策给出建议，并向白宫汇报。

二、阅读理解

解析 该句中的动词有evolved、stems from、had和is，其中evolved、stems from和had在从句引导词whether和that之后，作从句的谓语动词，故排除。因此主句的谓语动词是is，两个whether引导的从句并列作主句主语，an unanswered question是表语，句子结构可简化为Whether...or whether...is an unanswered question。四个选项中虽然都有个别单词在原文中复现，但只有A选项中的an uncertain source能与句子主干的an unanswered question对应，故选择A项。

参考译文 这种公平意识是卷尾猴和人类各自独立进化而来的，还是起源于3,500万年前物种共同的祖先，至今仍是一个悬而未决的问题。

"主干家族"精讲

Day 02

上一节课我们已经对语法的概念以及学习考研英语语法的重要性有了大致的了解。从这一课开始，我们将进入到具体的语法理论及应用的学习。这节课我们主要讲解：

❶ 词性、句子成分、基本句型；❷ 并列句。

要系统学习考研英语语法理论并娴熟运用，我们首先需要了解"主干家族"到"修饰集团"这一系列概念，在脑海里筑起整个语法体系的"地基"。然后，我们在此"地基"之上"添砖加瓦"，并把所学的语法基础知识应用到考研英语阅读、翻译、写作等各个题型中。

一、词性、句子成分、基本句型

在句子中，词与词之间有一定的组合关系，按照不同的关系，可以把句子分为不同的成分。英语句子的基本成分有七种，分别为：主语（Subject）、谓语（Predicate）、表语（Predicative）、宾语（Object）、定语（Attribute）、状语（Adverbial）和补语（Complement）。句子成分可由词、词组或从句充当。

无论句子有多长，结构有多复杂，我们都可以把它们分为两个部分："主干家族"和"修饰集团"。如果说"主干家族"是一棵大树的树干，支撑起了整个句子的结构，那么"修饰集团"便是树上的枝叶，让句子更丰满。

在本节课中，我们主要讲解"主干家族"的五大基本句型：主谓、主谓宾、主系表、主谓双宾、主谓宾宾补。区分句型的关键在于谓语动词，不同的句型使用不同的谓语动词。下面我们逐一说明。

❶ 基本句型1：主谓

主语是谓语的陈述对象，是句子所要说明的人或物，或是谓语动作的发起者，通常由名词、代词、数词、动词不定式、动名词或主语从句等来充当。

谓语是用来说明主语发出的动作或具有的特征和状态，通常由动词或动词短语来充当，一般位于主语之后。主谓句型中，谓语动词是不及物动词（Intransitive Verb, *vi.*），不带宾语，动词本身就能表达完整的意思。需要注意的是，划分句子成分时，谓语动词不一定是一个单独的动词，有时也会以复合谓语的形式出现。复合谓语，通常为"情态

11

动词/助动词+实义动词"形式，用于表示时态、语态、情态、疑问、否定等意义时，其整体应被划归为谓语。例如：

例1　I came. I saw. I conquered. 我来了。我见了。我征服了。　　　　　　(凯撒名言)
　　　主谓　主谓　主　谓

例2　Industry pays. 天道酬勤。　　　　　　　　　　　　　　　　　　　(谚语)
　　　主　　谓

例3　Pleasure can vanish. 快乐会消失。　　　　　　　　　　　　　(2005年阅读)
　　　主　　谓

解析 该句中的can vanish就是一个复合谓语，由情态动词can和不及物动词vanish构成。

简单的主谓句型在考研英语中出现的频率虽不高，但却是长难句变化的基础。下面我们对主谓句型的成分及其相对应的词性或形式做一个总结：

成分	词性或形式
主语：谓语的陈述对象	名词、代词、数词、动词不定式、动名词或主语从句等
谓语：对主语动作、状态或特征的陈述说明	不及物动词

② 基本句型2：主谓宾

此句型中的谓语动词是主语发出的动作，但不能表达完整的意思，必须跟有一个宾语，句意才能完整。这类动词一般是及物动词（Transitive Verb, *vt.*），也可以由"某些不及物动词+介词"充当。

宾语是动作、行为的对象，是动作的承受者，一般由名词、代词、数词、动词不定式、动名词、名词化的形容词（如the rich"富人"、the important"重要人士"等）或宾语从句等充当。宾语通常位于及物动词或介词之后，在介词之后的称作介词宾语。来看下面几个例子：

例1　I love you. 我爱你。
　　　主谓　宾

例2　He refused to accept the apology. 他拒绝接受道歉。
　　　主　谓　　　　宾

例3　Memory depends on processing. 记忆力取决于信息处理。　　　(2007年阅读)
　　　主　　　谓　　　宾

解析 该句中的depends是不及物动词，需要加上介词on后再加动名词processing作宾语。

下面我们对主谓宾句型的谓宾成分及其相对应的词性或形式进行总结：

成分	词性或形式
谓语：动作	及物动词、某些不及物动词+介词
宾语：动作承受者	名词、代词、数词、动词不定式、动名词、名词化的形容词或宾语从句等

当谓语动词后还跟有其他成分时，主谓宾句型与主谓句型往往难以分辨，其区别的关键在于谓语动词的属性，以下表作为总结：

句型	区别	充当谓语的词性或形式
主谓	谓语不能跟宾语	不及物动词
主谓宾	谓语必须跟宾语	及物动词、某些不及物动词+介词

注意 某些动词既可以是及物动词，又可以是不及物动词。例如：

I live a peaceful life.（主谓宾）

I live peacefully.（主谓）

解析 第一句中，live为及物动词，意为"过（……样的生活）"，后接宾语a peaceful life。第二句中，live为不及物动词，意为"生活"，后面不需要接宾语，副词peacefully作状语，修饰动词live。

③ 基本句型3：主系表

此句型中，谓语动词必须加上一个表明主语身份或状态的表语构成复合谓语，才能表达完整的意思。这类动词叫作系动词（Linking Verb）。常见的系动词除了be动词外，可以分为以下五组：

- 变化系动词：become、come、fall、get、go、grow、run、turn等，表示"变成""成为"。
- 持续系动词：continue、hold、keep、lie、remain、stand、stay等，表示"保持着某一状态"。
- 表象系动词：appear、look、seem等，表示"看起来""好像"。
- 感官系动词：feel、smell、sound、taste等，表示"某种官能"。
- 终止系动词：prove、turn out等，表示"证实""结果是"。

表语在系动词之后表示主语的性质、特征、状态或身份，通常由名词、代词、形容词、副词、数词、介词短语、动词不定式、动名词、分词或表语从句等充当。例如：

例1 He is a loser. 他是个失败者。
　　 主 系 表

例2 Elizabeth looks pretty. 伊丽莎白看起来很美。
　　 主　　系　表

例3 The industry was on the ropes. 该产业命悬一线。　　　　　　(2000年阅读)
　　 主　　　系　　表

下面我们对主系表句型的系表成分及其相对应的词性或形式进行总结：

成分	词性或形式
系动词：连接主语和表语	be动词等
表语：补充说明主语的性质、特征、状态或身份等	名词、代词、形容词、副词、数词、介词短语、动词不定式、动名词、分词或表语从句等

主谓宾句型与主系表句型在形式上很相像，都有三个核心成分。区分的关键在于谓语动词后的成分与主语之间的关系，以及能充当该成分的词性或形式，以下表作为归纳：

句型	成分	词性或形式
主谓宾	宾语≠主语	宾语不能为形容词或介词短语
主系表	表语≈主语	表语可以为形容词或介词短语

例如 I taste the fish. （主谓宾）

　　 The fish tastes delicious. （主系表）

解析 第一句中，谓语动词taste意为"品尝"，是实义动词，后跟名词短语the fish作宾语，宾语≠主语，I做出taste的动作，其施加对象是the fish，为主谓宾句型。第二句中，谓语动词tastes意为"尝起来"，是系动词，后跟形容词delicious作表语，表语≈主语，即delicious是对The fish的味道的补充说明，为主系表句型。

4 基本句型4：主谓双宾（主语+谓语+间接宾语+直接宾语）

此句型中的谓语动词是及物动词，但是必须跟两个宾语才能表达完整的意思。两个宾语中前一个为间接宾语，往往为某人，是动作的行为所指向的人；后一个为直接宾语，往往为某事物，是动作的承受者。一般顺序为：主+谓+间宾+直宾，若要将间接宾语位置后移，则必须在它的前面加上相应的介词，一般为to或for。例如：

例 1 I found you a dog. = I found a dog for you. 我给你找了条狗。
　　　主 谓　间宾 直宾

例 2 I will teach you a lesson. = I will teach a lesson to you. 我打算教训你。
　　　主　谓　　间宾 直宾

例 3 The district is giving students a pass.　　　　　　　　　　　(2012年英语二阅读)
　　　　主　　　　谓　　　 间宾　 直宾

　　= The district is giving a pass to students. 该地区让学生们通过。

下面我们对主谓双宾句型中的双宾成分及其相对应的词性或形式进行总结：

成分	词性或形式
直接宾语：动作承受者（something）	名词、代词、数词、不定式、宾语从句等
间接宾语：动作接受者（somebody）	名词、宾格代词

5 基本句型5：主谓宾宾补（主语+谓语+宾语+宾语补足语）

此句型中的谓语动词虽然是及物动词，但是只跟一个宾语还不能表达完整的意思，必须加上一个补足语，才能使意思完整。宾语补足语通常紧跟在宾语之后，对宾语的性质、状态等作出补充说明，可由名词、形容词、副词、动词不定式、分词或介词短语等充当。在宾语加宾语补足语构成的复合宾语中，宾语与宾语补足语之间存在着逻辑上（即意义上）的主谓或主系表关系。例如：

例 1 I find the girl <beautiful>.
　　　主谓　宾　　 宾补

参考译文 我发现这个女孩很漂亮。

逻辑检验 "The girl is beautiful." 宾语the girl和beautiful之间存在逻辑上的主系表关系。

例 2 The students find homework <to be unimportant>.　　　　(2012年英语二阅读)
　　　主　　　谓　　 宾　　　 宾补

参考译文 这些学生认为家庭作业不重要。

逻辑检验 "Homework is unimportant." 宾语homework和unimportant之间存在逻辑上的主系表关系。

例 3 These men believed in journalism <as a calling>.　　　　　(2010年英语一阅读)
　　　主　　　　谓　　　宾　　　　宾补

参考译文 这些人认为新闻写作是一种职业使命。

逻辑检验 "Journalism was a calling." 宾语journalism和a calling之间存在逻辑上的主系表关系。

下面我们对主谓宾宾补句型中的宾补成分及其相对应的词性或形式进行总结：

成分	词性或形式
宾补：对宾语的补充说明	名词、形容词、副词、代词、动词不定式、分词、介词短语或从句等

下面我们对主谓双宾和主谓宾宾补句型的区别进行总结：

句型	区别	
主谓双宾	间接宾语可去掉	双宾不能是形容词或介词短语
主谓宾宾补	宾补不能去掉	宾补可以是形容词或介词短语

判断下列句子所属的基本句型，并翻译：

例 1 I made you happy.

解析 谓语动词made后跟有人称代词you和形容词happy，从形式上来看，形容词只能充当宾语补足语，宾语you和宾语补足语happy之间存在逻辑上的主系表关系，即you were happy，因此此句型为主谓宾宾补。

参考译文 我让你开心。

例 2 I made you coffee.

解析 谓语动词made后跟有人称代词you和名词coffee，you是动作行为所指向的人，是间接宾语，coffee是动作的直接承受者，是直接宾语。间接宾语you和直接宾语coffee之间不存在逻辑上的主系表关系。此外，间接宾语you去掉后，"I made coffee." 句子结构依然成立，因此此句型为主谓双宾。

参考译文 我给你们冲了咖啡。

例 3 I made you my assistant.

解析 谓语动词made后跟有人称代词you和名词短语my assistant，my assistant用来补充说明宾语you的身份，是宾语补足语，两者之间存在逻辑上的主系表关系，即you were my assistant。此外，宾补不能去掉，否则句意不完整。因此此句型为主谓宾宾补。

参考译文 我让你做了我的助理。

学习了考研英语语法中的五个基本句型后，我们对于主语、谓语、宾语、表语和宾语补足语等成分有了基本的了解，它们是简单句的核心成分，是句子的"骨骼"。下面我们对各个核心成分常见的词性/形式进行总结：

核心成分——词性/形式对照表

词性 / 形式 ＼ 成分	主语	谓语	宾语	表语	宾语补足语
动词		✓			
名词	✓		✓	✓	✓
代词	✓		✓	✓	✓
数词	✓		✓	✓	
副词				✓	✓
形容词				✓	✓
不定式	✓		✓	✓	✓
V-ing	✓		✓	✓	✓
V-ed				✓	✓
介词短语				✓	✓
从句	✓		✓	✓	✓

二、并列句

学习完"主干家族"的五大基本句型，我们如何向更长、更难一点的句子进阶呢？其中一个方法就是添加并列连词，将两个简单句连接成一个并列句。并列连词是用来连接两个相互对等的词、词组或分句的，不能单独作句子成分，也没有词形变化。常见的并列连词主要有以下几类：

- 表示并列关系：and（和），both...and...（……和……都），not only...but also...（不仅……而且……），neither...nor...（既不……也不……）
- 表示转折关系：but（但是），yet（然而），while（然而），whereas（然而）
- 表示选择关系：or（或者），either...or...（或者……或者……），or else（否则），not...but...（不是……而是……）
- 表示因果推理关系：so（因此），for（因为）

我们来看几个例句：

例 1 Researchers should improve their standards, but journals should also take a tougher line.

(2015年英语一阅读)

解析 并列连词but前后连接两个主谓宾结构的简单句，主语、谓语均不相同，因此没有省略部分。

参考译文 研究者应提高其标准，而期刊杂志也应该采取更强硬的立场。

例 2 Most journals are weak in statistical review, and this damages the quality of what they publish.

(2015年英语一阅读)

解析 并列连词and连接前后两个独立的句子。句一Most journals are weak in statistical review为主系表结构；句二this damages the quality of what they publish为主谓宾结构，主语为this，谓语为damages，宾语为the quality，后接介词短语作quality的后置定语。

参考译文 大部分期刊在数据审查方面比较薄弱，而这会有损其出版内容的水准。

例 3 Most archaeological sites have been located by means of careful searching, while many others have been discovered by accident.

(2014年英语一新题型)

解析 并列连词while连接两个主谓结构的简单句，前后句存在"对比"关系，且两个句子的谓语都为现在完成时的被动语态。

参考译文 大部分考古遗址都是通过仔细搜寻才找到的，还有很多其他的遗址是偶然间发现的。

 课后练习

一、判断以下简单句句型及句中各部分成分

1. We forget these writers.

2. These writers are forgotten.

3. I taste the apple.

4. The apple tastes good.

5. I found the book easily.

6. I found the book easy.

7. He got wet.

8. Both children and adults got presents.

9. He got her a present.

10. He got his shoes and socks wet.

11. They elected him the chairman of the Students' Union.

二、在空格处填入合适的并列连词

1. It always interested Richard, _____ he decided to find out for sure.

2. Long-distance relationships are hard, _____ a couple has found a creative way to deal with physical separation.

3. Ms Brooks may have had suspicions, _____ she asked no questions.

4. Either Entergy never really intended to live by those commitments, _____ it simply didn't foresee what would happen.

📝 参考答案

一、判断以下简单句句型及句中各部分成分

1. <u>We</u> <u>forget</u> <u>these writers</u>.
   　主　　谓　　　宾

   解析 人称代词we作主语，及物动词forget作谓语，名词短语these writers作宾语。

2. <u>These writers</u> <u>are forgotten</u>.
   　　主　　　　　　谓

   解析 名词短语These writers作主语，及物动词forget的被动语态形式are forgotten作谓语。

3. I taste the apple.
   主谓　　宾

   解析 人称代词I作主语，及物动词taste作谓语，名词短语the apple作宾语。

4. The apple tastes good.
   　主　　　系　　表

   解析 名词短语the apple作主语，tastes是系动词，意为"尝起来"，形容词good作表语。

5. I found the book [easily].
   主谓　　宾　　状

   解析 人称代词I作主语，及物动词found作谓语，名词短语the book作宾语，副词easily作状语，修饰found。

6. I found the book <easy>.
   主谓　　宾　　宾补

   解析 人称代词I作主语，及物动词found作谓语，名词短语the book作宾语，形容词easy作宾语补足语，不能去掉，否则句意表达不准确。宾语与宾补之间存在逻辑上的主系表关系，即the book is easy。

7. He got wet.
   主 系 表

   解析 人称代词he作主语，got是系动词，意为"变得"，形容词wet作表语。

8. Both children and adults got presents.
   　　　　主　　　　　　谓　宾

   解析 名词短语Both children and adults作主语，及物动词got作谓语，意为"获得"，名词presents作宾语。

9. He got her a present.
   主 谓 间宾 直宾

   解析 人称代词he作主语，及物动词got作谓语，人称代词her作间接宾语，是got这个动作指向的对象，名词短语a present作直接宾语，是动作的直接承受者。

10. He got his shoes and socks <wet>.
    主谓　　宾　　　　宾补

    解析 人称代词he作主语，及物动词got作谓语，名词短语his shoes and socks作宾语，形容词wet作宾语补足语，补充说明宾语的状态。

11. They elected him <the chairman of the Students' Union>.

　　主　　谓　　宾　　　　　　　　宾补

解析 人称代词they作主语，及物动词elected作谓语，人称代词him作宾语，名词短语the chairman of the Students' Union作宾语补足语，补充说明宾语的身份。

二、在空格处填入合适的并列连词

1. **答案** so

   解析 逗号前后均为主谓宾结构的简单句，语义上形成因果逻辑关系，因此用表示因果关系的并列连词so。

   参考译文 它总是让理查德很感兴趣，所以他决定找出端倪。

2. **答案** but

   解析 逗号前后分别为主系表结构和主谓宾结构的简单句，语义上形成转折关系，因此用表示转折关系的并列连词but。

   参考译文 异地恋是很艰难的，但是一对情侣找到了一种解决异地问题的富有创意的方法。

3. **答案** but

   解析 逗号前后均为主谓宾结构的简单句，语义上形成转折关系，因此用表示转折关系的并列连词but。

   参考译文 布鲁克斯女士或许曾有过疑问，但她什么也没有问。

4. **答案** or

   解析 逗号前为主谓宾句型。逗号后为复合句，结构为"主谓+宾语从句"。前后两句在语义上形成选择关系，并列连词either...or...为固定用法，表示选择。

   参考译文 要么安特吉公司从来没有真正打算要遵守这些承诺，要么它根本没有预料到将来会发生什么。

"主干家族" 应用

上节课我们学习了"主干家族"语法理论，本节课我们来了解"主干家族"在考研英语阅读、翻译及写作拓句中的应用。快速定位句子的主干部分能够迅速把握句子的核心内容，在作答考研英语阅读题和翻译题时达到事半功倍的效果。

一、"主干家族"在翻译中的应用

快速确定1~4句主干部分所用的基本句型并翻译。

例 1 The longest bull run ended. (2010年英语二阅读)

解析 该句为主谓结构，其中the longest bull run作主语，意为"最长的牛市"，这里run作名词用，表示"一段时期"，不及物动词ended作谓语动词。

参考译文 最长的牛市期结束了。

例 2 The department stores of the 19th century played a role.

解析 该句为主谓宾结构，其中the department stores of the 19th century作主语，及物动词played作谓语动词，a role作宾语。

参考译文 19世纪的百货大楼产生了一定影响。

例 3 Spending became unfashionable. (2010年英语二阅读)

解析 该句为主系表结构，其中Spending作主语，became为系动词，形容词unfashionable作表语，意为"过时的；不合时宜的"。

参考译文 消费变得不合时宜。

例 4 He gave the world the final and polished work. (2019年英语二翻译)

解析 该句为主谓双宾结构，其中he作主语，gave作谓语动词，the world作间接宾语，the final and polished work作直接宾语（形容词短语final and polished译为"最终润色了的"，修饰work）。

参考译文 他给这个世界呈现了最终润色的作品。

以上四个句子均为简单句，句型比较容易判断。那么对于更长、结构更复杂的句子，我们该如何快速找到主干并判断句型呢？虽然句子长度增加，但底层逻辑是一致的，可以运用之前学到的"主干公式"：首先，找到所有动词；然后，去掉非谓语动词；最后，去掉从句的谓语动词。根据以上方法，我们来快速确定5~10句主干部分所用的基本句型，并翻译主干部分。

例 5 Powerful memory doesn't make my emotions acute or vivid.

解析 该句为主谓宾宾补结构，其中名词短语powerful memory作主语，doesn't make作谓语动词，my emotions作宾语，形容词短语acute or vivid（敏锐或清晰）作宾补。

参考译文 强大的记忆力并没有使我的情感变得敏锐或清晰。

例 6 The finding that the high rate of depression in British teenage girls is correlated to time spent on social media will be published.

解析 该句中的动词有is correlated to、spent和will be published，其中is correlated to在从句引导词that之后，故排除；spent为动词spend的过去式和过去分词形式，有可能排除；will be published为punish的一般将来时的被动语态，无法排除，因此确定其为谓语，该句主干部分为The finding will be published。

参考译文 这一发现即将被公布。

例 7 These days the Net, which has already re-made such everyday pastimes as buying books and sending mail, is reshaping Donovan's vocation.   (2003年阅读)

解析 该句中的动词有has re-made、buying、sending和is reshaping，其中has re-made在从句引导词which之后，故排除；buying和sending为非谓语动词，故排除。因此确定谓语为is reshaping，该句主干部分为the Net is reshaping Donovan's vocation。

参考译文 网络正在改变多诺万的职业。

例 8 At a time when Thomas Piketty and other economists are warning of rising inequality and the increasing power of inherited wealth, that wealthy aristocratic families should be the symbolic heart of modern democratic states is bizarre.   (2015年英语一阅读)

解析 该句中的动词有are warning、should be和is，其中are warning和should be分别在从句引导词when和that之后，故均排除。因此确定谓语为is，该句主干部分为that...is bizarre。

参考译文 这件事很奇怪。

例 9 I define "journalism" as "a term of contempt applied by writers who are not read to writers who are read."   (2010年英语一阅读)

解析 该句中的动词有define、applied、are not read和are read，其中applied为动词apply的过去式和过去分词形式，有可能排除；are not read在从句引导词who之后，故排除；从句时态为一般现在时，说明主句也为一般现在时，因此排除applied，确定谓语为define，该句主干部分为I define "journalism" as "a term of contempt"。

参考译文 我把"新闻写作"定义为一种"轻蔑之词"。

例 10 The bodies playing major professional sports have changed over the years, and managers have been adjusting team uniforms to fit the growing numbers of bigger, longer frames.

(2008年阅读)

解析 该句是由and连接的并列句，前一分句中的动词有playing和have changed，其中playing是非谓语动词，故排除，因此确定前一分句的谓语动词为have changed，其主干为主谓结构，即The bodies have changed；后一分句中的动词有have been adjusting和to fit，其中to fit是非谓语动词，故排除，因此确定后一分句的谓语动词为have been adjusting，其主干为主谓宾结构，即managers have been adjusting team uniforms。

参考译文 身材发生了变化并且经理们也一直在调整队服。

二、"主干家族"在阅读中的应用

例如 Epley found no significant gender difference in responses. Nor was there any evidence that those who self-enhanced the most (that is, the participants who thought the most positively doctored picture were real) were doing so to make up for profound insecurities. In fact, those who thought that the images higher up the attractiveness scale were real directly corresponded with those who showed other markers for having higher self-esteem. "I don't think the findings that we have are any evidence of personal delusion," says Epley. "It's a reflection simply of people generally thinking well of themselves." If you are depressed, you won't be self-enhancing.

(2014年英语二阅读)

Epley found that people with higher self-esteem tended to _____.

[A] underestimate their insecurities   [B] believe in their attractiveness

[C] cover up their depressions   [D] oversimplify their illusions

定位 根据题干中的higher self-esteem定位到原文的第三句：In fact, those who thought that the images higher up the attractiveness scale were real directly corresponded with those who showed other markers for having higher self-esteem. （事实上，那些认为更有吸引力的照片才是自己真实的照片的人，与那些在其他方面表现出更强自尊心的人正好一致。）

解析 该句中的动词有thought、were、corresponded with、showed和having，其中thought、were和showed分别在从句引导词who和that之后，作从句的谓语动词，故排除；having是非谓语动词，故排除。因此该句主干的谓语动词为corresponded with，主干部分是those...corresponded with those...。题干中的people with higher self-esteem（自尊心更强的人）即对应文中those who showed other markers for having higher self-esteem（那些在其他方面表现出更强自尊心的人），这一群人与句中前半部分提及的those who thought that the images higher up the attractiveness scale were real（那些认为更有吸引力的照片才是自己真

实的照片的人）恰好是一致的，也就是说，自尊心更强的人往往相信自己的吸引力，故选择B项。

参考译文 从（受试者的）反应中，艾普里并未发现显著的性别差异。也没有任何证据表明，那些自我拉抬最甚者（即那些认为修改得最好看的照片才是自己真实的照片的受试者），这样做是为了弥补内心强烈的不安全感。事实上，那些认为更有吸引力的照片才是自己真实的照片的人，与那些在其他方面表现出更强自尊心的人正好一致。艾普里说："我认为我们得到的研究结果并不能证明这是个人妄想。这只是反映了人们通常会自我感觉良好。"如果你感到沮丧，你就不会进行自我拉抬。

三、"主干家族"在写作中的应用

确定句子主干不仅是翻译、阅读板块中正确理解句意的核心所在，也是我们在写作板块中拓展出长句子的基础，更是写出正确句子的前提。下面我们来看一看主干句型如何运用在写作板块中。根据前面所学的五种主干句型，翻译下列句子。

例 1 这一数字从2010年到2020年增加了。

解析 该句为主谓结构，其中"这一数字"作主语，"增加"作谓语动词，"从2010年到2020年"作时间状语，翻译时谓语动词要使用过去式。

参考译文 The number increased from 2010 to 2020.

例 2 文化融合已经产生了重大影响。

解析 该句为主谓宾结构，其中"文化融合"作主语，"已经产生了"作谓语动词，使用现在完成时，"重大影响"作宾语。

参考译文 Cultural integration has exerted a great influence.

例 3 他成了一位有名的钢琴家。

解析 该句为主系表结构，其中"他"作主语，"成为了"作系动词，使用一般过去时，"一位有名的钢琴家"作表语。

参考译文 He became a famous pianist.

例 4 新时代正带给我们机遇和挑战。

解析 该句为主谓双宾结构，其中"新时代"作主语，"正带给"作谓语动词，使用现在进行时，"我们"作间接宾语，"机遇和挑战"作直接宾语。

参考译文 The new era is bringing us chances and challenges.

例 5 合作将使得这个社会繁荣昌盛。

解析 该句为主谓宾宾补结构，其中"合作"作主语，"将使得"作谓语动词，使用一般将来时，"这个社会"作宾语，"繁荣昌盛"作宾语补足语。

参考译文 Cooperation will make this society prosperous.

在以上5个句子的翻译过程中我们了解到，谓语动词有时态、语态、情态等不同的变化形式，常见的语法书中给我们介绍了16种时态，而在考研英语写作的实际应用中，最常用到的是6种时态（一般现在时、一般过去时、一般将来时、现在进行时、现在完成时、过去完成时），以及情态和被动语态。下列两表分别对此进行了总结：

谓语动词的16种时态

	一般时	进行时	完成时	完成进行时
现在	do/does; am/is/are	am/is/are doing	have/has done	have/has been doing
过去	did; was/were	was/were doing	had done	had been doing
将来	will do/ be going to do/ be (about) to do	will be doing	will have done	will have been doing
过去将来	would do	would be doing	would have done	would have been doing

谓语常见时态的标志词和谓语动词形式总结

	标志词	谓语动词形式
一般现在时	today, nowadays	do/does; am/is/are
一般过去时	yesterday, ...ago, in 1885	did; was/were
一般将来时	soon, future	will do/ be going to do/ be (about) to do
现在进行时	at the moment, now	am/is/are doing
现在完成时	so far, recently, yet, already, since	have/has done
过去完成时	by the end of +过去的时间点	had done
情态	if... order/suggest that... it is necessary that...	can/could/may/might/must/need/ would/should do
被动	by sth./sb.	be done

在考研英语写作板块中，时态的应用是一个考查重点。谓语动词时态混淆是我们写句子时最容易犯的错误之一。

请根据句子中的时态标志词写出下列句子中谓语动词的正确形式：

例1 Recently, there _____ (be) a growing concern over the topic of the choice after graduation.

答案 has been

解析 副词recently作时间状语，表示"最近，近来"，谓语动词be应使用现在完成时has been，表示最近这段时间以来一直在关注某个话题。

参考译文 最近，人们越来越关注毕业后的选择这个话题。

例2 No agreement _____ (reach) by the two sides in the past.

答案 was reached

解析 介词短语in the past作时间状语，表示"在过去"，谓语动词reach使用一般过去时态，此外，主语no agreement与谓语动词reach之间存在被动关系，即"没有协议被达成"，故应使用reach的被动语态was reached。

参考译文 过去，双方没有达成协议。

例3 But the trend _____ (continue) in the near future.

答案 will continue

解析 介词短语in the near future作时间状语，表示"在不久的将来"，谓语动词continue使用一般将来时will continue。

参考译文 但是在不久的将来，这种趋势将继续下去。

在写作中，正确把握句子的主干能让我们写出语法结构完整、核心意义清晰的基本句型。在此基础之上，我们再"添砖加瓦"，就可以写出更长、更难、更漂亮的佳句。如果暂时不能写出长难句，至少要保证自己能写出正确的句子，遵循"守门员"法则，守住底线，不犯简单错误。

"守门员"法则 ┌ 1. 守动词，定唯一谓语（及物与不及物）
     ├ 2. 守名词，定主干（可数与不可数、单数与复数）
     └ 3. 守主谓一致（数的一致）

课后练习

一、阅读理解

Of all the components of a good night's sleep, dreams seem to be least within our control. In dreams, a window opens into a world where logic is suspended and dead people speak.

A century ago, Freud formulated his revolutionary theory that dreams were the disguised shadows of our unconscious desires and fears; by the late 1970s, neurologists had switched to thinking of them as just "mental noise"—the random byproducts of the neural-repair work that goes on during sleep. Now researchers suspect that dreams are part of the mind's emotional thermostat, regulating moods while the brain is "off-line." And one leading authority says that these intensely powerful mental events can be not only harnessed but actually brought under conscious control, to help us sleep and feel better. "It's your dream," says Rosalind Cartwright, chair of psychology at Chicago's Medical Center. "If you don't like it, change it."

(2005年阅读)

Researchers have come to believe that dreams _____.

[A] can be modified in their courses   [B] are susceptible to emotional changes

[C] reflect our innermost desires and fears   [D] are a random outcome of neural repairs

二、用所给动词的正确形式翻译下列句子

1. 原因列举如下。(list)

2. 不久将举办一个活动。(host)

3. 已经得出一个结论。(draw)

三、改错

1. You explained that your parents had been ill at that moment yesterday.

(1999年改错)

2. All those sound greatly in theory.

(1999年改错)

3. The girl like Chinese culture. Cultures around the world is becoming similarly today. The cultural communication make more foreigner know China. China has opened its door to the world in 1979. More people visit China, become interested in Chinese culture. They communicate more with people belong to other cultures.

(2002年写作)

一、阅读理解

答案 A

解析 题干询问研究者们已经开始相信梦_____，应选择他们现在的想法，用一般现在时描述，该段第四至六句介绍了目前对梦的最新研究。目前研究的观点是，梦是可以控制和改变的，故选A。第四句中提到，梦是大脑情绪自动调节系统的一部分（part of the mind's emotional thermostat），当大脑处于"离线"状态时，梦会调节情绪（regulating moods），因此B选项"（梦）易受情绪变化的影响"与原文所述相反，故排除。C选项reflect our innermost desires and fears对应原文第三句A century ago, Freud formulated...that dreams were...our unconscious desires and fears，该句使用的时间状语a century ago以及动词formulated、were均表明C选项描述的应是发生在过去的事情，而题干中问的是研究者们现在的观点，二者不符，故排除。同理，D选项也存在时态混淆的问题，原文中by the late 1970s, neurologists had switched...the random byproducts of the neural-repair work...也使用了表过去的时间状语by the late 1970s以及动词的过去完成时态had switched，不符合题目要求。

参考译文 在一夜好眠的所有因素中，梦似乎是最无法控制的。在梦中，有一扇窗通向逻辑暂时失效、死人开口说话的世界。一个世纪前，弗洛伊德创立了他的革命性理论——梦是人们无意识的欲望和恐惧所伪装的影子；到了20世纪70年代末，神经学家们转而认为梦仅仅是"精神噪音"——睡眠期间持续进行的神经修复活动的随机副产品。现在，研究者觉察到梦是大脑情绪自动调节系统的组成部分，当大脑处于"离线"状态时对情绪进行调整。一位有影响力的权威人士认为，这种异常重要的精神活动不仅能加以利用，事实上还可以将其置于有意识的控制之下，以使得我们的睡眠质量更高、心情更好。芝加哥医疗中心心理部主任罗莎琳德·卡特赖特说："这是你的梦。若不喜欢它，就改变它。"

二、用所给动词的正确形式翻译下列句子

1. **解析** The reasons为可数名词复数形式，且谓语动词list（列举）和主语The reasons（原因）构成逻辑上的被动关系，即原因是被列举出来的，所以使用are listed。

   参考译文 The reasons are listed as follows.

2. **解析** 因为"将举办一个活动"，故谓语动词使用一般将来时，且activity（活动）和host（举办）构成逻辑上的被动关系，即活动是被举办的，所以使用will be hosted。

   参考译文 An activity will be hosted soon.

3. 解析 因为"已经得出"，故谓语动词使用现在完成时，且conclusion（结论）和draw（得出）构成逻辑上的被动关系，即结论被得出，所以使用has been drawn。

参考译文 A conclusion has been drawn.

三、改错

1. 答案 had been改为were

   解析 宾语从句that your parents...中的介词短语at that moment yesterday作时间状语，表示"昨天那个时刻"，是过去的短暂时刻，因此谓语动词不可使用过去完成时，应改为一般过去时。

2. 答案 greatly改为great

   解析 sound作系动词，意为"听起来"，后接形容词作表语，但greatly为副词，需改为形容词。

3. 答案 like改为likes；is改为are；similarly改为similar；make改为makes；foreigner改为foreigners；has opened改为opened；become前面添加and；belong改为belonging或who belong。

   解析 The girl为第三人称单数形式，故like改为likes；Cultures为复数形式，故is改为are；become是系动词，故副词similarly改为形容词similar；communication此处理解为"交流，交际"，为不可数名词，故make改为makes；形容词more此处作many的比较级，修饰可数名词foreigner，故foreigner应改为复数形式；in 1979表示过去的时间点，故谓语动词open使用一般过去时；谓语动词的并列需要添加并列连词，故become前面添加and；一个句子若使用多个谓语动词，必须采用并列或从属两种手段处理多个谓语动词，故可将belong改为非谓语动词belonging，作people的后置定语（避免使用两个及以上的谓语动词而无连词的情形），或在belong前添加who，将之改为定语从句（使用从属手段）。

"修饰集团"之定语精讲

Day 04

本节课我们将探讨：

1 定语的作用；**2** 定语的形式；**3** 定语的位置。

在前面讲到的五个基本句型中，主语、谓语、宾语、表语、宾语补足语等成分是句子的核心成分，是"主干家族"的成员，通过组合可以表达出一件完整的事情。但要把一件事情描述得更加充分具体，光靠"主干家族"是不够的，需要引入"修饰集团"，使"主干"上长出茂密的枝叶来，让整个句子变得更丰满。定语便是"修饰集团"中的重要一员，所有的简单句都可以通过叠加定语的方式变得更加具体。如何在纷繁复杂的定语的掩盖中抓到句子主干，找准定语修饰的对象，理清定语的顺序，是这节课要学习的重点。

一、定语的作用

定语是用来修饰、限定、说明名词的品质与特征的成分，汉语中常用"……的"表示。下面这首《再别康桥》（节选）中有哪些词是作定语的?

轻轻地我走了，
正如我轻轻地来；
我轻轻地招手，
作别西天的云彩。
那河畔的金柳，
是夕阳中的新娘；
波光里的艳影，
在我的心头荡漾。

以上带有"的"的几个词，例如"西天的""河畔的""夕阳中的""波光里的""我的"，都是定语，修饰限定后面的名词。

31

二、定语的形式

　　除了上文中的"……的"这样的形容词之外，还有多种形式可以作定语，包括名词、代词、数词、单个的动名词或现在分词、单个的过去分词、现在分词短语、过去分词短语、动词不定式短语、介词短语、形容词短语以及定语从句等。名词、代词、数词等作定语修饰名词时，我们通常将其合并成一个名词短语，在此不作进一步分类。

三、定语的位置

　　前置定语一般比较简单，往往是单词。后置定语更为复杂，可以是短语和句子。为了方便大家记忆，我们把前置定语的三种形式和后置定语的六种形式称为"三姑六婆"。"三姑"较易，"六婆"较难，我们从易到难来学习如何把握定语和被修饰对象之间的位置关系。

1 "三姑"——单词前置

a. 形容词（*adj.*）

例如 a tough guy 硬汉　　a suspicious face 可疑的脸　　the rosy clouds 彩云

b. 单个的动名词或现在分词（V-ing）

例如 a sleeping bag 一个睡袋　　a running man 在奔跑的男士　　emerging economies 新兴的经济体

c. 单个的过去分词（V-ed）

例如 profit-driven businessmen 为利润驱使的商人　　published books 已出版的图书

注意区别：V-ing表用途、主动、进行。V-ed表被动、完成。

2 "六婆"——短语、句子后置

a. 现在分词短语（V-ing...）

例如 a man running on the sports field 在操场跑步的男人

economies emerging from Asia 从亚洲新兴的经济体

b. 过去分词短语（V-ed...）

例如 businessmen driven by profits 为利润驱使的商人

books published in the 20th century 在20世纪出版的书籍

c. 动词不定式短语（to do...）

例如 the ability to pay 支付的能力　　a way to boost profits 增加利润的方式

d. 介词短语（*prep. ...*）

例如 clouds in the western sky 西天的云彩

the readers under the age of forty 四十岁以下的读者

e. 形容词短语（*adj. ...*）

例如 a girl kind to me 对我友善的女孩　　food necessary to us 对我们必要的食物

f. 定语从句（that/wh- ...）

例如 the girl who is beautiful 那个美丽的女孩

the changes that took place 那些过去发生的变化

若名词由多个定语修饰，可借助以下公式帮助理解：

多重定语公式 ── ① 识别定语：找出"三姑六婆"
② 识别中心词：找到"三姑"之后或"六婆"之前的名词
③ 翻译："三姑"位置不变，"六婆"层层向前，
调整语序，中心词最后翻译

下面我们根据所学知识，识别下列表达中的定语并翻译。

例 1 the marketing of products for children

解析 此短语中有两个后置定语，分别为of products和for children，均为介词短语。中心名词是marketing。翻译时后置定语层层向前，从最后的for children逆序向前翻译到of products再到中心名词marketing。

参考译文 儿童用品的营销策略

例 2 the changes taking place in newspapers during the past century （2010年英语一阅读）

解析 此短语中有两个后置定语，分别是现在分词短语taking place in newspapers和介词短语during the past century。中心名词是changes。翻译时后置定语层层向前，从最后的during the past century逆序向前翻译到中心名词changes。

参考译文 上世纪报纸中发生的变化

例 3 one more reason not to lose sleep over the rise in oil prices （2002年阅读）

解析 此短语中有一个前置定语，为形容词more，三个后置定语分别是动词不定式短语not to lose sleep和两个介词短语over the rise、in oil prices。中心名词是reason。翻译时前置定语位置不变，后置定语层层向前，从最后的in oil prices逆序向前翻译到中心名词reason。"油价上涨不为此失眠的另一个原因"不符合汉语将否定前置的表达习惯，调整语序，将否定提到前面。

参考译文 不为油价上涨而失眠的另一个原因

例 4 the inexorable decline in the seriousness of their arts coverage (2010年英语一阅读)

解析 此短语中有一个前置定语，为形容词inexorable，两个后置定语分别为介词短语in the seriousness和of their arts coverage。中心名词是decline。翻译时前置定语保留在所修饰名词的前面，位置不变，后置定语层层向前，从最后的of their arts coverage逆序向前翻译到中心名词decline。

参考译文 文学报道严肃性的必然衰退

例 5 physicians frustrated by their inability to cure the disease

解析 此短语的中心名词是physicians，过去分词短语frustrated by their inability to cure the disease作其后置定语，其中，动词不定式短语to cure the disease又作名词inability的后置定语，往前译为"治愈疾病的无能"，不符合汉语的表达习惯，可将名词inability转译为动词，译为"不能治愈疾病"。

参考译文 因不能治愈疾病而受挫的医生们

例 6 physicians fearing loss of hope in the patient

解析 此短语的中心名词是physicians，现在分词短语fearing loss of hope in the patient作其后置定语，其中，介词短语of hope和in the patient又分别作名词loss和名词hope的后置定语，往前译为"病人的希望的失去"，不符合汉语的表达习惯，可将名词loss转译为动词，译为"病人失去希望"。

参考译文 担心病人失去希望的医生们

 课后练习

一、找出下列表达中的定语，并翻译

1. the revival of the U.S. economy in the 1990s

2. intimate shops catering to a knowledgeable elite

3. the background of general commodity-price inflation and global excess demand

(2002年阅读)

4. the unfocused reviews published in England

(2010年英语一阅读)

二、翻译下列短语

1. 避免麻烦的最好办法

2. 创新需要的第一样东西

3. 奢靡的生活品味

4. 用来养活自己和家人的关键收入

5. 界定女性形体美的绝对权利

参考答案

一、找出下列表达中的定语，并翻译

1. the revival (of the U.S. economy in the 1990s)

   解析 此短语中，介词短语of the U.S. economy in the 1990s作中心名词revival的后置定语，其中in the 1990s又作名词economy的后置定语，从后向前，层层翻译。

   参考译文 20世纪90年代美国经济的复苏

2. (intimate) shops (catering to a knowledgeable elite)

   解析 此短语中有一个形容词intimate、一个现在分词短语catering to a knowledgeable elite，分别作中心名词shops的前置定语和后置定语，翻译时后置定语位置前移，前置定语位置不变。

   参考译文 迎合知识分子的精品店铺

3. the background (of general commodity-price inflation and global excess demand)

   解析 此短语中有一个介词短语of general commodity-price inflation and global excess demand作中心名词background的后置定语，翻译时位置前移。

   参考译文 一般商品价格通货膨胀和全球需求过剩的背景

4. the (unfocused) reviews (published in England)

   解析 此短语中有一个形容词unfocused、一个过去分词短语published in England，分别作中心名词reviews的前置定语和后置定语，翻译时后置定语位置前移，前置定语位置不变。

   参考译文 在英国出版的没有焦点的评论

二、翻译下列短语

1. the best way to avoid trouble

2. the first thing needed for innovation

3. an expensive taste of lifestyle

4. the crucial income to feed yourself and your family

5. an absolute right to define physical beauty for women

"修饰集团"之定语应用

Day 05

从理论层面把握了定语的作用、形式、位置和分析公式后，接下来我们看看定语在真题翻译、阅读和写作中的具体应用。

在考研英语真题中，一个名词前后可能存在多个定语起修饰、限定的作用，这极大地增加了理解的难度。但只要我们能把握好句子的主干，利用"三姑六婆"原则，将多个定语准确划分，不难理清句子结构。还是以《再别康桥》里的两行诗为例：

> The golden willows by the riverside are young brides in the setting sun.
>
> 那河畔的金柳，是夕阳中的新娘；
>
> Their reflections on the shimmering waves always linger in the depth of my heart.
>
> 波光里的艳影，在我的心头荡漾。

第一个句子的主干为The willows are brides，属于简单句中的主系表句型。句子长度变长是因为两个名词前后存在多个定语，形容词golden和介词短语by the riverside分别作willows的前置定语和后置定语，形容词young和介词短语in the setting sun分别作brides的前置定语和后置定语。

第二个句子的主干为Their reflections linger，属于简单句中的主谓句型。其中介词短语on the shimmering waves作后置定语修饰reflections，状语in the depth of my heart中的名词depth由介词短语of my heart作其后置定语。

下面我们看看多重定语在考研英语翻译、阅读以及写作板块中的应用。

一、多重定语翻译应用

面对多重定语，我们用以下步骤思考：

1 主干公式

　　a. 找出所有动词；

　　b. 去掉非谓语动词；

　　c. 去掉从句的谓语动词。

2 多重定语公式

a. 识别定语；

b. 识别中心词；

c. 翻译。

下面我们根据以上步骤，完成以下几个句子的翻译。

例 1 The loss of U.S. predominance in the world economy in the 1980s is manifested in the fact. (2000年阅读)

解析 首先抓句子的主干，主语是the loss of U.S. predominance in the world economy in the 1980s，谓语动词是is manifested，句型是主谓结构。主语中有三个介词短语of U.S. predominance、in the world economy和in the 1980s，均作后置定语，中心名词是loss，翻译时层层向前，译为"20世纪80年代的世界经济中美国主导地位的丧失"，由于"丧失"一词在汉语里常被用作动词，这里可将名词loss转译为动词，译成"美国丧失了主导地位"。谓语动词is manifested直译为"被表明"也不符合汉语里少用被动句的特点，因此翻译时可将"被"直接去掉。

参考译文 这一事实表明美国在20世纪80年代的世界经济中丧失了主导地位。

例 2 A shift to other fuels and a decline in the importance of heavy, energy-intensive industries have reduced oil consumption. (2002年阅读)

解析 首先抓句子的主干，主语是a shift to other fuels and a decline in the importance of heavy, energy-intensive industries，谓语动词是have reduced，宾语是oil consumption，句型是主谓宾结构。主语中心词是由and连接的两个并列名词shift和decline。其中，介词短语to other fuels作名词shift的后置定语，介词短语in the importance of heavy, energy-intensive industries作名词decline的后置定语，翻译时将后置定语位置提前，译为"其他燃料的更换"和"能源密集型重工业的重要性的降低"。由于"更换"和"降低"一词在汉语里常被用作动词，在翻译时可将名词shift和decline转译为动词，译成"更换其他燃料"和"降低能源密集型重工业的重要性"。

参考译文 更换其他燃料以及降低能源密集型重工业的重要性都降低了油耗。

例 3 People are absorbed into "a culture of consumption" launched by the 19th-century department stores. (2006年阅读)

解析 首先抓句子的主干，动词有are absorbed into和launched。are absorbed into是动词的被动语态，可作谓语动词，launched是非谓语动词，可排除。主语是people，宾语是"a culture of consumption" launched by the 19th-century department stores，句型是主谓宾

结构。介词短语of consumption作culture的后置定语，过去分词短语launched by the 19th-century department stores作a culture of consumption的后置定语，翻译时前置，译为"被19世纪的百货商店发起的'消费文化'"。由于谓语are absorbed into直译为"被……吸引"和过去分词短语launched by the 19th-century department stores"被百货商店发起的"不符合汉语里少用被动句的特点，翻译时可将"被"去掉，转换为主动说法。

参考译文 人们沉迷于19世纪百货商店发起的"消费文化"之中。

例 4 Physicians frustrated by their inability to cure the disease and fearing loss of hope in the patient often offer aggressive treatment. (2003年阅读)

解析 首先抓句子的主干，句中动词有frustrated、to cure、fearing和offer。其中，frustrated、to cure和fearing是非谓语动词，故排除。因此谓语动词是offer，主语是physicians frustrated by their inability to cure the disease and fearing loss of hope in the patient，宾语是aggressive treatment，句型是主谓宾结构。主语的中心名词是physicians，and连接的过去分词短语frustrated by...和现在分词短语fearing...作后置定语，并列限定physicians。其中，过去分词短语frustrated by...中，动词不定式短语to cure the disease又作名词inability的后置定语，往前译为"治愈疾病的无能"，不符合汉语的表达习惯，可将名词inability转译为动词，译为"不能治愈疾病"；现在分词短语fearing...中，介词短语of hope和in patient作名词loss的后置定语，往前译为"病人的希望的失去"，不符合汉语的表达习惯，可将名词loss转译为动词，译为"病人失去希望"。

参考译文 医生由于不能治愈这种疾病而感到沮丧，同时又担心病人失去希望，因此常常采用极端大胆的治疗方法。

二、多重定语在阅读中的应用

根据前面所学的翻译多重定语的步骤，理解以下句子，并翻译主干部分。

例 1 Any fair-minded assessment of the dangers of the deal between Britain's National Health Service (NHS) and DeepMind must start by acknowledging that both sides mean well.

(2018年英语一阅读)

解析 此句中的动词有must start、acknowledging和mean，其中，acknowledging是非谓语动词，mean在从句引导词that之后，故均排除，因此主句谓语动词是must start。主语any fair-minded assessment of the dangers of the deal between Britain's National Health Service (NHS) and DeepMind中有多重定语，前置定语为形容词fair-minded，后置定语为三个介词短语of the dangers、of the deal、between Britain's National Health Service (NHS) and

DeepMind，中心词是assessment，主句主干为any assessment...must start by...。主语部分将后置定语层层向前，翻译为"任何对英国国民医疗服务体系与深度思考公司之间的交易风险的公正评估"。

参考译文 主干：任何（对……之间的交易风险）的评估必须以……开始

整句：要想公正地评估英国国民医疗服务体系与深度思考公司之间的交易风险，必须首先承认双方都怀有好意。

翻译结束后，我们看看下面这道阅读题是如何利用上句中的定语来设置干扰选项的。

What is true of the agreement between the NHS and DeepMind?

[A] It caused conflicts among tech giants.

[B] It failed to pay due attention to patients' rights.

[C] It fell short of the latter's expectations.

[D] It put both sides into a dangerous situation.

解析 题目的D选项"它（协议）将双方置于危险的境地"是针对主语的定语部分设置的干扰项，偷换了定语中dangers的概念，原文of the dangers修饰的是assessment，而不是选项中的situation。

例2 People are absorbed into "a culture of consumption" launched by the 19th-century department stores that offered "vast arrays of goods in an elegant atmosphere." Instead of intimate shops catering to a knowledgeable elite, these were stores that "anyone could enter, regardless of class or background. This turned shopping into a public and democratic act." The mass media, advertising and sports are other forces for homogenization.   (2006年阅读)

According to the author, the department stores of the 19th century _____.

[A] played a role in the spread of popular culture

[B] became intimate shops for common consumers

[C] satisfied the needs of a knowledgeable elite

[D] owed its emergence to the culture of consumption

解析 第一句中，介词短语of consumption作名词culture的后置定语，过去分词短语launched by the 19th-century department stores作a culture of consumption的后置定语，前半句意为"人们被19世纪的百货商店掀起的'消费文化'所同化"。D选项"（19世纪百货商店）的出现归功于消费文化"曲解了原句后置定语中过去分词短语的被动关系，可被排除。第二句中，现在分词短语catering to a knowledgeable elite作intimate shops

的后置定语，意为"迎合知识精英需求的精品店"。但instead of（代替，而不是）这个短语将intimate shops catering to a knowledgeable elite和these were stores...置于相反的逻辑关系，意为"19世纪的百货商店不是迎合知识精英需求的精品店"，因此C选项"满足了知识精英的需求"与原文不符。B选项"成为面向普通消费者的精品店"中，除了精品店这一说法有误外，原文后半句中还补充说明"anyone could enter, regardless of class or background"，即任何阶层或背景的人都能进入，不仅限于普通消费者，故排除B选项和C选项。A选项"在传播大众文化方面发挥了作用"与文意相符，为正确选项。

参考译文 人们被19世纪的百货商店掀起的"消费文化"所同化，这些商店"在优雅的环境中提供琳琅满目的商品"。与那些迎合知识精英需求的精品店不同，这些商店"不论其阶级或背景，任何人都可以进入。这使得购物转变为一种公开的、大众的行为"。大众传媒、广告和体育赛事是同化的其他推动力。

三、多重定语在写作中的应用

定语在考研英语写作中经常被用到，常见于提出解决问题的原因、导致变化的因素等。下面我们具体来看看如何在考研英语写作中正确地使用定语。下面是使用定语的两种情形：

1 单词：*adj.*/V-ing/V-ed

单个单词作定语一般放在所修饰的名词或代词前，作前置定语。常见的形式有形容词、单个的现在分词和过去分词。

例如 帅气的男孩 → a (handsome) boy   善良的女孩 → a (kind) girl
小红花 → a (little red) flower

2 短语：V-ing.../V-ed.../to do.../*prep.* .../*adj.* ...

短语作定语一般放在所修饰的名词或代词后面，作后置定语。常见的形式有现在分词短语、动词不定式短语、过去分词短语、形容词短语和介词短语。其中，现在分词短语作后置定语时，与所修饰的词之间存在主谓关系，即由该名词或代词主动发出动作。过去分词短语作后置定语时，与所修饰的词之间存在动宾关系，即该名词或代词为动作的承受者。动词不定式短语作定语时，其逻辑主语为该名词或代词，一般表目的或时间上将要发生的动作。

下面我们根据以上规则，翻译下列短语。

例 1 读艺术专业的男孩

解析 "读艺术专业"非形容词，是短语，只能作boy的后置定语，由于"男孩"和"读"之间存在逻辑上的主谓关系，故应使用现在分词短语majoring in Art。

参考译文 a boy (majoring in Art)

例 2 坐在他旁边的女孩

解析 "坐在他旁边"是短语，作girl的后置定语，由于"女孩"和"坐"之间存在逻辑上的主谓关系，故应使用现在分词短语sitting beside him。

参考译文 a girl (sitting beside him)

例 3 高中的女孩

解析 "高中"即"在高中"，是短语，需作后置定语放在"女孩"后，故应使用介词短语in high school。

参考译文 a girl (in high school)

例 4 一朵他亲自做的花

解析 "他亲自做"是短语，需作后置定语放在"花"后面，由于"花"和"他亲自做"之间存在逻辑上的动宾关系，即"花被他亲自做"，故应使用过去分词短语made by him。

参考译文 a flower (made by him)

将以上短语以正确的句子主干结构连接起来，便能写出一个漂亮的写作长难句。试着翻译这个句子：

一个帅气的[1]读艺术专业的[2]男孩送给那个高中[3]坐在他旁边的[4]善良的[5]女孩一朵他亲自做的[6]小[7]红[8]花。

解析 本句主干为"男孩送给女孩花"，是一个主谓双宾句型。主语中心词"男孩"由"帅气的"和"读艺术专业的"两个定语修饰，连接起来为A handsome boy majoring in Art。间接宾语"女孩"由"高中""坐在他旁边的""善良的"三个定语修饰，连接起来为the kind girl sitting beside him in high school。直接宾语"花"由三个定语"亲自做的""小""红"修饰，连接起来为a little red flower made by him。

参考译文 A (handsome)[1] boy (majoring in Art)[2] sent the (kind)[5] girl (sitting beside him)[4] (in high school)[3] a (little)[7] (red)[8] flower (made by him)[6].

以上句子中的名词主语boy，间接宾语girl和直接宾语flower，便是通过在其前面添加"三姑"、后面添加"六婆"的方式变得更长、更丰满，下面我们用一个表格对这种多重定语的添加方式进行总结：

"三姑"			中心名词	"六婆"					
adj.	V-ing	V-ed	*n.*	V-ing...	V-ed...	to do...	*prep.* ...	*adj.* ...	that/wh-...

下面我们继续学习写作中常用的定语该如何表达。试着翻译以下短语：

例 1 解释问题的原因

解析 "解释问题（account for the problem）"是动词短语，作定语修饰名词"原因（the reasons）"时需放在名词后面，由于动词短语与中心名词之间存在逻辑上的主谓关系，即"原因解释问题"，故应用现在分词短语accounting for the problem。

参考译文 the reasons accounting for the problem

例 2 导致变化的因素

解析 "导致变化（lead to the changes）"是动词短语，作定语修饰名词"因素（the factors）"时需放在名词后面，由于动词短语与中心名词之间存在逻辑上的主谓关系，即"因素导致变化"，故应用现在分词短语leading to the changes。

参考译文 the factors leading to the changes

例 3 要解决的问题

解析 "解决（address）"是动词，作定语修饰名词"问题（a problem）"时需放在名词后面，由于"要解决"是时间上将要发生的动作，且problem和address之间存在逻辑上的动宾关系，即"问题要被解决"，故应用动词不定式的被动语态to be addressed。

参考译文 a problem to be addressed

例 4 教育扮演的角色

解析 "教育扮演（education plays）"是动词短语，作定语修饰名词"角色（the role）"时需放在名词后面，由于动词短语与中心名词之间存在逻辑上的动宾关系，即"角色被教育扮演"，故应用过去分词短语played by education。

参考译文 the role played by education

例 5 图片反映的现象

解析 "图片反映（the picture mirrors）"是动词短语，作定语修饰名词"现象（the phenomenon）"时需放在名词后面，由于动词短语与中心名词之间存在逻辑上的动宾关系，即"现象被图片反映"，故应用过去分词短语mirrored by the picture。

参考译文 the phenomenon mirrored by the picture

例 6 现象背后隐藏的原因

解析 名词"原因（the reasons）"由两个定语修饰，"现象背后（behind the phenomenon）"

是介词短语，应作后置定语，"隐藏的（invisible）"是形容词，应作前置定语。

参考译文 the invisible reasons behind the phenomenon

例7 要考虑的最重要的因素

解析 名词"因素（factor）"由两个定语修饰，"考虑（consider）"是动词，应作后置定语，"要"是时间上将要发生的动作，且consider和factor之间存在逻辑上的动宾关系，即"因素要被考虑"，故应用动词不定式的被动语态to be considered。"最重要的（the most important）"是形容词最高级，应作前置定语。

参考译文 the most important factor to be considered

例8 图片反映的现象背后的驱动力

解析 名词"驱动力（the driving force）"由两个定语修饰，"图片反映（the picture mirrors）"是动词短语，"现象背后（behind the phenomenon）"是介词短语，都应作后置定语。遵循翻译时后置定语层层向前的原则，将"现象背后"放在名词后的第一个位置。

参考译文 the driving force behind the phenomenon mirrored by the picture

下面我们看看如何利用以上的一些短语，将定语应用于一篇完整的考研英语作文中。请根据下图内容，用英语写出以下内容：

这一现象背后隐藏的原因是什么？首先，要考虑的最重要的因素是全面发展。其次，我们应该密切关注教育扮演的角色。这两个原因是图片反映的现象背后的驱动力。

参考范文 So what are the invisible/intangible reasons behind the phenomenon[6]? Firstly, the most important factor to be considered[7] is all-round development. Secondly, close attention should be paid to the role played by education[4]. The two factors are the driving force behind the phenomenon mirrored by the picture[8].

课后练习

一、英译汉

1. The creation of the "statistics board" was motivated by concerns with the application of statistics and data analysis in scientific research.　　　　(2015年英语一阅读)

2. Works of several historians reveal the moral compromises made by the nation's early leaders and the fragile nature of the country's infancy.　　　　(2008年阅读)

二、阅读理解

One more reason not to lose sleep over the rise in oil prices is that, it has not occurred against the background of general commodity-price inflation and global excess demand.　　(2002年阅读)

The writer seems _____.

[A] optimistic　　　　　　　　　　[B] sensitive

[C] gloomy　　　　　　　　　　　　[D] scared

三、写作

1. 表示祝愿的新年礼物拉近了人们之间的距离。　　　　(2015年英语二写作)

2. 图中站在左边的那个人露出了不满和失望的表情。　　　　(2012年英语一写作)

3. 有一个把崇拜写在脸上的狂热小粉丝。

4. 这个讲座传达的主题是青春与梦想的完美的融合。

一、英译汉

1. **解析** 首先抓句子的主干，句子的谓语动词是was motivated，句型是主谓结构。主语是the creation of the "statistics board"，介词短语of the "statistics board" 修饰中心名词the creation。状语是by concerns with the application of statistics and data analysis in scientific research，其中介词短语with the application和of statistics and data analysis分别作名词concerns和application的后置定语，翻译时层层向前，译为"对科学研究中数字统计和数据分析应用的担忧"。

   参考译文 对科学研究中数字统计和数据分析应用的担忧，促进了统计数据委员会的组建。

2. **解析** 首先抓句子的主干，句子中的动词有reveal和made。made是非谓语动词，故排除。由此确定谓语动词是reveal，句型是主谓宾结构。主语是works of several historians，介词短语of several historians作名词works的后置定语，译为"数位历史学家的作品"。宾语是the moral compromises made by the nation's early leaders and the fragile nature of the country's infancy，由连词and连接两个并列宾语，中心词分别为compromises和nature。其中，compromises由形容词moral作前置定语，过去分词短语made by the nation's early leaders作后置定语，翻译时前置，直译为"被国家早期领导人做出的道德妥协"，由于汉语少用被动，故转译为主动语态"国家早期领导人做出的道德妥协"。nature由形容词fragile作前置定语，由介词短语of the country's infancy作后置定语，翻译时前置，译为"国家初建时的脆弱本质"。

   参考译文 数位历史学家的作品揭示了国家早期领导人所做出的道德妥协和国家初建时的脆弱本质。

二、阅读理解

解析 本句中的动词有to lose、is和has not occurred，由于to lose是非谓语动词，has not occurred跟在从句引导词that后，故均排除。由此确定谓语动词是is，本句的主干为One more reason...is that...，that引导表语从句。其中不定式短语not to lose sleep、介词短语over the rise和in oil prices均为主语中心名词reason的后置定语。over意为"以……为原因"，翻译时将否定前移，定语从后往前层层译为"不因油价上涨而失眠的原因"。句中表语从句的主语为it，谓语动词是不及物动词has not occurred，介词短语against the background of general commodity-price inflation and global excess demand作状

46

语，意为"在……背景之下"，介词against后的宾语中心词是background，由介词短语of general commodity-price inflation and global excess demand作后置定语，翻译时前置。"不因此失眠"说明作者的态度是乐观的，A选项正确。

参考译文 不因油价上涨而失眠的另一个原因是其并非发生在物价普遍上涨及全球需求过旺的背景之下。

三、写作

1. 解析 该句主干部分为"新年礼物拉近了距离"，是主谓宾结构。"表示祝愿的"作主语中心词"新年礼物（New Year presents）"的定语，由于"表示祝愿（express wishes）"是动词短语，只能作后置定语，且"礼物"和"表示"之间存在逻辑上的主谓关系，故应使用现在分词短语expressing wishes。谓语"拉近了"使用及物动词shorten。"人们之间的"作宾语中心词"距离"的定语，"人们之间（among people）"是介词短语，应放在被修饰名词的后面。写完句子后注意用"守门员法则"验证，检查谓语动词是否唯一，名词单复数是否正确，以及主谓是否一致。

参考译文 New Year presents expressing wishes shorten the distance among people.

2. 解析 该句主干部分为"那个人露出了表情"，是主谓宾结构。"图中站在左边的"作主语中心词"那个人（the person）"的定语，由于"站在左边（stand on the left）"是动词短语，只能作后置定语，且"人"和"站"之间存在逻辑上的主谓关系，故应使用现在分词短语standing on the left。"图中（in the picture）"是介词短语，也只能作后置定语。按照翻译时后置定语层层向前的原则，就近翻译定语，将"站在左边的"放在"那个人"后的第一个位置。谓语"露出了"使用及物动词show或更特别一点的air。宾语"不满和失望的表情"，可采用形容词作前置定语的译法，译作discontented and disappointed expression。也可采用介词短语作后置定语的译法，译作the expression of discontent and disappointment。

参考译文 The person standing on the left in the picture airs the expression of discontent and disappointment.

3. 解析 该句主干部分为"有一个粉丝"，是一种表示"存在"的句式，常用there be结构表示。"把崇拜写在脸上的狂热小粉丝"的中心词"粉丝"由多重定语修饰，"狂热（crazy）"和"小（little）"作为形容词可直接作前置定语，"把崇拜写在脸上"表面上看是动词短语，但实际上就是"脸上挂着崇拜"，用一个with短语（with worship on his face）就可以表示，也作后置定语，译为fan with worship on his face。

参考译文 There is a crazy little fan with worship on his face.

47

4. 解析 该句主干部分为"主题是融合",是主系表结构。"这个讲座传达的"作主语中心词"主题（the theme）"的定语，由于"讲座传达（the lecture convey）"是动词短语，只能作后置定语，且"主题"和"传达"之间存在逻辑上的动宾关系，故使用过去分词短语conveyed by the lecture。"青春与梦想的完美的"作表语中心词"融合（combination）"的定语，其中"完美的（perfect）"为形容词作前置定语，"青春与梦想的"用介词短语of youth and dream作后置定语。

参考译文 The theme conveyed by the lecture is a perfect combination of youth and dream.

"修饰集团"之状语精讲

Day 06

学习完定语的基本语法理论和它在考研英语翻译、阅读、写作等板块中的应用后，接下来我们来认识一下定语在"修饰集团"中的小伙伴——状语。

除定语外，状语是"修饰集团"中的另一"主力干将"。通过定语和状语的多重叠加修饰，简单句可能会变得极为复杂，主干被多片树叶（定语和状语）掩盖了真实的模样。因此，在分析句子时，我们需要对定语和状语进行抽丝剥茧般的归类。只有严格区别这两种不同的语法成分，搞清楚它们各自的作用，才能在把握句子主干的同时正确理解句子。在本节课中，我们将从状语的作用、形式、位置以及状语和定语的区别等多个方面对状语进行全面系统的学习。

一、状语的作用

状语是句子的重要修饰成分，在句中修饰动词、形容词、副词或整个句子等。可以说，除定语以外的修饰语都是状语，也就是"非定即状"。状语用来说明地点、时间、原因、目的、结果、条件、让步、比较、方式、方向、程度和伴随状况等。

二、状语的形式

状语与定语类似，常见的形式除了"……地"这样的副词之外，还有现在分词短语、过去分词短语、动词不定式短语、形容词短语、介词短语、状语从句等多种形式。下面我们分别举例说明。

1 单词作状语：副词，常以-ly结尾

副词和形容词一样，在句中主要作修饰成分，不同的是，副词可以修饰动词、形容词、副词和句子等，而形容词一般修饰名词。来看下面这些例子：

例 1 She is very beautiful. I really like her very much. She is the very woman.

解析 副词very修饰形容词beautiful，副词really和副词短语very much均修饰动词like。注

意the very woman中的very不是副词作状语，而是形容词作名词woman的前置定语，意为"正是的，恰好的"，不要误译为"她是个'狠'女人"。

参考译文 她很美。我非常爱她。她是我的"梦中情人"。

例2 Mental health is perfectly ordinary.　　　　　　　　　　　　(2016年英语一翻译)

解析 副词perfectly修饰形容词ordinary。

参考译文 心理健康非常普遍。

例3 It's all deliciously ironic.　　　　　　　　　　　　　　　　(2006年阅读)

解析 副词deliciously修饰形容词ironic。翻译时可根据汉语习惯将形容词ironic译成名词"讽刺"，并将副词译成形容词。

参考译文 它是一种绝妙的讽刺。

2 短语作状语：V-ing.../V-ed.../to do.../adj. .../prep. ...（=后置定语的5种形式）

与后置定语的表现形式一样，现在分词短语、过去分词短语、动词不定式短语、形容词短语和介词短语也可以作状语。

例如 In Chengdu, I loved a girl.

解析 介词短语in Chengdu作状语，修饰整个句子，表示地点。

参考译文 在成都，我爱过一个女孩。

3 句子作状语：状语从句

状语从句用来说明时间、地点、原因、结果、目的、条件、让步、比较、方式等。

例如 You say it best when you say nothing at all.

解析 when引导时间状语从句。

参考译文 此时无声胜有声。

三、状语的位置

由于状语可以修饰多种类型的词和句子，因此状语的位置并不固定，可以位于句首、句中或句末。副词修饰形容词或副词时，通常放在该形容词或副词的前面。副词修饰动词时，通常位于动词之后，如有宾语则位于宾语之后。表示否定或频度的副词则通常置于动词之前，但要放在助动词或系动词之后，以前面的两个句子为例：

例1 She is very beautiful.

解析 副词very修饰形容词beautiful，放在形容词之前。

例 2 I really like her very much.

解析 副词really修饰动词like，由于really是程度副词，所以需放在动词like之前；副词短语very much修饰动词like，放在其后面，由于有宾语her，所以放在宾语her之后。

那么短语作状语时，应放在哪儿呢？来看下面这四个句子：

In Chengdu, I loved a girl.

In Chengdu I loved a girl.

I loved a girl, in Chengdu.

I loved a girl in Chengdu.

请先作思考，再继续往下看。

四、状语与定语的重要区别

状语和定语在形式上大致相同，在考研英语中我们应该如何区分这两种修饰成分呢？以既可作定语也可作状语的介词短语为例，我们来看二者的区别。请看下面五个句子，判断一下句中的介词短语"in Chengdu""in 2021"分别作什么成分？

In Chengdu, I loved a girl.

In Chengdu I loved a girl.

I loved a girl, in Chengdu.

I loved a girl in Chengdu.

I loved a girl in 2021.

首先需要清楚的一点：区分一个短语是作定语还是状语关键在于是否修饰名词。若短语前没有名词，则一定是状语；若短语前有名词，则通过短语与名词之间是否存在修饰关系来判断是定语还是状语。定语与名词必须构成修饰，且位置固定，而状语与名词不构成修饰，位置自由。定语和状语的区别总结如下表：

形式	定语	状语
前无名词	绝不是	必须是
前有名词	与名词必须构成修饰； 位置不自由	与名词不能构成修饰； 位置自由

掌握了定语和状语的区别后，我们再来分析一下上面的例句：

例1 In Chengdu, I loved a girl.

解析 介词短语in Chengdu前无名词，作地点状语。

参考译文 在成都，我爱过一个女孩。

例2 In Chengdu I loved a girl.

解析 介词短语in Chengdu前无名词，作地点状语。

参考译文 在成都，我爱过一个女孩。

例3 I loved a girl, in Chengdu.

解析 介词短语in Chengdu前无名词，作地点状语。

参考译文 我爱过一个女孩，在成都。

例4 I loved a girl in Chengdu.

解析 介词短语in Chengdu前有名词girl，且构成限定关系，优先作后置定语，译为"成都的女孩"，句意通顺。

参考译文 我爱过一个成都的女孩。

例5 I loved a girl in 2021.

解析 介词短语in 2021前有名词girl，若作后置定语译为"2021年的女孩"，句意不通，二者无法构成修饰关系。因此该句中in 2021作时间状语。

参考译文 在2021年，我爱过一个女孩。

在考研英语中，一个句子可能带有多个起修饰作用的定语或状语，难以辨别，但只要把握住"定状"公式，便能将二者区分开来，正确理解句意。下面我们用两个真题例句来进行具体分析。

例1 In the past, workers with average skills, doing an average job, could earn an average lifestyle.

(2013年英语二阅读)

解析 本句中有两个介词短语in the past、with average skills和一个现在分词短语doing an average job。其中，介词短语with average skills前有名词workers，作其后置定语，对其起修饰作用，意为"具备一般技能的工人"。介词短语in the past和现在分词短语doing an average job未修饰名词，作时间状语和伴随状语。

参考译文 在过去，工人只要具备一般的技能，做一份普通的工作，就能过上中等的生活。

例2 Students without experience can catch up after a few introductory courses.

(2016年英语二阅读)

解析 本句中有两个介词短语without experience和after a few introductory courses。其中，介词短语without experience前有名词students，作其后置定语，意为"没有经验的学生"。介词短语after a few introductory courses前无名词，作状语，意为"在上一些入门课程后"。

参考译文 没有经验的学生在上一些入门课程后就能赶上。

五、非谓语动词作状语的时态及语态

非谓语动词在考研英语中的应用十分广泛，不同的形式对应着不同的时态和语态。不论是作定语还是作状语，形式本身所具备的时态和语态含义都如下表所示：

形式	时态	语态
V-ing	进行	主动
to do	将来	主动
V-ed	完成	被动
having V-ed	完成	主动
being V-ed	进行	被动

请找出下列句子的状语，确定时态及语态，并将句子翻译成中文。

例1 Lifting my eyes, I watch the bright moon.

解析 现在分词短语lifting my eyes作状语，时态上表示进行，语态上表示逻辑主语I和动词lift之间是主动关系。

参考译文 举头望明月。

例2 Watching the moon, I was drowned in homesickness.

解析 现在分词短语watching the moon作状语，时态上表示进行，语态上表示逻辑主语I和动词watch之间是主动关系。

参考译文 望明月，思故乡。

例3 To revitalize China, I work hard.

解析 不定式短语to revitalize China作状语，时态上表示将来，语态上表示逻辑主语I和动词revitalize之间是主动关系。

参考译文 为中华之崛起，我努力奋斗。

例 4 To pass the test, I study hard.

解析 不定式短语to pass the test作状语，时态上表示将来，语态上表示逻辑主语I和动词pass之间是主动关系。

参考译文 为了通过考试，我努力学习。

例 5 Having made their wealth and their reputations elsewhere, they presumably have enough independence to disagree with the chief executive's proposals. (2011年英语二阅读)

解析 现在分词短语having made their wealth and their reputations elsewhere作状语，时态上表示完成，语态上表示逻辑主语they和动词make之间是主动关系。

参考译文 他们已在其他领域获得了财富和声誉，想必有足够的独立性来反对首席执行官的提议。

通过上述分析，我们发现遇到状语一般可按如下公式处理：

状语公式 ┤
1. 区分定状
2. 调整语序，添加逻辑（因为……/伴随……）
* 标点符号（也可直接判断，但有局限性）

下面我们以两个真题句子为例，看看"状语公式"如何帮助我们找出状语，理清句子结构，正确翻译句子。

例 1 Hearing allegations of cruelty to animals in research settings, many are perplexed that anyone would deliberately harm an animal. (2003年阅读)

解析 此句中有一个现在分词短语hearing allegations，前无名词，故为状语。三个介词短语of cruelty、to animals、in research settings前均有名词，作后置定语层层修饰，直译为"研究中对动物的残忍行为的指控"。按照汉语表达习惯，"对动物的残忍行为"可转译为动宾结构，译作"虐待动物"。副词deliberately作状语，修饰动词harm。"听到……指控"与"许多人对……感到困惑"之间存在时间上的伴随关系，翻译时可加上"当……时"。

参考译文 当听到研究中虐待动物的指控时，许多人都不解为何会有人故意伤害动物。

例 2 Declaring his opposition to the technology, he asked an independent panel of experts chaired by Princeton President Harold Shapiro to report back to the White House in 90 days with recommendations for a national policy on human cloning. (1999年阅读)

解析 此句中有现在分词短语declaring his opposition，前无名词，故为状语。介词短语to the technology前有名词opposition，作其后置定语，直译为"对该技术的反对"，可转译成动宾结构"反对该技术"。介词短语of experts前有名词panel，作其后置定语，译为"专家小组"。其后的过去分词短语chaired by Princeton President Harold Shapiro作该名

54

词短语panel of experts的后置定语，译为"由普林斯顿大学校长哈罗德·夏普罗主持的专家小组"。介词短语to the White House前无名词，作状语。介词短语in 90 days和with recommendations前虽有名词the White House和days，但若当作后置定语，译为"90天内的白宫"和"推荐的90天"，语意不通，故只能作状语。介词短语for a national policy和on human cloning前有名词recommendations和policy，作其后置定语，译为"关于克隆人的国家政策的建议"。

参考译文 他宣称反对该技术，要求由普林斯顿大学校长哈罗德·夏普罗主持的独立专家小组在90天内对有关克隆人的国家政策给出建议，并向白宫汇报。

 课后练习

一、 判断下列句子中的非谓语动词短语是定语还是状语，并翻译该句子

1. Having watched Beijing Winter Olympics, I became interested in winter sports.

2. I teach students majoring in English.

3. I talked with an Englishman to improve English.

4. I found a way to improve English.

二、找出句中的状语，并翻译该句子

1. Oversleeping in spring I missed the dawn.

2. Being established at 30 and being no longer perplexed at 40, understanding the will of heaven at 50 and listening to everything without feeling unhappy at 60, a man seizes the time.

3. Having seen the vastness of an ocean, one will never content himself with a pool of water.

4. Having viewed the clouds over the Wu Mount, one will call nothing else a cloud.

5. With three men walking together, one of them must be qualified to be my teacher.

6. The going getting tough, the tough get going.

参考答案

一、判断下列句子中的非谓语动词短语是定语还是状语，并翻译该句子

1. [Having watched Beijing Winter Olympics], I became interested in winter sports.

   解析 现在分词短语having watched Beijing Winter Olympics前无名词，作状语。

   参考译文 看了北京冬奥会之后，我开始对冬季运动感兴趣。

2. I teach students (majoring in English).

   解析 现在分词短语majoring in English前有名词students，作其后置定语，意为"英语专业的学生"。

   参考译文 我教英语专业的学生。

3. I talked with an Englishman [to improve English].

   解析 动词不定式短语to improve English前有名词Englishman，若作其后置定语，意为"为了提高英语的英国人"，不合逻辑，故to improve English对Englishman不构成修饰作用，是状语，表目的。

   参考译文 我和一个英国人聊天以提高英语。

4. I found a way (to improve English).

   解析 动词不定式短语to improve English前有名词way，作其后置定语，意为"提高英语的方法"。

   参考译文 我找到了一个提高英语的方法。

二、找出句中的状语，并翻译该句子

1. [Oversleeping in spring] I missed the dawn.

   解析 现在分词短语oversleeping in spring前无名词，作状语。

   参考译文 春眠不觉晓。

2. [Being established at 30 and being no longer perplexed at 40, understanding the will of heaven at 50 and listening to everything without feeling unhappy at 60], a man seizes the time.

   解析 四个现在分词短语being established at 30、being no longer perplexed at 40、understanding the will of heaven at 50以及listening to everything without feeling unhappy at 60前均无名词，作状语。

   参考译文 三十而立，四十不惑，五十知天命，六十耳顺，把握时机。

3. [Having seen the vastness of an ocean], one will never content himself with a pool of water.

【解析】现在分词短语having seen the vastness of an ocean前无名词，作状语。

【参考译文】曾经沧海难为水。

4. [Having viewed the clouds over the Wu Mount], one will call nothing else a cloud.

【解析】现在分词短语having viewed the clouds over the Wu Mount前无名词，作状语。

【参考译文】除却巫山不是云。

5. [With three men walking together], one of them must be qualified to be my teacher.

【解析】with three men walking together是由名词加上其他成分等构成的一种独立结构，用于修饰整个句子。当句中出现现在分词短语或过去分词短语作状语时，一般来说其逻辑主语应与句子的主语一致。如果不一致，也就是说分词短语的逻辑主语并不是句子主语，而有自己单独的主语的话，必须用独立主格结构来表示，即在分词前面加上它自己的逻辑主语。这里的句子主语是one of them，而现在分词短语walking together的逻辑主语是three men，因此，需用with加上three men构成独立主格结构作状语。

【参考译文】三人行必有我师。

6. [The going getting tough], the tough get going.

【解析】the going getting tough是独立主格结构作状语，句子的主语是the tough，"the+形容词"表示一类人，这里指"坚强的人或勇者"，现在分词短语getting tough的逻辑主语是the going。

【参考译文】路漫漫其修远兮，吾将上下而求索。

"修饰集团"之状语应用

在全面系统地学习了状语的作用、形式、位置以及状语和定语的区别后，接下来我们看看状语在真题中的具体应用。

一、状语在翻译中的应用

我们先来看两个真题例句：

例 1 Arguing from the view that humans are different from animals in every relevant respect, extremists of this kind think that animals lie outside the area of moral choice. (1997年翻译)

解析 此句中有四个动词：arguing、are、think和lie。由于arguing是非谓语动词，are和lie在从句引导词that之后，故均排除，据此确定句子的谓语动词是think，句子主干为extremists think that...。现在分词短语arguing from the view that...前无名词，整体作原因状语，其中that引导的从句作view的同位语。介词短语of this kind作名词extremists的后置定语。think后的that引导宾语从句，其中介词短语outside the area of moral choice为地点状语。翻译时，that引导的同位语从句可与前面的现在分词短语arguing...合译为"认为……"，view省略不译。翻译that引导的宾语从句（that animals lie...）时，可译为汉语中的"无主"句，即"对待动物无须考虑道德问题"。

参考译文 这类极端主义者认为人与动物在各相关方面都不同，因此对待动物无须考虑道德问题。

例 2 We reach for them mindlessly, setting our brains on auto-pilot and relaxing into the unconscious comfort of familiar routine. (2009年阅读)

解析 此句中有三个动词：reach、setting和relaxing，由于setting和relaxing是非谓语动词，故均排除，据此确定句子的谓语动词是reach，句子主干是we reach for them。副词mindlessly修饰动词reach，作方式状语。由and并列的两个现在分词短语setting our brains...和relaxing into...前无名词，整体作伴随状语。其中，介词短语on auto-pilot若修饰名词brains，意为"自动导航的大脑"，语意不通，故应为状语。介词短语of familiar routine作名词comfort的后置定语。

参考译文 我们无意识间养成了它们（习惯），将我们的大脑设置为自动导航状态，放松地进入由熟悉的日常事物带来的不自觉的舒适状态。

二、状语在阅读中的应用

再来看状语的判定对于阅读理解解题的帮助。

例 1 In order to make the most of our focus and energy, we also need to embrace downtime, or as Newport suggests, "be lazy." "Idleness is not just a vacation, an indulgence or a vice; it is as indispensable to the brain as Vitamin D is to the body...idleness is, paradoxically, necessary to getting any work done," he argues.

(2018年英语二阅读)

According to Newport, idleness is _____.

[A] a desirable mental state for busy people

[B] a major contributor to physical health

[C] an effective way to save time and energy

[D] an essential factor in accomplishing any work

解析 本题问纽坡特对idleness（闲散）的看法，关键句可对应到原文引语的最后一句。副词paradoxically（自相矛盾地）不是对系动词is或表语形容词necessary的否定，而是作为插入语修饰整个句子，翻译时可前置于句首。Idleness is necessary to getting any work done对应选项D中的an essential factor in accomplishing any work，说明"闲散是完成任何工作所必需的"，因此D项正确。

参考译文 若要充分利用自身专注力和精力，我们还需要"拥抱闲暇时间"，或如纽坡特所说，"偷偷懒。"他认为，"闲散不仅仅是一个假期、一种放纵或一种恶习；它对大脑就像维生素D对身体一样，不可或缺……矛盾的是，闲散是完成任何工作所必需的。"

例 2 This rule is made by L.A. Unified, meant to address the difficulty for poor students in completing their homework. But the policy is unclear and contradictory. Certainly, no homework should be assigned that students cannot complete on their own or that they cannot do without expensive equipment. But if the district is essentially giving a pass to students who do not do their homework because of complicated family lives, it is going riskily close to the implication that standards need to be lowered for poor children.

(2012年英语二阅读)

L.A. Unified has made the rule about homework mainly because poor students _____.

[A] tend to have moderate expectations for their education

[B] have asked for a different educational standard

[C] may have problems finishing their homework

[D] have voiced their complaints about homework

解析 本题要求考生找到规定出台的原因，本段首句即提到相关信息。首句主干为This rule is made by L.A. Unified，逗号后的过去分词短语meant to address the difficulty...作目的状语，意为"旨在/目的是……"。由此可知，规定出台的原因是address the difficulty for poor students in completing their homework（解决贫困学生在完成作业方面的困难），其中介词短语for poor students作状语，介词短语in completing their homework作名词difficulty的后置定语。由此确定C项（可能很难完成作业）为本题答案。

参考译文 洛杉矶联合学区出台的这项规定旨在解决贫困学生在完成作业方面的困难。但是该政策阐述得不够清晰而且自相矛盾。当然，学生难以独立完成的作业，或者需要昂贵的设备才能完成的作业，都是不应该布置的。但是，如果学区真的要让那些由于家庭生活状况复杂而不能完成作业的学生通过的话，那么这极有可能在暗示：需要对贫困学生降低学习标准。

例 3 Shielded by third-party payers from the cost of our care, we demand everything that can possibly be done for us, even if it's useless. The most obvious example is late-stage cancer care. Physicians—frustrated by their inability to cure the disease and fearing loss of hope in the patient—too often offer aggressive treatment far beyond what is scientifically justified.

(2003年阅读)

The author uses the example of cancer patients to show that _____.

[A] medical resources are often wasted

[B] doctors are helpless against fatal diseases

[C] some treatments are too aggressive

[D] medical costs are becoming unaffordable

解析 题目问作者用癌症患者的例子来说明什么，根据行文逻辑，例子往往是用来论证前面阐述的观点，因此本段首句为关键解题句。该句中有四个动词：shielded、demand、can be done和is。由于shielded是过去分词，can be done和is分别位于从句引导词that和even if之后，故demand是主句的谓语动词。这是由一个带有定语从句的主句和一个状语从句构成的复合长句，主句主干是we demand everything。that引导定语从句，修饰everything；even if则引导让步状语从句。本句的阅读重点是抓出最主干的成分之后，了解分词短语作状语的用法。shielded by...our care是过去分词短语作状语，表原因，其逻辑主语是主句的主语we。shield...from...表示"保护……免遭……"，句中直译为"我们受到第三方支付者的保护，免于支付医疗费用"，可结合实际意义，理解为"医疗费用由第三方支付"。因此，D选项"医疗费用变得难以承受"表述错误。让步状语从句even if it's useless表明，人们往往要求医生用尽一切办法，即使这些方法不起作用，这是浪费医疗资源的表现。后面作者用癌症晚期患者为例，指出医生们往往采取一些极端大胆的乃至缺乏科学根据的治疗方法。因此我们可以推断出作者的意图，即不应该浪费医疗资源。正确选项为A。

参考译文 由于医疗费用由第三方支付，我们常常要求用尽所有可用的医疗手段，即使它们不会有任何作用。最明显的例子就是癌症晚期的治疗。医生由于不能治愈这种疾病而感到沮丧，同时又担心病人失去希望，因此常常采用极端大胆的乃至缺乏科学根据的治疗方法。

例 4 But with homework counting for no more than 10% of their grades, students can easily skip half their homework and see very little difference on their report cards.　(2012年英语二阅读)

　　One problem with the policy is that it may _____.

　　[A] result in students' indifference to their report cards

　　[B] undermine the authority of state tests

　　[C] restrict teachers' power in education

　　[D] discourage students from doing homework

解析 本句有三个动词：counting、can skip和see。counting是非谓语动词，可排除。由此可知本句的谓语部分是由and连接的两个并列谓语来充当。第一个谓语是can skip，副词easily作状语，宾语是half their homework。第二个谓语是see，宾语是very little difference。介词短语on their report cards表示范围，因此作状语。句首是由with引导的独立主格结构，作原因状语，因为counting的逻辑主语是homework，与主句主语students不一致。题目问该政策可能会导致什么问题，注意A选项的students' indifference to their report cards（学生对成绩单漠不关心）与原文的students...see little difference on their report cards（学生看到他们的成绩单差别不大）形式虽相近，但意思不同。原文是说学生可以轻易地逃掉一半的作业而成绩单却几乎不会有变化，也就是说，这一政策不鼓励学生做作业，正确答案是D选项。

参考译文 然而，由于家庭作业仅占学业成绩的10%，学生大可轻易地逃掉一半的作业，而成绩单却几乎不会有变化。

三、状语在写作中的应用

　　写作中如果能合理、正确地使用状语，不但能使英文表达更地道，而且还能使文章结构更加严谨、美观。我们常采用的方式是在句子主干前后加上一些短语作状语。注意，若用非谓语动词短语，则动词短语与主语的逻辑关系决定了短语的形式：如果句子的主语是动作的执行者，则用现在分词短语；如果句子的主语是动作的承受者，则用过去分词短语；表示目的、意图时，常用动词不定式短语；如果动作与句子的主语无关，有另外的执行者或承受者，则需使用独立主格结构。除此之外，形容词短语、介词短语也可以作状语。

我们可以通过下面的例子，看看如何将几个短语改写成状语，揉合进一句话。

例1 温故 review the past

知新 gain new insights

可以为师矣 one is fit to be a teacher

解析 one是句子的主语，是动词review和gain的动作执行者，因此将review...和gain...这两个动词短语改写为状语时，应采用现在分词形式。

参考组句 Reviewing the past and gaining new insights, one is fit to be a teacher. / Having reviewed the past and having gained new insights, one is fit to be a teacher.

例2 在就业压力下 under job-hunting pressure

寻求竞争力 seek for competitiveness

越来越多的大学生选择考研（postgraduate entrance exams）而非就业

(2013年英语二写作)

解析 "大学生"是句子的主语，是就业压力的承受者，因后者为名词，用一个介词短语即可表达大学生处于就业压力之下，因此利用介词under，组成介词短语作状语表明大学生所面临的情况。"寻求竞争力（seek for competitiveness）"表示目的，故采用动词不定式形式。

参考组句 Under job-hunting pressure, to seek for competitiveness, more and more college students choose postgraduate entrance exams instead of jobs.

例3 谭剑波在讲课 Tangible is teaching

看着学生 look at students

同时一个麦克风发出哔哔声 a microphone is beeping

解析 "谭剑波"是句子的主语，是动词"看着"的动作执行者，因此将look at students改写为状语时，采用现在分词形式。"发出"哔哔声的是"麦克风"，与句子主语"谭剑波"无关，因此需采用独立主格结构。

参考组句 Tangible is teaching, looking at students, with a microphone beeping.

例4 一只母鸡仰望着天空 A hen looks up into the sky

拿了张纸 hold a piece of paper

同时文字显示了承诺 the caption shows the promise

(1998年写作)

解析　"母鸡"是句子的主语,是动词"拿"的动作执行者,因此将hold a piece of paper改写为状语时,应采用现在分词形式。"显示"是"文字"发出的动作,与句子主语"母鸡"无关,因此需采用独立主格结构。

参考组句　A hen looks up into the sky, holding a piece of paper, with the caption showing the promise.

　　下面我们来看看如何通过状语的使用,写出作文的主体段落。

例1　首先,随着改革开放政策得以实施,中国文化逐渐吸引了越来越多来自世界各地的人。

解析　句子主干是"中国文化逐渐吸引了越来越多来自世界各地的人"。"随着改革开放政策得以实施"作伴随状语,用with结构翻译。

参考译文　First of all, with the implementation of the reform and opening-up policy, Chinese culture has gradually attracted more and more people from all over the world.

例2　此外,有些人将外国文化看作时尚,投入所有的精力和热情去体验其他文化。

解析　句子主干是"有些人将外国文化看作时尚",动词短语"投入所有精力和热情去……"可采用现在分词短语的形式,作状语。

参考译文　In addition, some people regard foreign culture as a fashion, devoting all their energy and passion to experiencing other cultures.

例3　最后,信息技术的兴起是另一个幕后推动力,传播不同文化的信息。

解析　句子主干是"信息技术的兴起是另一个幕后推动力",动词短语"传播不同文化的信息"可采用现在分词短语的形式,作状语。

参考译文　Finally, the rise of information technology is another push behind the scene, spreading information of different cultures.

 课后练习

一、标出句中的状语,并翻译该句子

1. Being interested in the relationship of language and thought, Whorf developed the idea that the structure of language determines the structure of habitual thought in a society.

(2004年阅读)

2. By offering on-trend items at dirt-cheap prices, these brands have hijacked fashion cycles, shaking an industry accustomed to a seasonal pace.

(2013年英语一阅读)

二、阅读理解

Homework has never been terribly popular with students and even many parents, but in recent years it has been particularly scorned. School districts across the country, most recently Los Angeles Unified, are revising their thinking on this educational ritual. Unfortunately, L.A. Unified has produced an inflexible policy which mandates that with the exception of some advanced courses, homework may no longer count for more than 10% of a student's academic grade.

(2012年英语二阅读)

It is implied in paragraph 1 that nowadays homework _____.

[A] is receiving more criticism　　　　[B] is gaining more preferences

[C] is no longer an educational ritual　　[D] is not required for advanced courses

三、将括号中单词的正确形式填入句中

1. _____ (broaden) your horizons and _____ (enrich) extracurricular experiences, the Students' Union will host an activity.

2. I am an undergraduate in a university, _____ (major) in Art.

3. With all the analyses _____ (consider), a conclusion can be made.

四、合并短语并翻译成句

1. (1) 一个可爱的美国女孩

   (2) 穿着传统中国服装

   (3) 同时微笑挂在脸上

(2003年写作)

2. (1) 农村的贫困人口数量

   (2) 正剧烈地下降

   (3) 同时城市的人口迅速上升

(2014年英语二写作)

一、标出句中的状语，并翻译该句子

1. [Being interested in the relationship of language and thought], Whorf developed the idea that the structure of language determines the structure of habitual thought [in a society].

   解析 此句中的状语有：现在分词短语being interested in...thought，表原因；介词短语in a society，表地点。其余三个介词短语of language and thought、of language和of habitual thought前都有名词，作它们的后置定语。主句的谓语动词是developed，是主谓宾结构，主干是Whorf developed the idea。

   参考译文 （由于）沃尔夫对语言和思维的关系很感兴趣，于是他逐渐形成了这样一种观点：语言的结构决定了一个社会中习惯性思维的结构。

2. [By offering on-trend items at dirt-cheap prices], these brands have hijacked fashion cycles, [shaking an industry accustomed to a seasonal pace].

   解析 此句中的状语有：介词短语by offering...prices，表方式；现在分词短语shaking an industry...，表结果。过去分词短语accustomed to a seasonal pace前有名词industry，作其后置定语。主句的谓语动词是have hijacked，是主谓宾结构，主干是these brands have hijacked fashion cycles。

   参考译文 这些品牌通过超低价售卖流行商品，控制了时尚周期，动摇了这个随季节而变化的行业。

二、阅读理解

   解析 题目询问"如今的家庭作业_____"，由nowadays和homework对应到第一段第一句话（Homework...in recent years...）。题干中的nowadays对应该句的in recent years，因此可进一步定位到该句的后半部分。该部分指出，最近几年来，家庭作业更是饱受诟病（in recent years it has been particularly scorned），副词particularly作状语，修饰动词scorn，表示程度。由此可知，A选项"遭受了更多批评"符合文意。

   参考译文 家庭作业从来就不太受学生欢迎，甚至很多家长也不喜欢，但最近几年来，家庭作业更是饱受诟病。全国各地的学区，最近一次是洛杉矶联合学区，纷纷改变了他们对这项教育惯例的看法。不幸的是，洛杉矶联合学区制定了一项硬性政策，该政策规定除了一些高级课程外，家庭作业在学生的学业成绩中所占的比例不得超过10%。

三、将括号中单词的正确形式填入句中

1. 答案 To broaden；(to) enrich

   解析 句子主干是the Students' Union will host an activity，为主谓宾结构，句子成分完整。因此，括号中的两个动词需采用非谓语动词的形式，根据句意，应该用动词不定式to broaden...和to enrich...作目的状语。注意，当两个或两个以上的不定式并列时，除去第一个不定式必须带to，后面的不定式标志to可以省略。

   参考译文 为了开阔你们的视野，丰富课外经历，学生会将举办一场活动。

2. 答案 majoring

   解析 句子主干是I am an undergraduate，为主系表结构，句子成分完整。因此，括号中的动词需采用非谓语动词的形式。由于主语I和动词major之间存在主谓（主动）关系，故应选择现在分词形式majoring，作伴随状语。

   参考译文 我是一名大学本科生，主修艺术。

3. 答案 considered

   解析 句子主干是a conclusion can be made，为主谓结构，句子成分完整。因此，括号中的动词需采用非谓语动词的形式。with引导独立主格结构，此结构中的主语analyses与动词consider之间存在逻辑上的动宾（被动）关系，且表示已完成的动作，故应选择过去分词形式considered。

   参考译文 综合所有分析，可以得出一个结论。

四、合并短语并翻译成句

1. 解析 本句中有两个动词："穿"和"挂"。"一个可爱的美国女孩"是主语，"挂"是"微笑"发出的动作，与主语"女孩"无关，因此需采用with结构作伴随状语，用with a smile on her face就可以表示"微笑挂在她的脸上"。

   参考译文 A lovely American girl wears the traditional Chinese costume, with a smile on her face.

2. 解析 本句中有两个动词："下降"和"上升"。"下降"是主语"农村的贫困人口数量"发出的动作，因此作谓语。"上升"是"城市的人口"发出的动作，与主语"农村的贫困人口数量"无关，因此需采用独立主格结构，用"with+名词+现在分词"形式表示。

   参考译文 The rural population in poverty is decreasing dramatically, with the urban population increasing rapidly.

"从句家族"之名词性从句精讲（上）

本节课我们将学习：

❶ 名词性从句的作用；❷ 名词性从句的形式；

❸ 名词性从句的种类。

在前面的学习中，我们掌握了简单句的"主干家族"和"修饰集团"。那么还有哪些方式能让句子变得更难、更长呢？很常见的一种方法是引入从句，在"主干"上生出新的"枝叶"，也就是将简单句变为复合句。复合句，又叫主从复合句，表达主要意思的就是主句，表达次要意思的就是从句。从句前一般都有连接词引导，作为从句的标志。从句对主句起到修饰限定、补充说明或在主句中充当成分的作用。按照它们在复合句中所起的作用，从句通常可以分成这三类：名词性从句、定语从句和状语从句。我们先来看看名词性从句的用法。

英国前首相丘吉尔有句名言是这样说的：

> It is no use doing what you like; you have got to like what you do.
> 不能爱哪行才干哪行，要干哪行爱哪行。

这句话除了给我们考研的同学精神上的激励外，它的语法结构也值得我们探讨。翻译时前一分句中的主语it去哪儿了？为什么不翻译成"它是没有用的……"呢？原因在于，这一分句使用了it作形式主语，而真正的主语是doing what you like这个动名词短语。为什么除了主干的两个谓语is和have got to like外，还有两个动词like和do呢？原因是这句话中有两个宾语从句，分别是what you like和what you do。宾语从句是什么？它是名词性从句的一种。下面我们将从名词性从句的作用、形式和种类这三个方面进行具体讲解。

一、名词性从句的作用

名词性从句指在复合句中所起的作用相当于名词的从句，是主干的延伸，可被看作"大号的名词"。由于在多数情况下，主语、宾语、表语、同位语这四种句子成分都由名词性词类充当，所以我们把这些作用相当于名词的从句统称为名词性从句，把充当主语、宾语、表语、同位语的从句分别称为主语从句、宾语从句、表语从句、同位语从句。名词性从句不是对整个句子的修饰，不是定语或状语，而是充当句子的核心成分。

二、名词性从句的形式

名词性从句由连接词（或关联词）引导。从句都要写成陈述句语序，即"引导词+主语+谓语"。陈述句、一般疑问句、特殊疑问句改写为名词性从句时有不同的变化形式，具体如下：

1 陈述句改写为名词性从句

陈述句变为名词性从句，语序不变，前面加上从句引导词that即可。

I love you. → **that** I love you （加that变成"大号的名词"）

a. It is the reason.	That I love you is the reason.
b. You know it.	You know that I love you.
c. The reason is it.	The reason is that I love you.
d. You know the fact (it).	You know the fact that I love you.

2 一般疑问句改写为名词性从句

一般疑问句，即通常用yes或no回答的疑问句，在改写为名词性从句时，用whether或if作从句引导词，表示"是否"，不可以省略。

Is it true? → **whether** it is true

a. It is the question.	Whether it is true is the question.
b. I want to know it.	I want to know whether it is true.
c. The question is it.	The question is whether it is true.
d. You need to answer the question (it).	You need to answer the question whether it is true.

❸ 特殊疑问句改写为名词性从句

特殊疑问句，即不是一般疑问句的问句，常见的特殊疑问词有what、when、where、who、which、why、how等，在改写为名词性从句时，就用原句的疑问词作引导词，后跟上"主语+动词原来的时态"。

Why is he late? → **why** he is late

a. It is unknown.	Why he is late is unknown.
b. I don't know it.	I don't know why he is late.
c. The question is it.	The question is why he is late.
d. I can't answer the question (it).	I can't answer the question why he is late.

三、名词性从句的种类

❶ 主语从句

在复合句中充当主语成分的句子叫主语从句。在判断从句类型时，如果发现引导词出现在句首，且和主句的谓语动词之间没有逗号，则此从句为主语从句。其基本结构为：

that/who/whose/what/where/when/whether/which/how...从句谓语...主句谓语...

注意，主语从句中的that只起引导作用，不作任何成分，但不能省略。为便于大家理解，我们来看两个改编过的真题句子里的主语从句。

例 1 That the money and attention come to science rather than go elsewhere is surely a good thing.

(2014年英语一阅读)

步骤	译文
1) 主干：...is surely a good thing. (主系表)	……当然是一件好事。
2) 从句：That the money and attention come to science rather than go elsewhere (主谓宾)	金钱和注意力来到科学而非其他地方 调整：财力和精力放在科学而非其他方面

步骤	译文
3) 整合	财力和精力放在科学而非其他方面当然是一件好事。
4) 应用	财力和精力放在某方面而非其他方面当然是一件好事。 That the money and attention come to sth. rather than go elsewhere is surely a good thing.
	a. 财力和精力放在全面发展而非其他方面当然是一件好事。 That the money and attention come to all-round development rather than go elsewhere is surely a good thing.
	b. 财力和精力放在读书而非其他方面当然是一件好事。 That the money and attention come to reading books rather than go elsewhere is surely a good thing.
	c. 财力和精力放在保护环境而非其他方面当然是一件好事。 That the money and attention come to protecting the environment rather than go elsewhere is surely a good thing.

例 2 Whether such a sense of fairness evolved independently in capuchins and humans, or whether it stems from the common ancestor is an unanswered question. (2005年阅读)

步骤	译文
1) 主干：...is an unanswered question. (主系表)	……是个未知的问题。
2) 从句：Whether such a sense of fairness evolved independently in capuchins and humans, whether it stems from the common ancestor (主谓+or+主谓宾)	这种公平意识是卷尾猴和人类各自独立进化而来的，还是来自共同的祖先
3) 整合	这种公平意识是卷尾猴和人类各自独立进化而来的，还是来自共同的祖先，是个未知的问题。

步骤	译文
4) 应用	是……，还是……，是个……问题。 Whether..., or whether...is a...question/problem/issue.
	a. 孩子是应该独立思考，还是应该合作，是个要解决的问题。 Whether children should think independently, or whether they should cooperate is a problem to be addressed.
	b. 大学生是应该创业，还是应该求职，是个热门问题。 Whether college students should start their own business, or whether they should find a job is a hot issue.

前面我们所讲的是常规的主语从句，通常位于主句的谓语动词之前。但由于主语从句往往较长，易使句子头重脚轻，英语中通常使用it来作形式主语，把真正的主语移到句子后边去，以使全句结构前后平衡。此时it并无实际意义，移到后面的that等引导的从句才是真正的主语，为主语从句。这和动词不定式短语作主语时，也常使用it作形式主语十分类似。来看下面这两个例句：

例 1 It is said that in England death is pressing.　　　　　　　　　　　　(2003年阅读)

步骤	译文
1) 主干：It is said... (主谓)	据说……
2) 从句：that in England death is pressing (主系表)	在英国，死亡是紧迫的
3) 整合	据说在英国，死亡是紧迫的。

例 2 It is now beyond dispute that the plates are moving.

步骤	译文
1) 主干：It is now beyond dispute (主系表)	这是无可争议的
2) 从句：that the plates are moving (主谓)	各大板块在移动
3) 整合	毫无疑问，各大板块在移动。

② 宾语从句

在复合句中充当宾语成分的句子叫宾语从句。及物动词、介词之后都可以带有宾语从句。需要注意的是，及物动词后的宾语从句中，连词that往往可以被省略。我们来看下面三个例句：

例 1 I think (that) hot hot hot is sensational.

步骤	译文
1) 主干：I think (that)... (主谓宾)	我觉得……
2) 从句：hot hot hot is sensational (主系表)	麻辣烫很火
3) 整合	我觉得麻辣烫很火！

例 2 Declaring that he was opposed to using this unusual animal husbandry technique to clone humans, he ordered that federal funds should not be used for such an experiment. (1999年阅读)

步骤	译文
1) 主干：he ordered that... (主谓宾)	他命令……
2) a. 宾语从句1：that he was opposed to using this unusual animal husbandry technique to clone humans (主谓宾)	他反对利用这种不同寻常的畜牧业技术去克隆人类
b. 宾语从句2：that federal funds should not be used for such an experiment (主谓)	联邦基金不应该用于这样一个实验
3) 整合	他宣称反对利用这种不同寻常的畜牧业技术去克隆人类，下令禁止使用联邦基金做这样的实验。

例 3 The boy is convinced that he can explore as many career paths as he likes.

(2018年英语二翻译)

步骤	译文
1) 主干：The boy is convinced that... (主谓宾)	这个男孩相信……
2) 从句：that he can explore as many career paths as he likes (主谓宾)	他能够随心所欲地探索多样化的职业道路

| 3) 整合 | 这个男孩相信，他能够随心所欲地探索多样化的职业道路。 |

注意，某些形容词或过去分词后也可以接宾语从句，这类形容词或过去分词有sure、glad、certain、pleased、happy、afraid、surprised、satisfied等，若其后的宾语从句由that引导，则连词that可省略。如：

I am not sure what I ought to do. 我不能确定我该做什么。

I'm afraid (that) you don't understand what I said. 恐怕你没领会我说的意思。

I'm surprised (that) I didn't see all that before. 我很惊讶，我以前没看到过。

Mother was very pleased (that) her daughter had passed the exams. 妈妈为她的女儿通过了考试而感到高兴。

 课后练习

找出下列句子中的名词性从句，判断从句类型，并翻译句子

1. What was important to her was her family.

2. He decided to see whether it got any better.

3. We've agreed on when and where we will go out for a picnic.

4. It is known to us all that the earth is round.

5. That people have failed to detect the massive changes is the notion.

6. It is noticed that people have failed to detect the massive changes.

📝 **参考答案**

找出下列句子中的名词性从句，判断从句类型，并翻译句子

1. What was important to her was her family.

   解析 本句中有两个动词was、was。第一个was前有从句引导词what，且位于句首，因此What was important to her是主语从句。

   参考译文 对她来说，重要的是她的家庭。

2. He decided to see whether it got any better.

   解析 本句中的动词有decided、to see和got。to see是非谓语动词，故排除。got位于从句引导词whether后，是从句的谓语动词，因此decided是主句的谓语动词，whether it got any better是非谓语动词to see后的宾语从句。

   参考译文 他决定看看情况是否变好了。

3. We've agreed on when and where we will go out for a picnic.

   解析 本句中的动词有have agreed和will go out。其中，will go out位于从句引导词when and where后，因此主句谓语动词为have agreed，when and where we will go out for a picnic是位于介词on之后的宾语从句。

   参考译文 我们在野餐的时间和地点上达成了一致意见。

4. It is known to us all that the earth is round.

   解析 本句中的动词有is known和is。其中is位于从句引导词that后，是从句的谓语动词，且it为形式主语，因此that the earth is round是主语从句。

   参考译文 众所周知，地球是圆的。

5. That people have failed to detect the massive changes is the notion.

   解析 本句中的动词有have failed、to detect和is。其中，have failed前有从句引导词that，to detect是非谓语动词，因此is是主句的谓语动词。主句主干为That...is the notion。that people have failed to...位于句首，因此是主语从句。

   参考译文 人们已经不能察觉出巨大的变化这一点是要表达的意思。

6. It is noticed that people have failed to detect the massive changes.

   解析 本句中的动词有is noticed、have failed和to detect。其中have failed位于从句引导词that后，to detect是非谓语动词，因此is noticed是主句的谓语动词，it为形式主语，因此that people have failed to...是主语从句。

   参考译文 人们已经不能察觉出巨大的变化这一点被注意到了。

"从句家族"之名词性从句精讲（下）

在上一课中我们介绍了名词性从句家族中的两名成员：主语从句和宾语从句。接下来我们来介绍另外两名成员：表语从句和同位语从句。

一、表语从句

在复合句中充当表语成分的句子叫表语从句，位于主句的连系词之后，从句的语序为陈述句语序。考研英语中表语从句常出现在be动词后，我们结合三个改编过的真题例句来看下：

例 1 The notion is that people have failed to detect the massive changes. (2006年阅读)

步骤	译文
1) 主干：The notion is... (主系表)	该观念在于……
2) 从句：that people have failed to detect the massive changes (主谓宾)	人们已经不能察觉巨大的变化
3) 整合	该观念在于人们已经不能察觉巨大的变化。

例 2 The wonderful thing about failure is that we decide how to look at it. (2020年英语二翻译)

步骤	译文
1) 主干：The wonderful thing about failure is that... (主系表)	失败的美妙之处在于……
2) 从句：that we decide how to look at it (主谓宾)	我们决定如何看待失败
3) 整合	失败的美妙之处在于由我们决定如何看待失败。
4) 应用	成功的美妙之处在于由我们决定如何取得成功。The wonderful thing about success is that we decide how to achieve it.

例 3 The reason is that both globalization and the information technology revolution advance.

(2013年英语二阅读)

步骤	译文
1) 主干：The reason is that... (主系表)	原因就是……
2) 从句：that both globalization and the information technology revolution advance (主谓)	全球化和信息技术革命都在发展
3) 整合	原因就是全球化和信息技术革命都在发展。

二、同位语从句

同位语从句是对名词的内容做具体、详细的说明。句子作某一名词或名词性短语的同位语时，一般位于其后。常在后面接同位语从句的名词一般是抽象名词，如：idea、fact、feeling、chance、possibility、phenomenon、proof、notion、claim等。同位语从句常用的引导词为that，仅起连接作用，无词义，不作从句成分，但不可省略。有时也用when、where等疑问词作引导词。

例 1 Is there any chance that Cardus's criticism will enjoy a revival?

(2010年英语一阅读)

步骤	译文
1) 主干：Is there any chance...? (主系表)	……有任何可能吗？
2) 从句：that Cardus's criticism will enjoy a revival (主谓宾)	卡尔德斯的评论再受欢迎
3) 整合	卡尔德斯的评论有可能再受欢迎吗？

例 2 It is the surest proof that the article does what is claimed for it, and that it represents good value.

(1995年阅读)

步骤	译文
1) 主干：It is the surest proof... (主系表)	这是最有力的证明：……

2) 从句：that the article does what is claimed for it, and that it represents good value (主谓宾+and+主谓宾)	这个产品做到了它所宣称的事情并且它代表了高价值 调整：这个产品确实名副其实并且价值很高
3) 整合	这是最有力的证明：这个产品确实名副其实并且价值很高。
4) 应用	这一现象是最有力的证明：财力和精力投入到读书而非其他一定是好事。 The phenomenon is the surest proof that it is surely a good thing that money and attention come to reading books rather than go elsewhere.

例 3 The loss of U.S. predominance in the world economy in the 1980s is manifested in the fact that the American auto industry had lost part of its domestic market. (2000年阅读)

步骤	译文
1) 主干：The loss of U.S. predominance in the world economy in the 1980s is manifested in the fact that... (主谓)	……这一事实表明，美国在20世纪80年代的世界经济中丧失了主导地位
2) 从句：that the American auto industry had lost part of its domestic market (主谓宾)	美国汽车产业已经失去国内部分市场
3) 整合	美国汽车产业已经失去国内部分市场这一事实表明，美国在20世纪80年代的世界经济中丧失了主导地位。

在全面认识名词性从句后，我们可以通过如下公式，快速定位并理解名词性从句：

名从公式

1. 抓谓语，定主干

2. 辨从句，分层次

* 辨别方法：先找that/wh-，向前看

(1) 无/主语为it→主从

(2) *v./prep.* →宾从

(3) be/系动词→表从

(4) 抽象 *n.* →同从

* 翻译方法：一般采用顺译法

(1) 形式主语/宾语可顺译，it省略不翻译或还原前置翻译

(2) 同位语从句可顺译，添加标点"冒号/破折号"或指代词"即/也就是"；
也可前置翻译

下面我们以几个改编过的真题句子为例，看看"名从公式"如何应用到考研真题中。

例 1 That the seas are being overfished has been known for years.
(2006年阅读)

解析 句子中有两个谓语动词：are being overfished和has been known，句子开头有that，往前看，没有主语，因此that引导主语从句。

参考译文 海洋生物被过度捕捞这个事实已经被知道很多年了。

例 2 Last year, the Transportation Security Administration (TSA) found that undercover investigators were able to sneak weapons past airport security.
(2017年英语一阅读)

解析 句子中有两个谓语动词：found和were able to，that前是动词found，因此that引导宾语从句。

参考译文 去年，美国运输安全管理局发现，卧底调查员能将武器偷运过机场安检。

例 3 One reason is that they cut across the insistence by top American universities.
(2011年英语一阅读)

解析 句子中有两个谓语动词：is和cut，that前是系动词is，因此that引导表语从句。

参考译文 原因之一是它们违背了美国一流大学的一贯主张。

 课后练习

找出下列句子中的名词性从句，判断从句类型，并翻译句子

1. Is there any possibility that you could pick me up at the airport?

2. What worries him is how he can finish so difficult a job within a week.

3. The notion is that people have failed to detect the massive changes.

4. The notion that people have failed to detect the massive changes is important.

📝 参考答案

找出下列句子中的名词性从句，判断从句类型，并翻译句子

1. Is there any possibility {that you could pick me up at the airport}?

   解析 本句中的动词有is和could pick up。其中，could pick up位于从句引导词that后，且that从句在名词possibility的后面，解释说明其内容，因此that you could pick me up at the airport是同位语从句。

   参考译文 你有可能去机场接我一下吗?

2. What worries him is how he can finish so difficult a job within a week.

   解析 本句中的动词有worries、is和can finish。其中，worries位于从句引导词what后，且从句位于句首，因此What worries him是主语从句；can finish在从句引导词how之后，且从句在系动词is之后，因此how he can finish so difficult a job within a week是表语从句。

   参考译文 让他担忧的是他如何能在一周内完成这么困难的工作。

3. The notion is that people have failed to detect the massive changes.

   解析 本句中的动词有is、have failed和to detect。其中，have failed前有从句引导词that，to detect是非谓语动词，因此is是主句的谓语动词。主句主干为：The notion is that...。that people have failed to...跟在系动词is后，因此是表语从句。

   参考译文 该观念在于人们已经不能察觉出巨大的变化。

4. The notion {that people have failed to detect the massive changes} is important.

   解析 本句中的动词有have failed、to detect和is。其中，have failed前有从句引导词that，to detect是非谓语动词，因此is是主句的谓语动词，主句主干为The notion is important。that people have failed to...跟在名词notion后，解释说明其具体内容，因此是同位语从句。

   参考译文 人们已经不能察觉出巨大的变化这一观念是重要的。

"从句家族"之名词性从句应用

前两节课我们学习了名词性从句的作用、形式和种类，下面我们来看看名词性从句在考研英语翻译、阅读和写作中的应用。

一、名词性从句在翻译中的应用

名词性从句在考研英语翻译板块中很常见。由于名词性从句大多可以直接按照原文的顺序翻译成相应的汉语译文，因此，在翻译中只要能将之辨认出来，就不需要太繁杂的技巧去调整语序。需要注意的是，由于汉语中没有同位语从句这个成分，因此同位语从句翻译时需要进行语序上的分析和调整。这点在后面章节具体句子中会给大家讲解，这里不再单独举例。下面来看两个经典真题例句：

例 1 What is harder to establish is whether the productivity revolution that businessmen assume they are presiding over is for real.

(1998年阅读)

步骤	译文
1) 主干：What...is whether... (主系表)	……是……
2) a. 主语从句：What is harder to establish (主系表) b. 表语从句：whether the productivity revolution is for real (主系表) c. 定语从句：that businessmen assume... (主谓宾) d. 宾语从句：they are presiding over (the productivity revolution) (主谓宾)	a. 什么是更难确定的 调整：更难确定的事情 b. 是否生产力革命是真的 调整：生产力革命是否真实存在 c. 商人认为…… d. 他们正在主导生产力革命
3) 整合	更难确定的事情是商人认为他们正在主导的生产力革命是否真实存在。

例 2 Whether the government should increase the financing power of pure science at the expense of technology or vice versa often depends on which issue is seen as the driving force.

(1994年翻译)

步骤	译文
1) 主干：...(often) depends on... (主谓宾)	……（经常）依靠/取决于……
2) a. 主语从句：Whether the government should increase the financing power of pure science at the expense of technology or vice versa (主谓宾) b. 宾语从句：which issue is seen as the driving force (主谓宾)	a. 是否政府应该增加纯科学的金融力量（财力）以技术为代价或反之亦然 调整：是否政府应该以技术为代价增加纯科学的财力或反之亦然 高光版调整：政府是应该增加纯科学还是技术的财力 b. 哪个问题被看作是驱动力
3) 整合	政府是应该增加纯科学还是技术的财力经常取决于哪个问题被看作是驱动力。
4) 应用	某人是应该A还是B，经常取决于哪个问题被看作sth.(重点) Whether sb. should A (do...) at the expense of B (doing...) or vice versa often depends on which issue is seen as sth.
	a. 大学生是应该求职还是创业经常取决于哪个问题被看作他们的首要关注。 Whether college students should hunt for jobs at the expense of starting their own business or vice versa often depends on which issue is seen as their top concern.
	b. 我们是应该坚持还是及时止损经常取决于哪个问题将有更好的结果。 Whether we should persist at the expense of stopping loss in time or vice versa often depends on which issue will get a better result.

81

二、名词性从句在阅读中的应用

名词性从句的考查在考研英语阅读中也是屡见不鲜，阅读题的答案往往隐藏在长难句里，若不能理清句子结构，划分出主句与从句，便很难正确理解句意并保证做题的正确率。下面我们以真题为例，进行实战演练。

例 1 The system also failed to regularly include women on juries until the mid-20th century. Although women first served on state juries in Utah in 1898, it was not until the 1940s that a majority of states made women eligible for jury duty. Even then several states automatically exempted women from jury duty unless they personally asked to have their names included on the jury list. This practice was justified by the claim that women were needed at home, and it kept juries unrepresentative of women through the 1960s.
(2010年英语二阅读)

Even in the 1960s, women were seldom on the jury list in some states because _____.

[A] they were automatically banned by state laws

[B] they fell far short of the required qualifications

[C] they were supposed to perform domestic duties

[D] they tended to evade public engagement

解析 由题干中的1960s定位到原文最后一句话。该句为and连接的并列句，共有三个动词：was justified、were needed和kept。其中，were needed前有从句引导词that，故排除，因此两个并列分句的谓语分别是was justified和kept。第一个分句中，主语为this practice，谓语为was justified，后接介宾结构by the claim作状语，解释justified的方式，其后接that引导的同位语从句，对claim的内容做进一步说明。第二个分句中，主语it指代前一个分句中的this practice，谓语为kept，宾语为juries，后接形容词短语unrepresentative...作宾语补足语，对juries的状态进行补充说明，句末的through the 1960s是时间状语，说明kept的时间背景。C选项"她们被认为要履行家庭责任"与同位语从句的内容相符，是正确选项。

参考译文 直到20世纪中期，该制度才定期将女性纳入陪审团成员中。虽然1898年犹他州首次出现了女性陪审员，但是一直到20世纪40年代，大多数州才赋予女性加入陪审团的资格。当时甚至还有几个州自动将女性除名，除非她们亲自要求将其名字加在陪审团名单上。他们为这种做法辩解，声称家里需要女性，这使得整个20世纪60年代陪审团都没有女性代表。

例 2 Education in any society is a mirror of that society. In that mirror we can see the strengths, the weaknesses, the hopes, the prejudices, and the central values of the culture itself.

The great interest in exceptional children shown in public education over the past three decades indicates the strong feeling in our society that all citizens, whatever their special conditions, deserve the opportunity to fully develop their capabilities. (1994年阅读)

The reason that the exceptional children receive so much concern in education is that _____.

[A] they are expected to be leaders of the society

[B] they might become a burden of the society

[C] they should fully develop their potentials

[D] disabled children deserve special consideration

解析 由题干中的exceptional children定位到第三句。该句有四个动词：shown、indicates、 deserve和to develop。其中shown、to develop为非谓语动词，deserve前有从句引导词that，故均排除。因此主句谓语动词为indicates，主句主干为The great interest...indicates the strong feeling...。其中，介词短语in exceptional children和过去分词短语shown in public education作名词interest的后置定语。介词短语over the past three decades作时间状语。位于抽象名词feeling之后的that引导同位语从句，解释说明其内容，两者之间的介词短语in our society作状语。同位语从句中，动词不定式短语to fully develop their capabilities作名词opportunity的后置定语。C选项的"他们应该充分发展自己的能力"与同位语从句描述的内容相符，是正确选项。

参考译文 在任何社会里面，教育都是这个社会的一面镜子。在这面镜子里，我们能看到优点、弱点、希望、偏见和文化本身的核心价值观。过去三十年间，公共教育中表现出的对于特殊儿童的巨大关注表明了我们的社会中存在一种强烈的感受：所有公民，无论他们的情况如何特殊，都应该获得全面发展其能力的机会。

三、名词性从句在写作中的应用

名词性从句在写作中经常被用到。将句中的名词性成分适当改写成名词性从句，可使句式更多样，增强文章语言的简洁性和语法使用的广度。以下是常用的几个包含由that引导的名词性从句的写作句型：

1 It is known to us all that...（主语从句）

众所周知，……

2 It is universally acknowledged that...（主语从句）

人们普遍认为……

3 There is no doubt/denying that...（同位语从句）

毫无疑问，……

4 There is no doubt in saying that...（宾语从句）

毫无疑问，……

5 The main point is that...（表语从句）

重点是……

6 It is indispensable and inevitable for me to mention that...（宾语从句）

我不可避免地要提及……

7 It can be seen that...is one of the most important factors in deciding...（主语从句）

看得出来，……在决定……方面是最重要的因素之一。

8 It is no exaggeration to say that...brings a great influence on...（宾语从句）

毫不夸张地说，……给……带来了巨大影响。

9 This picture epitomizes a common phenomenon that...（同位语从句）

该图集中体现了一种普遍现象：…………

下面是由一篇完整的作文拆分成的单句，我们试着将它们用名词性从句或it作形式主语的方式翻译出来。

a. 如今，五十岁以上的中国人很难去想象这样一个时代。

b. 大学生是应该创业还是应该求职，是个热门问题。

c. 原因就是竞争越来越激烈。

d. 首先，大学生是应该求职还是创业经常取决于他们首要关注哪个问题。

e. 此外，成功的美妙之处在于由我们决定如何取得成功。

f. 将财力和精力放在努力奋斗而非其他方面肯定会是一件好事.

g. 综上所述，我相信，我们能够随心所欲地探索多样化的职业道路。

参考译文

a. It is difficult for Chinese people above the age of 50 today to imagine such an era.（it作形式主语，不定式作真正的主语）

b. Whether college students should start their own business or whether they should hunt for jobs is a heated issue.（主语从句）

c. The reason is that the competition is increasingly fierce.（表语从句）

d. Firstly, whether college students should hunt for jobs at the expense of starting their own business or vice versa often depends on which issue is seen as their top concern.（主语从句；宾语从句）

e. Besides, the wonderful thing about success is that we decide how to achieve it.（表语从句）

f. It is surely a good thing that money and attention come to working hard rather than go elsewhere.（主语从句）

g. With all the analyses mentioned above, I am convinced that we can explore as many career paths as we like.（宾语从句）

 课后练习

一、找出下列句子中的名词性从句，判断从句类型，并翻译该句子

1. In its latest survey of CEO pay, *The Wall Street Journal* finds that "a substantial part" of executive pay is now tied to performance.　　　　　　　　(2019年英语一阅读)

2. Just how people think is still far too complex to be understood.　　　　　　(2019年英语一阅读)

3. It's a tremendous luxury that BuzzFeed doesn't have a legacy business.　　(2016年英语一阅读)

4. We cannot help considering whether or not we are forming the powers which will secure this ability.　　　　　　　　　　　　　　　　　　　　　　(2009年翻译)

5. What they found is that the human brain's roughly one hundred billion nerve cells are much more talented.　　　　　　　　　　　　　　　　　　　(2002年阅读)

二、阅读理解

The use of privacy law to curb the tech giants in this instance feels slightly maladapted. This practice does not address the real worry. It is not enough to say that the algorithms DeepMind develops will benefit patients and save lives. What matters is that they will belong to a private monopoly which developed them using public resources. If software promises to save lives on the scale that drugs now can, big data may be expected to behave as a big pharma has done. We are still at the beginning of this revolution and small choices now may turn out to have gigantic consequences later.

(2018年英语一阅读)

According to the last paragraph, the real worry arising from this deal is _____.

[A] the vicious rivalry among big pharmas

[B] the ineffective enforcement of privacy law

[C] the uncontrolled use of new software

[D] the monopoly of big data by tech giants

三、用名词性从句合并句子并翻译

1. (1) 他们所不知道的是
   (2) 身教胜于言传

(2016年英语一写作)

2. (1) 极少学生选择创业是一个事实
   (2) 这一事实显示出
   (3) 如今，在做开创性的工作方面，大学毕业生缺乏自信和勇气去面对困难

(2019年英语二写作)

◇ 参考答案

一、找出下列句子中的名词性从句，判断从句类型，并翻译该句子

1. In its latest survey of CEO pay, *The Wall Street Journal* finds that "a substantial part" of executive pay is now tied to performance.

   解析 谓语动词finds后面的that引导宾语从句。

   参考译文 《华尔街日报》在其最近的CEO薪酬调查中发现，如今高管薪酬的"很大一部分"与业绩挂钩。

2. Just how people think is still far too complex to be understood.

解析 how people think位于系动词is之前，因此是主语从句。too...to...意为"太……以至于……"。

参考译文 人们的思维方式仍然太复杂，以至于难以理解。

3. It's a tremendous luxury that BuzzFeed doesn't have a legacy business.

解析 句子开头的it无实际意义，作形式主语，that引导的从句是真正的主语，为主语从句。正常语序应为That BuzzFeed doesn't have a legacy business is a tremendous luxury.

参考译文 BuzzFeed公司没有传统业务，这实在是巨大的奢侈。

4. We cannot help considering whether or not we are forming the powers which will secure this ability.

解析 whether位于非谓语动词considering后，因此引导宾语从句。宾语从句中，which will secure this ability为定语从句，限定修饰名词powers。

参考译文 我们不禁会思考：我们是否正在形成使他们获得这种能力的力量。

5. What they found is that the human brain's roughly one hundred billion nerve cells are much more talented.

解析 what引导的从句位于系动词is之前，因此是主语从句；that引导的从句位于系动词is之后，因此是表语从句。

参考译文 他们发现，人脑中大约一千亿个神经细胞比以前想象的更有天赋。

二、阅读理解

解析 定位到原文第四句 "What matters is that they will belong to a private monopoly which developed them using public resources."。What matters是主语从句，that they will...是表语从句，其中，which又引导定语从句修饰先行词monopoly。该句意为"真正让人担忧的是科技公司开发的算法属于垄断企业，而这些垄断企业使用的又是公共资源。"D选项"科技巨头对于大数据的垄断"是原文这层意思的同义改写。故为正确选项。

参考译文 在这种情况下，利用隐私法来遏制科技巨头似乎不太合适，因为它不能解决问题的真正痛点。仅仅说深度思考公司开发的算法将使患者受益并挽救生命是不够的。关键是，这些算法将属于利用公共资源对其进行开发的私人垄断企业。如果软件能够像药品那样大规模地挽救病人的生命，届时大数据也有望发挥和大型医药公司一样的作用。我们尚处于这场改革的起步阶段，现在任何一个微小的决定都可能会对将来产生巨大影响。

三、用名词性从句合并句子并翻译

1. 解析 这句话看起来虽简短，实际应用两个从句来翻译："他们所不知道的"用what引导主语从句来表示，"是"用系动词is来表示，"身教胜于言传"用that引导表语从句来表示。

   参考译文 What they don't know is that example is better than precept.

2. 解析 "事实"的内容"极少学生选择创业"用the fact后接that引导的同位语从句来表示，动词"显示出"后跟宾语从句，翻译出(3)的内容。同位语从句和宾语从句的结合使用，可以让句子看起来更高级。

   参考译文 The fact that few students choose to start their own business shows that now university graduates lack the confidence and courage to face hardships in terms of doing pioneering work.

"从句家族"之定语从句精讲

本节课我们来学习：

❶ 定语从句的作用；❷ 定语从句的形式；

❸ 定语从句和同位语从句的区别；❹ 定语从句的省略。

作为三大从句之一，定语从句是英语学习的难点，也是考研英语考查的重点。如果能够在拆解长难句时快速准确地锁定定语从句，对于理清主从句的逻辑关系，弄清句意，可达到事半功倍的效果。下面我们来对定语从句进行具体讲解。

一、定语从句的作用

我们在前面讲过，定语指的是用来修饰、限定、说明名词或代词的品质与特征的成分。那么定语从句也是一样，是用来说明主句中某一名词或代词（有时也可说明整个主句或主句中的一部分）而起定语作用的句子，可将这个句子看作一个"大号的定语"。由于它在句中起到的作用相当于形容词，因此又被称为形容词性从句。

二、定语从句的形式

定语从句可被分为限制性定语从句和非限制性定语从句。区别两者最简单的方法就是看从句引导词前有没有逗号：若没有逗号，则是限制性定语从句；若有逗号，便是非限制性定语从句。限制性定语从句与先行词的关系非常密切，是先行词在意义上不可缺少的定语，起到说明先行词性质、身份、特征等状况的作用，从句引导词常用that和wh-等。而非限制性定语从句仅起补充说明作用，即使缺少也不会影响全句的理解，往往不用that作从句引导词，只用wh-或as。来看下面的例子：

例 1 I respect the lady (that/who is a teacher).（限制性定语从句）

例 2 I love my mother, (who is a teacher).（非限制性定语从句）

引导词that/which/as的区别：

引导词	先行词	作用
that	人/物	特指，限定
which	物	泛指，限定/非限定，不能放在句首
as	人/物	限定/非限定，位置可前后

三、定语从句与同位语从句的区别

由于定语从句和同位语从句都是跟在一个名词后的从句，都可用that引导，因此非常容易混淆。我们可以根据以下几点主要区别来区分：

1 从定义上来看，定语从句用来说明名词的性质、特征、身份等，翻译时可前置先行词翻译，译为"……的"，若太长，则可顺译，添加指代词"这/那"；而同位语从句用以解释名词的具体内容，翻译时可前置抽象名词翻译或顺译，添加标点"冒号/破折号"或指代词"即/也就是"等。

2 引导定语从句的that是关系代词，在从句中充当成分，作宾语和表语时可省略；而引导同位语从句的that不充当任何成分，但不能省略。

3 同位语从句的先行词数量有限，如fact、news、idea、truth、hope、suggestion、question、problem、doubt、fear、thought、promise、order、belief、concern等包含某种信息的抽象名词；而定语从句的先行词则无限制。

从句	形式	翻译方法
同位语从句	抽象n.+引导词（在从句中不作成分；去掉that完整）	a. 前置抽象名词翻译 b. 顺译，添加标点"冒号/破折号"或指代词"即/也就是"
定语从句	n.+引导词（在从句中作成分；去掉that不完整）	a. 前置先行词翻译 b. 顺译，添加指代词"这/那"

请依据以上表格，判断以下画线的句子是同位语从句还是定语从句：

1 The reason that I explain is true.

2 The reason that I feel so tired is true.

3 I don't know the reason why I feel so tired.

正确答案：

1 定语从句

参考译文 我解释的原因是真的。

2 同位语从句

参考译文 我筋疲力尽这一原因是真的。

3 定语从句

参考译文 我不知道我筋疲力尽的原因。

下面我们来分析两个改编过的真题例句，进一步掌握定语从句的特点并灵活应用：

例 1 These leaders are living proof that we can manage the health problems that come naturally with age.

(2003年阅读)

步骤	译文
1) 主干：These leaders are living proof (主系表)	这些领导者是活生生的证据
2) a. 同位语从句：that we can manage the health problems (主谓宾) b. 定语从句：that come naturally with age (主谓)	a. 我们能处理好健康问题 b. 伴随年龄自然而来的
3) 整合	这些领导者是活生生的证据：我们能处理好伴随年龄自然而来的健康问题。
4) 应用	这些成功人士（名人、知识分子、企业家等）/ 这些事（现象、行为、结果等）是活生生的证据：人们能…… These celebrities/ knowledgeable elites/ entrepreneurs/ phenomena/ behaviors/ consequences are living proof that people can do sth. ...
	a. 这些团队是活生生的证据：他们能应对伴随工作和生活自然而来的挑战。 (2008年写作) These teams are living proof that they can deal with challenges that come naturally with work and life.

	b. 这些精英是活生生的证据：他们很乐观/他们有乐观的态度，这会对个人的学业、职业前景及社会的进步产生至关重要的影响。
	(2012年英语一写作)
	These elites are living proof that they are optimistic/they have optimism, which exerts fundamental and instrumental influence on personal academic performance, career prospects and social progress.

例 2 Social science is the branch of intellectual enquiry which seeks to study humans and their endeavors in the reasoned, orderly, systematic and dispassioned manner that natural scientists use for the study of natural phenomena.

(2003年翻译)

步骤	译文
1) 主干：Social science is the branch of intellectual enquiry (主系表)	社会科学是知识探索的分支
2) a. 定语从句：which seeks to study humans and their endeavors in the reasoned, orderly, systematic and dispassioned manner (主谓宾) b. 定语从句：that natural scientists use for the study of natural phenomena (主谓宾)	a. 这个分支（社会科学）寻求研究人类及其努力通过理性的、有序的、系统的和冷静的方式 调整：这个分支（社会科学）力图通过理性、有序、系统和客观的方式研究人类及其行为 b. 自然科学家使用（这种方式）为了自然现象的研究 调整：自然科学家使用这种方式来研究自然现象
3) 整合	社会科学是知识探索的分支，这个分支（社会科学）力图通过理性、有序、系统和客观的方式研究人类及其行为，自然科学家使用这种方式来研究自然现象。

四、定语从句的省略

从句引导词that在定语从句中作宾语、表语时可以省略。划分从句时我们可使用"名名"法则，即如果句中出现了"*n.(pron.)+n.(pron.)+v.*"的结构，则后一个"*n.(pron.)+v.*"是省略了从句引导词的定语从句。以下面两个句子为例：

例 1 That is the way it is. = That is the way (that) it is.

解析 主句的谓语是第一个is，主语是that，表语是the way。it is是省略了引导词that的定语从句，修饰先行词the way。一旦识别不出来省略，可能翻译时句子结构就会出现混乱。怎么识别定语从句中是否省略了从句引导词呢？我们可以用"名名"法则。the way it is符合"名名"法则，所以it is前省略了从句引导词that，that在从句中作表语。

参考译文 道法自然。

例 2 I never feel overwhelmed with the amount of information my brain absorbs.

(2013年英语二翻译)

解析 主句的谓语是feel overwhelmed with，主语是I，宾语是the amount of information。my brain absorbs是省略了从句引导词that的定语从句，修饰information。information my brain absorbs符合"名名"法则，所以第一个名词information的后面省略了从句引导词that，它在从句中作宾语。这个定语从句比较短，可以前置到先行词information前面翻译，加个"的"即可。

参考译文 我从不会因大脑吸收的信息量过大而感到难以承受。

在全面认识定语从句后，我们可以通过如下公式，快速定位并理解定语从句：

定从公式

1. 抓谓语，定主干

2. 辨从句，分层次（that/wh- 往前看）

* 翻译方法：还原至先行词前翻译；成分复杂或非限定时则顺译，需添加指代词

下面我们以几个真题句子为例，看看定从公式如何帮助我们找出定语从句，理清句子结构，正确翻译句子。

例 1 It is difficult to the point of impossibility for the average reader under the age of forty to imagine a time when high-quality arts criticism could be found in most big-city newspapers.

(2010年英语一阅读)

[解析] 除去非谓语动词to imagine外，该句有两个动词：is和could be found。其中，could be found位于从句引导词when之后，是从句的谓语动词。因此主句的谓语动词是is，主干为It is difficult...to imagine a time...，其中，it为形式主语，而真正的主语是不定式结构to imagine a time...。介词短语to the point of impossibility是理解的难点，它是一个程度状语，说明了difficult的程度。介词短语for the average reader说明了imagine这个动作的逻辑主语，其后的介词短语under the age of forty作后置定语，修饰reader。句尾有一个when引导的定语从句，修饰名词time。

[参考译文] 有一个时代是40岁以下的普通读者难以想象的，在那个时代，大多数大城市的报纸都有高质量的艺术评论。

例2 In a world where average is officially over, there are many things we need to do to support employment, but nothing would be more important than passing some kind of G.I. Bill for the 21st century that ensures that every American has access to post-high school education.

(2013年英语二阅读)

[解析] 除去非谓语动词to do、to support和passing外，该句有六个动词：is、are、need、would be、ensures、has。其中，is、ensures和has前分别由从句引导词where、that和that引导，可排除。many things we need符合"名名"法则，we need是一个省略引导词的定语从句，因此need可排除。只剩下动词are和would be作主句的谓语动词。主句是由but连接的并列句，即there are many things...but nothing would be more important than...。句子开头的in a world where...中，where引导定语从句修饰先行词world，整个结构作句子的地点状语。前一个分句中，由省略引导词that的定语从句修饰many things，不定式短语to support employment作目的状语。后一个分句中，句子主干为nothing would be more important，为主系表结构，紧跟than引导的比较状语，在这个比较状语中，that ensures that...为定语从句，限定说明some kind of G.I. Bill，确保的内容为句子，因此紧跟的that every American has access to post-high school education为ensures的宾语从句。

[参考译文] 在一个平庸已无法立足的世界里，我们需要做很多事情以扶持就业，但对21世纪来讲，最重要的事情莫过于出台《退伍军人权利法案》之类的法案，以确保每个美国人都有机会接受高中后的教育。

注：G.I. Bill，全称为G.I. Bill of Rights，正式名称为Servicemen's Readjustment Act of 1944《退伍军人权利法案》，这一法案规定为退役军人提供极低利率的住房贷款，更重要的是给退伍军人提供申请大学或者进入职业学校的便利，以帮助他们重新融入社会。

例 3 Changes in the economy that lead to fewer job opportunities for youth and rising unemployment in general make gainful employment increasingly difficult to obtain.

(2004年完形)

解析 除去非谓语动词rising、to obtain外，该句有两个动词：lead to、make。其中，lead to在从句引导词that后，是定语从句的谓语动词，该定语从句修饰名词changes，介词短语in the economy也修饰changes，作它的后置定语。因此主句主语为changes，谓语为make，宾语为gainful employment，形容词短语increasingly difficult to obtain为宾语补足语。

参考译文 经济的变化导致年轻人就业机会减少，且失业率普遍上升，这导致赚钱的工作越来越难找。

例 4 The rise of a commercial culture in which happiness is not just an ideal but an ideology almost exactly tracks the emergence of mass media. (2006年阅读)

解析 该句有两个动词：is、tracks。其中，is在从句引导词which后，是从句的谓语动词。因此主句的谓语动词是tracks，主干是The rise of a commercial culture...tracks the emergence of...。主句主语为The rise，后置定语of a commercial culture对其进行说明，宾语是the emergence，介词短语of mass media作其后置定语。in which引导的定语从句修饰a commercial culture。翻译时，由于定语从句较长，前置到先行词前容易导致表意不清，此时可重复先行词，进行拆分翻译。

参考译文 商业文化的兴起与大众传媒的出现几乎完全同步，在这种文化中，快乐不仅仅是一种理想，还是一种意识形态。

例 5 An important factor in a market-oriented economy is the mechanism by which consumer demands can be expressed and responded to. (1994年阅读)

解析 该句有三个动词：is、can be expressed和responded to，但can be expressed和responded to在从句引导词by which后，故主句的谓语动词为is。本句的主干是An important factor...is the mechanism，两个并列的动词can be expressed和responded to是由by which引导的定语从句中的谓语动词，定语从句修饰名词mechanism。

参考译文 在市场导向型经济中，一个重要的因素就是使消费者的需求得以表达和反馈的机制。

一、在空格中填入正确的定语从句引导词

1. On display here are various fantasy elements _____ reference, at some basic level, seems to be the natural world. (2013年英语一翻译)

2. But there are few places _____ clients have more grounds for complaint than America. (2014年英语一阅读)

3. The other reason _____ costs are so high is the restrictive guild-like ownership structure of the business. (2014年英语一阅读)

4. Cline introduced her ideal, a Brooklyn woman named Sarah Kate Beaumont, _____ since 2008 has made all of her own clothes—and beautifully. (2013年英语一阅读)

5. The parliament also agreed to ban websites _____ "incite excessive thinness" by promoting extreme dieting. (2016年英语一阅读)

二、判断下列that引导的从句是定语从句还是同位语从句，并翻译全句

1. Many leading American universities want their undergraduates to have a grounding in the basic canon of ideas that every educated person should possess. (2011年英语一阅读)

2. However, the conventional view that education should be one of the very highest priorities for promoting rapid economic development in poor countries is wrong. (2009年阅读)

3. Many Americans regard the jury system as a concrete expression of crucial democratic values, including the principle that defendants are entitled to trial by their peers. (2010年英语二阅读)

4. It identifies the undertreatment of pain and the aggressive use of "ineffectual and forced medical procedures" that may prolong and even dishonor the period of dying as the twin problems of end-of-life care. (2002年阅读)

一、在空格中填入正确的定语从句引导词

1. 答案 whose

   解析 先行词为elements，从句主语为reference，两者为所属关系，即"元素的参照物"，因此关系代词用whose，相当于elements'，在定语从句中作名词reference的定语。

   参考译文 在这里展示的是各种各样奇幻的元素，其参照依据，就某种基本层面来说，似乎都是大自然。

2. 答案 where / in which

   解析 由于空格前有表地点的名词few places，因此用关系副词where来引导定语从句，修饰限定few places。where在从句中作地点状语，相当于in which。

   参考译文 但是，几乎没有哪个国家的委托人要比美国的委托人更有理由抱怨。

3. 答案 why / for which

   解析 先行词为reason，且空格后的从句costs are so high不缺成分，因此用关系副词why来引导，限定说明reason，why可以用for which代替。

   参考译文 （法律服务）费用如此之高的另一个原因是该行业类似于行会性质的限制性所有权结构。

4. 答案 who

   解析 句子主干为Cline introduced her ideal。a Brooklyn woman named Sarah Kate Beaumont是her ideal的同位语，为了进一步介绍Sarah Kate Beaumont的信息，用who引导的非限制性定语从句进行补充，who在从句中充当主语。

   参考译文 克莱因介绍了她的偶像，一位名叫萨拉·凯特·博蒙特的布鲁克林女性，她从2008年起就亲手制作自己所有的衣服——而且做得很漂亮。

5. 答案 that/which

   解析 先行词为websites，指物，应用that或which引导定语从句，对其起修饰限定作用，that或which代替先行词在从句中作主语。

   参考译文 议会还同意取缔那些通过宣扬极端节食来"煽动过度瘦身"的网站。

二、判断下列that引导的从句是定语从句还是同位语从句，并翻译全句

1. 答案 定语从句

   解析 此句中ideas为抽象名词，后既可以接同位语从句，也可以接定语从句，that引导的从句中，possess为及物动词，可知从句缺宾语成分，需由that充当。由于同位语从

句的引导词不在从句中充当成分，因此此句为定语从句。

参考译文 许多美国的一流大学都希望他们的本科生对每个受过教育的人都应该掌握的基本思想准则有基本的认识。

2. 答案 同位语从句

解析 此句中view为抽象名词，后既可以接同位语从句，也可以接定语从句。that引导的从句不缺成分，因此that引导的是同位语从句，解释名词view的具体内容。

参考译文 然而，认为教育应该是促进贫穷国家经济快速发展的重中之重的传统观点是错误的。

3. 答案 同位语从句

解析 that引导的从句不缺成分，因此principle之后为that引导的同位语从句，对principle的内容进一步解释说明。

参考译文 许多美国人把陪审团制度看作是重要的民主价值观的具体体现，包括被告有权由同龄人进行审判这一原则。

4. 答案 定语从句

解析 that引导定语从句，修饰先行词procedures，从句缺主语成分，需由that充当。

参考译文 它指出了医院临终关怀护理中存在的两个问题：对病痛处理不足和不顾后果地使用"无效而强制性的医疗手段"，这些手段可能会延长死亡期，甚至会使病人在此期间饱受屈辱。

"从句家族"之定语从句应用

上一节课我们学习了定语从句的作用与形式、定语从句和同位语从句的区别、定语从句的省略，接下来我们来看看定语从句在真题中的应用。

一、定语从句在翻译中的应用

根据我们在上一节课所学的内容，翻译以下句子。

例1 His analysis should therefore end any self-contentedness among those who may believe that the global position of English is so stable that the young generations of the United Kingdom do not need additional language capabilities.

(2017年英语一翻译)

解析 句中的动词有should end、may believe、is和do not need。其中，may believe、is和do not need前分别有从句引导词who、that和that，因此主句的谓语动词是should end，主句主干为His analysis should therefore end any self-contentedness，是主谓宾结构。who引导定语从句who may believe...，修饰代词those。第一个that引导动词believe后的宾语从句the global position of English is so stable...，同时，该宾语从句中嵌套了so...that...结构，so...that引导结果状语从句。

参考译文 对于那些可能会认为英语的国际地位十分稳固，以至于英国的年轻人不需要掌握其他语言的人而言，他的分析可能因此会让这些人不再自满。

例2 Fundamentally, the USPS is in a historic squeeze between technological change that has permanently decreased demand for its bread-and-butter product, first-class mail, and a regulatory structure that denies management the flexibility to adjust its operations to the new reality.

(2018年英语一阅读)

解析 句中的动词有is、has decreased、denies和to adjust。其中，has decreased和denies前都有从句引导词that，to adjust为非谓语动词，故均排除。因此主句的谓语动词为is，主句主干为the USPS is in a historic squeeze，squeeze一般作动词，表示"挤压"，这里用作名词，需要意译，理解成"处于两者夹击的境地"。第一个that引导定语从句that has permanently decreased demand...，修饰change。bread-and-butter是习语，本意是"面包和黄油"，西方饮食中主食经常是抹了黄油的面包，属于"日常必需品"，因此该复合形容词代指"基本的"。第二个that引导定语从句that denies management the flexibility to...，修饰regulatory structure，that代替先行词在从句中作主语，从句是主谓双宾结构。其中，management作间接宾语，意为"管理层"，to adjust its operations作直接宾语the flexibility的后置定语。to the new reality作状语。还有一个难点在于介词结构between...and...，由于两个定语从句的存在，让这个结构间隔较大，划分时注意提炼关键词，理清楚是"……和……之间"，翻译时可重新断句。

参考译文 从根本上来说，美国邮政署正处于技术变革和监管架构的历史性双重夹击中。前者已经永久性地降低了对其基本产品（即一类邮件）的需求，而后者使管理层缺乏灵活性，无法根据新的现状灵活调整其经营活动。

例 3 Realistic optimists are those who make the best of things that happen, but not those who believe everything happens for the best. (2014年英语二翻译)

解析 句中的动词有are、make、happen、believe和happens。其中make、happen、believe前面均有从句引导词，故均排除。happens所在的从句前省略了引导词that，故也排除。因此主句的谓语动词是are，主句主干为Realistic optimists are those...but not those...，由but并列两个平行结构。第一个并列结构里，who引导的定语从句who make the best of things that happen修饰代词those，其中that happen也为定语从句，修饰things。第二个并列结构里，who引导的定语从句who believe everything happens for the best修饰代词those。其中，everything happens for the best是动词believe后省略了从句引导词that的宾语从句。翻译时，若译成"现实的乐观主义者是……的人，而不是……的人"则不够精练，可将"是……的人"删去，直接转译为动作。

参考译文 现实的乐观主义者会尽力从发生的事情中获得最大收获，而不是相信一切都是最好的安排。

例 4 Finally, there is perspective, which involves acknowledging that in the grand scheme of life, one lecture really doesn't matter. (2014年英语二翻译)

解析 除去从句引导词which和that后面的谓语动词involves、doesn't matter以及非谓语动词acknowledging，可知主句的谓语动词为is，主句主干为there is perspective，其后是关系代词which引导的非限制性定语从句，从句的主语是which，谓语是involves，宾语是动名词短语acknowledging...；其中嵌套that引导的名词性从句，作acknowledging的宾语，即宾语从句。

参考译文 最后是"观念态度"，要认识到在辽阔的人生道路上，一次讲座真的没什么大不了的。

例 5 After about 40 minutes of shopping, most people stop struggling to be rationally selective, and instead begin shopping emotionally—which is the point at which we accumulate the 50 percent of stuff in our cart that we never intended buying.　　　　　(2016年英语二翻译)

解析 除去非谓语动词struggling、shopping和buying，再去掉从句谓语动词is、accumulate和intended，确定主句的谓语动词为stop和begin，由连词and并列连接。主句主干为most people stop struggling to be selective, and begin shopping。句首的After about 40 minutes of shopping是时间状语，翻译时置于句首。破折号后面有which、at which和that引导的三个从句，which引导的which is the point...是定语从句，修饰前面的主句，翻译时顺译。point有"理由"之意，翻译时译为"理由/原因"均可。其中嵌套的另一个定语从句at which we accumulate...修饰point。最后一个从句引导词that引导的也是定语从句，修饰先行词stuff，而非cart，介词短语in our cart是stuff的后置定语。

参考译文 大多数人购物约40分钟之后就不会再费心地去理性选购了，而是开始冲动购物——而这时，我们的购物车里已经装了一半原本不打算买的东西了。

例 6 Social science is the branch of intellectual enquiry which seeks to study humans and their endeavors in the same reasoned, orderly, systematic and dispassioned manner that natural scientists use for the study of natural phenomena.　　　　　(2003年翻译)

解析 除去非谓语动词to study和从句谓语动词seeks、use，确定主句的谓语动词为is。主句主干是Social science is the branch of intellectual enquiry，是主系表结构。which引导定语从句，修饰先行词the branch of intellectual enquiry。从句中，介词短语in...manner作方式状语，其后接that引导的定语从句，修饰限定manner。翻译时定语从句要层层剥开，与主句分开译。方式状语in...manner在从句中可前置翻译。intellectual enquiry直译为"智力的询问"，意译为"知识探索"。endeavor作名词时意为"努力；尝试"，此处意译为"行为，活动"。in the same manner意为"以同样的方式"。

参考译文 社会科学是知识探索的一个分支，它力图像自然科学家研究自然现象那样，通过理性、有序、系统和客观的方式去研究人类及其行为。

二、定语从句在阅读中的应用

例 1 The southern states would not have signed the Constitution without protections for the "peculiar institution," which is including a clause that counted a slave as three fifths of a man for purposes of congressional representation.　　　　　(2018年英语一翻译)

判断正误：Slavery was regarded as a peculiar institution.

解析 除去从句谓语动词is including和counted，可确定主句的谓语动词为would not have signed。主句主干是The southern states would not have signed the Constitution，使用了虚拟语气，would not have signed表达的是与过去事实相反的假设。介词短语without protections for the "peculiar institution" 表达了隐含的条件，相当于if they had not had protections for the "peculiar institution"。which引导非限制性定语从句，对peculiar institution作进一步的解释，指出该特殊制度中包含一条规定，即在选举国会代表时，一个奴隶可算作五分之三个公民。其中that引导的定语从句修饰clause。题干Slavery was regarded as a peculiar institution意为"奴隶制度被视为一种特殊制度"，是利用原文提到的peculiar institution设置的错误表述，原文中该词组加有引号，代表特定含义，不能按照一般的字面意思进行解读。因此该表述错误。

参考译文 如果不保护他们的"特殊制度"，南方各州是不会签署联邦宪法的。"特殊制度"中有一条规定：在选举国会代表时，一个奴隶可算作五分之三个公民。

例 2 I also know that people in Japan and Sweden that spend far less on medical care have achieved longer, healthier lives than we have. (2003年阅读)

　　Japan and Sweden are funding their medical care _____.

　　[A] more flexibly　　　　　　　　[B] more extravagantly

　　[C] more cautiously　　　　　　　 [D] more reasonably

解析 本句中有四个动词：know、spend、have achieved和have。由于spend、have achieved和have分别在从句引导词that、that和than之后，都排除，因此主句的谓语动词为know，主句主干是I also know that...。that people in...we have是know后的宾语从句，从句的谓语动词是have achieved，其中又嵌套that引导的定语从句that spend far less on medical care，修饰名词短语people in Japan and Sweden。than we have是比较状语从句，从句谓语承前省略了achieved。题目问"日本人和瑞典人在医疗上花销……"，由定语从句that spend far less on medical care（在医疗开销上花费极少）可以看出，D选项"更合理"正确。

参考译文 我也深知在医疗开销少得多的日本和瑞典，其人民却更长寿，而且更健康。

例 3 Washington, who had begun to believe that all men were created equal after observing the bravery of the black soldiers during the Revolutionary War, overcame the strong opposition of his relatives to grant his slaves their freedom in his will. (2008年阅读)

　　Washington's decision to free slaves originated from his _____.

　　[A] moral considerations　　　　　 [B] military experience

　　[C] financial conditions　　　　　　[D] political stand

解析 除去非谓语动词to believe、observing和to grant，再除去从句谓语动词had begun和were created，可知主句的谓语动词为overcame，主句主干为Washington overcame the strong opposition...。who引导的非限制性定语从句修饰Washington，其中that引导的从句作believe的宾语，after...the Revolutionary War为时间状语。句尾的不定式to grant...结构作谓语overcame的目的状语。题目对应原文句子主干，问华盛顿释放奴隶这一决定是源于什么，也就是问原因，答案在非限制性定语从句里，从句中的after observing the bravery of the black soldiers during the Revolutionary War对应B选项"军事经历"。

参考译文 在目睹了黑人士兵在美国独立战争中的英勇表现之后，华盛顿开始相信人人生而平等。于是他不顾亲属们的强烈反对，立下遗嘱赋予他的奴隶自由。

三、定语从句在写作中的应用

定语从句是写作的常用句型，可以起到各种修饰和限定说明的作用，增强句子的紧凑感。但是很多同学对其用法一直模糊不清，常常出现很多错用现象。好的定语从句能体现出考生对句子较为精确的掌控能力，让我们看看如何将定语从句正确地应用在写作中。请完成下列练习：

例1 There are several research centers in China _____ COVID-19 is being studied.

[A] which　　　　[B] where　　　　[C] when　　　　[D] what

解析 从句_____ COVID-19 is being studied修饰的是名词短语research centers，表地点，从句引导词用where，故选择B项。

参考译文 在中国有多个研究新冠病毒的研究中心。

例2 I will never forget the day _____ you went away, _____ exerts a great influence on my life.

[A] when, which　　[B] that, which　　[C] which, that　　[D] when, that

解析 第一个从句_____ you went away修饰的是名词the day，表具体的日期，因此从句引导词用when。第二个从句_____ exerts a great influence on my life在逗号后，是非限制性定语从句，只能用which作从句引导词，故选择A项。

参考译文 我永远不会忘记你离开的那天，这对我的人生影响重大。

例3 _____ can be seen from the comparison of these figures, the principle involves the active participation of the patient in the modification of his condition. (1999年选择题)

[A] As　　　　　[B] What　　　　[C] That　　　　[D] It

解析 该句的主句为the principle involves the active participation...，前面的成分中也有谓语can be seen，所以要写成从句。由于有逗号隔开，只能作非限制性定语从句，由as引导，故选择A项。

参考译文 正如比较这些数据所见，这一原理需要病人的积极参与，才能使病人状况有所改善。

定语从句还可以应用于图片描述类作文中，例如：

1. as或which引导的非限制性定语从句

a. China is great, as/which is known to us all.

b. As is known to us all, China is great.

（注：as位置可前可后；which只能置后。as有"正如"之意。）

c. As is graphically depicted by the cartoon, a couple is boating, throwing rubbish into the lake.

d. As is logically demonstrated by the graph, there is a series of figures disclosing the changes in the number of sth., which is thought-provoking and deserves a further analysis.

2. that引导的限制性定语从句，that在从句中充当宾语时可以省略。例如：

例1 This picture epitomizes a common phenomenon that is known to us all.

解析 that引导定语从句，修饰先行词phenomenon。在从句中，that代替先行词phenomenon充当主语。

例2 The most important factor (that) we have to consider is how to save water.

解析 that引导定语从句，代替先行词factor在从句里充当consider的宾语，此时that可以省略。

课后练习

一、找出下列句子中的定语从句，并翻译句子

1. Most of the women she interviewed—but only a few of the men—gave lack of communication as the reason for their divorces.

(2010年英语二阅读)

2. Dickens worked in a shoe-polish factory, where the other working boys mocked him as "the young gentleman".

(2017年英语一新题型)

3. California has asked the justices to refrain from a sweeping ruling, particularly one that upsets the old assumptions that authorities may search through the possessions of suspects at the time of their arrest.

(2015年英语一阅读)

二、阅读理解

Grade inflation—the gradual increase in average GPAs (grade-point averages) over the past few decades—is often considered a product of a consumer era in higher education, in which students are treated like customers to be pleased. But another, related force—a policy often buried deep in course catalogs called "grade forgiveness"—is helping raise GPAs.

(2019年英语一阅读)

What is commonly regarded as the cause of grade inflation?

[A] The change of course catalogs.　　　　[B] Students' indifference to GPAs.

[C] Colleges' neglect of GPAs.　　　　　[D] The influence of consumer culture.

三、使用恰当的从句合并句子

1. (1) 我们需要一个拥有恰当资金来源的教育系统

    (2) 这个教育系统能保证

    (3) 所有儿童都能获得恰当的教育

2. (1) 自信是最重要的品质

    (2) 任何想要取得成功的人都要拥有这种品质

3. (1) 对于父母来说

    (2) 父母含辛茹苦把我们养育大

    (3) 这些礼物远远不是他们所期望的

◇ 参考答案

一、找出下列句子中的定语从句，并翻译句子

1. Most of the women (she interviewed)—but only a few of the men—gave lack of communication as the reason for their divorces.

    解析 she interviewed为省略关系代词的定语从句，修饰先行词women。

    参考译文 她采访的大多数女性——但只有少数男性——将缺乏沟通视为他们离婚的原因。

2. Dickens worked in a shoe-polish factory, (where the other working boys mocked him as "the young gentleman").

解析 where引导非限制性定语从句，修饰先行词factory。

参考译文 狄更斯在一家鞋油厂做工，在那里做工的其他男孩嘲笑他是"小绅士"。

3. California has asked the justices to refrain from a sweeping ruling, particularly one (that upsets the old assumptions that authorities may search through the possessions of suspects at the time of their arrest).

解析 此句中，代词one是前半句中a sweeping ruling的同位语。其后再跟一个定语从句修饰one。难点在于定语从句中又嵌套一个that引导的同位语从句，解释说明assumptions。

参考译文 加利福尼亚州已经要求法官们避免做出一刀切的裁决，尤其是这一裁决可能会颠覆人们一直以来的观念，即在逮捕嫌犯时当局可以搜查他/她的财物。

二、阅读理解

解析 第一句就解释了grade inflation "成绩膨胀"的含义，破折号之间的内容作插入语，指出grade inflation指的是过去的几十年中GPA（平均学分绩点）的逐渐升高。原文的is...a product of...是题干中cause的同义改写，指出"成绩膨胀"现象产生的原因是高校教育进入消费时代（consumer era），in which引导定语从句，补充说明学生们在这样的时代中被视为需要被取悦的消费者，所以教授们倾向于给学生打高分。因此D选项"消费文化的影响"为正确选项。

参考译文 "成绩膨胀"指的是在过去的几十年中，学生的平均学分绩点逐渐上升的现象。这一现象通常被认为是高等教育消费时代的产物，学生被视为需要被取悦的顾客。然而，还有另外一种相关力量也助长了这一现象。这种力量不易察觉，隐藏在学校的课程设置里，我们把它称为"成绩宽容"政策。

三、使用恰当的从句合并句子

1. We need a properly funded education system, which can guarantee that all children can receive proper education.

2. Self-confidence is the most essential quality that anyone who wants to achieve success should possess.

3. To the parents, who overcame a lot of difficulties to bring us up, those presents are far away from what they really hope for.

"从句家族"之状语从句精讲

本节课我们来学习：

❶ 状语从句的作用；❷ 状语从句的形式；

❸ 状语从句的省略。

我们前面讲到，除定语以外的修饰语都是状语。状语可修饰动词、形容词、副词或整个句子，用来说明地点、时间、原因、目的、结果、条件、方向、程度、方式和伴随状况等。状语与定语类似，常见的形式除了"……地"这样的副词之外，还可以由短语（如现在分词短语、过去分词短语、动词不定式短语、形容词短语、介词短语等）以及句子（状语从句）充当。本节中的状语不再是某个词或短语，而是一个句子，这个句子从属于它的主句，故得名"状语从句"。我们可将状语从句视为一个"大号的状语"。

一、状语从句的作用

状语从句用来说明主句的地点、时间、原因、目的、结果、条件、方向、程度、方式和伴随状况等。

二、状语从句的形式

状语从句的构成并不复杂，它由一个逻辑连接词和一个句子构成，其中的逻辑连接词按照不同的功能分类，如下表所示：

类型	逻辑连接词
时间状语从句	when/while（当……时）；as（随着；当……时）；before/after（在……之前/之后）；till/until（直到……）；since（自从）；as soon as / hardly...when...（一……就……）
地点状语从句	where（在哪里）；wherever（在任何地方）
原因状语从句	because/since/as/for（因为）
目的状语从句	so that / in order that（以便，为了）

结果状语从句	so that（以至于）； so/such...that...（如此……以至于……）
条件状语从句	If（如果）；unless（除非）；as/so long as / only if（只要）
让步状语从句	although/though/while/as（虽然；即使）
比较状语从句	as...as...（和……一样）；than（比……）
方式状语从句	as / just as（正如）；as if / as though（好像；仿佛）；(in) the way that（以……方式）

三、状语从句的省略

状语从句中，若主从句主语一致时，可省略从句主语。从句谓语动词根据与主语之间形成主动关系还是被动关系相应转化为现在分词V-ing（主动关系）或过去分词V-ed（被动关系）。具体改写规则如下：

- 主动关系：从句引导词+ sb. do/does/did..., sb.+... = 从属连词+V-ing..., sb.+...
- 被动关系：从句引导词+ sb. be done..., sb.+... = 从属连词+V-ed... , sb.+...

我们来看两个例子：

例 1 When I fell in love with you, I... = When falling in love with you, I...

当我爱上你时，我……

例 2 If properly handled, it may become a driving force. (2000年阅读)

= If it is properly handled, it may become a driving force.

如果（被）适当处理了，它也许会变成一种驱动力。

接着来做两个练习加以巩固：

1 翻译句子：如果被不当处理了，成功也许会变成一种阻碍。

_____

答案 If not properly handled, success may become a handicap.

2 选择填空：_____ with the other two groups, the satisfaction level is the highest.

(2012年英语二写作)

[A] When compared　　　　　　[B] Compare

[C] While comparing　　　　　　[D] Comparing

答案 A选项正确。When compared... = when the satisfaction level is compared...当与其他两组对比的时候，满意度是最高的。

在全面认识状语从句后，我们可以通过如下公式快速定位并理解状语从句：

状从公式

1. 抓谓语，定主干

2. 辨从句，分层次（9类）

* 翻译点拨

时间、地点、原因、方式等状语从句一般前置于主句之前。

若句子过长，也可以顺译，如"因为……"译为"之所以……是因为……"

下面我们以几个真题句子为例，看看"状从公式"如何帮助我们找出状语从句，理清句子结构，进而正确翻译句子。

例 1 Although mental health is the cure-all for living our lives, it is perfectly ordinary as you will see that it has been there to direct you through all your difficult decisions. (2016年英语一翻译)

解析 该句主干为it is perfectly ordinary，可译为"这再寻常不过了"；该句有一个让步状语从句和原因状语从句，分别由although和as引导。此外，在as引导的原因状语从句中，还包含一个that引导的宾语从句，作see的宾语。

参考译文 尽管心理健康是我们生活中的万能药，但它其实非常普通，因为你会发现在你难以做决定时，是它一直指引着你。

例 2 As families move away from their stable community, their friends of many years, their extended family relationships, the informal flow of information is cut off. (1995年翻译)

解析 该句主干为the informal flow...is cut off，谓语动词是is cut off（被切断）；句首是as引导的时间状语从句，该从句为主谓宾结构，谓语move away from意为"远离"，其宾语由三个名词短语（their..., their..., their...）充当。

参考译文 随着家庭成员远离稳定的社区、多年的朋友和大家庭的种种关系，非正式的信息交流就被切断了。

例 3 If you see an article consistently advertised, it is the surest proof I know that the article does what is claimed for it. (1995年阅读)

解析 该句主干为it is the surest proof，其中I know为省略了引导词that的定语从句，修饰proof，之后的that引导同位语从句，用于补充说明proof（证据）的内容，可译为"证明该产品确实如它所宣称的那样"；句首是由if引导的条件状语从句，其中过去分词advertised不是后置定语，而是宾语补足语，与宾语an article之间存在被动关系，译为"如果你看到一件产品一直在做广告"。

参考译文 如果你看到一件产品一直在做广告，那这就是我知道的最强有力的证据，证明该产品确实如它所宣称的那样。

例 4 If he had played last season, however, he would have been one of 42. (2008年阅读)

解析 该句结构较简单，包含一个由if引导的条件状语从句。however是插入语，if引导的条件状语从句用了过去完成时，主句用了would have done，表示对过去事实进行虚拟，与过去实际情况相反。事实上他没有参加上个赛季的比赛，他也不是四十二人之一。

参考译文 如果他参加了上个赛季的比赛，就可能会是四十二人之一了。

例 5 While producing large quantities of CO_2, these computers emit a great deal of heat, so the centres need to be well air-conditioned, which uses even more energy. (2011年英语二翻译)

解析 该句中的so作并列连词，连接前后两个分句。前一分句主干为these computers emit a great deal of heat，译为"这些计算机释放大量的热量"；While producing large quantities of CO_2是一个省略了主语的时间状语从句，其主语同后面主句的主语一致，都是these computers，且produce与主语是主动关系，所以用现在分词形式producing，此句译为"在排放大量的二氧化碳的同时"。后一分句主干为the centres need to be well air-conditioned，其中air-conditioned作动词，表示"提供空调环境（设备）"，主干译为"这些数据中心需要良好的空调设备"；which uses even more energy是定语从句，译为"这（么做）甚至会消耗更多的能源"。

参考译文 在排放大量的二氧化碳的同时，这些计算机还释放大量的热量，所以这些数据中心需要良好的空调设备，而这甚至会消耗更多的能源。

找出句子中的状语从句，判断从句类型，并翻译句子

1. As the cost to everyone else has become clearer, politicians have begun to clamp down.

    (2012年英语一阅读)

2. Overwhelming majorities of both groups said they believe it is harder for young people today to get started in life than it was for earlier generations. (2016年英语二阅读)

3. We're doing these things because we know they help people stay off benefits and help those on benefits get into work faster. (2014年英语一阅读)

4. In December 2010 America's Federal Trade Commission proposed adding a "do not track" option to internet browsers, so that users could tell advertisers that they did not want to be followed. (2013年英语一阅读)

5. Beethoven's music tends to move from chaos to order as if order were an imperative of human existence. (2014年英语一翻译)

找出句子中的状语从句，判断从句类型，并翻译句子

1. [As the cost to everyone else has become clearer], politicians have begun to clamp down.

   解析 句子出现两个动词has become和have begun，且无并列连词，为主从复合句。as引导时间状语从句，表示随着某件事的发生，另一件事也在进行中。

   参考译文 随着其他所有人付出的代价越来越明显，政客们已经开始镇压。

2. Overwhelming majorities of both groups said they believe it is harder for young people today to get started in life [than it was for earlier generations].

   解析 主句谓语动词said之后为省略引导词that的宾语从句；宾语从句谓语动词believe后为省略引导词that的又一个宾语从句，在该宾语从句中，than引导比较状语从句。

   参考译文 两个群体中的绝大多数人都表示，他们认为如今年轻人的人生起步比前几代人更难。

3. We're doing these things [because we know they help people stay off benefits and help those on benefits get into work faster].

   解析 主句为We're doing these things，连词because引导原因状语从句，该从句中又包含了省略引导词that的宾语从句they help...and help...，作know的宾语。

   参考译文 我们做这些事是因为我们知道，这样做有助于人们远离（失业）救济金，并帮助那些领取救济金的人尽快找到工作。

4. In December 2010 America's Federal Trade Commission proposed adding a "do not track" option to internet browsers, [so that users could tell advertisers that they did not want to be followed].

   解析 主句谓语为proposed，宾语为动名词短语adding a "do not track" option to internet browsers。so that引导目的状语从句，该从句为主谓双宾结构，从句谓语为could tell，advertisers作间接宾语，由that引导的宾语从句that they did not want to be followed作直接宾语。

   参考译文 2010年12月，美国联邦贸易委员会提议在网络浏览器中增加一个"拒绝跟踪"选项，这样用户就可以告诉广告商，自己不希望被追踪。

5. Beethoven's music tends to move from chaos to order [as if order were an imperative of human existence].

   解析 as if引导方式状语从句，表示"好像，仿佛"。当方式状语从句表示的情况是主观的想象或夸大性的比喻时，通常用虚拟语气。

   参考译文 贝多芬的音乐往往从混乱走向有序，仿佛秩序对人类的生存至关重要。

Day 14 "从句家族" 之状语从句应用

上一节课我们讲到了状语从句的形式和在句中定位状语从句的方法，下面我们来看看状语从句在考研英语完形、阅读和写作中的应用。

一、状语从句在完形中的应用

例 1 In fact, these commutes were reportedly more enjoyable compared with those without communication, which makes absolute sense, _____ human beings thrive off of social connections.

(2015年英语二完形)

　　[A] unless　　　　　　　　　　　[B] since

　　[C] if　　　　　　　　　　　　　[D] whereas

解析 通过四个选项可知，该题考查主从句之间的逻辑关系。主句主干为these commutes were reportedly more enjoyable，意为"据报道称，这种（有交流的）通勤更令人愉快"；过去分词短语compared with those without communication作比较状语，which makes absolute sense是非限制性定语从句，which代指前面的句子，意为"这是完全有道理的"；human beings thrive off of social connections作从句，意为"人类正是通过各种社会联系才能不断发展"，thrive off of表示"依托……而发展"。由主从句的逻辑关系可知，从句是主句的原因，故选择B项。

参考译文 实际上据报道称，同全程无交流的通勤相比，这种（有交流的）通勤更令人愉快。这是完全有道理的，因为人类正是通过各种社会联系才能够不断发展。

例 2 Some people with a high BMI are in fact extremely fit, _____ others with a low BMI may be in poor shape.

(2014年英语二完形)

　　[A] so　　　　　　　　　　　　[B] while

　　[C] since　　　　　　　　　　　[D] unless

解析 前句意为"有些人体脂率很高，实际上身材却非常好"，后句意为"有些人体脂率低，但身材可能不尽如人意"，前后两句的内容构成对比，四个选项中只有while有对比的含义，故选择B项。

参考译文 有些人体脂率很高，实际上身材却非常好，而有些人体脂率低，但身材却不尽如人意。

例 3 _____ this doesn't prove that happiness causes firms to invest more or to take a longer-term view, the authors believe it at least hints at that possibility. (2016年英语二完形)

[A] After　　　　[B] Until　　　　[C] While　　　　[D] Since

解析 前句主干为this doesn't prove that...，其中that引导宾语从句，前句意为"这并不能证明幸福会促使公司投入更多资金或把眼光放长远"。后句主干为the authors believe ...，believe后为省略了引导词that的宾语从句，后句意为"作者们认为这至少暗示了这种可能性"。由此可知，前后句之间存在让步转折关系，前句为让步状语从句，由while引导，故选择C项。

参考译文 尽管这并不能证明幸福会促使公司投入更多资金或把眼光放长远，但作者们认为这至少暗示了这种可能性。

例 4 Still, _____ every parent would like to be patient, this is no easy task. (2020年英语二完形)

[A] while　　　　[B] because　　　　[C] unless　　　　[D] once

解析 主句为this is no easy task，意为"这并非易事"，从句为every parent would like to be patient，意为"每个家长都希望有耐心"。由此可知，从句是主句的让步，由while引导，故选择A项。

参考译文 尽管每个家长都希望有耐心，但这并非易事。

例 5 As was discussed before, it was not _____ the 19th century that the newspaper became the dominant pre-electronic medium. (2002年完形)

[A] after　　　　[B] by　　　　[C] during　　　　[D] until

解析 该句考查not...until..."直到……才……"的用法。这里是not...until...句型与强调句句型it was...that...连用。

参考译文 正如之前所讨论的，直到19世纪，报纸才成为电子化之前的主流媒体。

例 6 In the United States, new cases seemed to fade _____ warmer weather arrived.

(2010年英语二完形)

[A] as　　　　[B] if　　　　[C] unless　　　　[D] until

解析 该句主干为new cases seemed to fade，意为"新的病例似乎逐渐减少"，从句为warmer weather arrived，意为"天气变暖"。主从句之间为时间上的伴随关系，由as引导，故正确答案为A项。

参考译文 在美国，随着天气变暖，新的病例似乎逐渐减少了。

二、状语从句在阅读中的应用

例 1 We are even farther removed from the unfocused newspaper reviews published in England between the turn of the 20th century and the eve of World War II, at a time when newsprint was dirt-cheap and stylish arts criticism was considered an ornament to the publications in which it appeared. In those far-off days, it was taken for granted that the critics of major papers would write in detail and at length about the events they covered. Theirs was a serious business, and even those reviewers who wore their learning lightly, like George Bernard Shaw and Ernest Newman, could be trusted to know what they were about. These men believed in journalism as a calling, and were proud to be published in the daily press. "So few authors have brains enough or literary gift enough to keep their own end up in journalism," Newman wrote, "that I am tempted to define 'journalism' as 'a term of contempt applied by writers who are not read to writers who are'."

(2010年英语一阅读)

Which of the following would Shaw and Newman most probably agree on?

[A] It is writers' duty to fulfill journalistic goals.

[B] It is contemptible for writers to be journalists.

[C] Writers are likely to be tempted into journalism.

[D] Not all writers are capable of journalistic writing.

解析 由题干人名Shaw and Newman可定位到原文该段第三至五句。解决该题的关键在于理解 "So few authors...to writers who are." 这句话。该句被连词so...that... （如此……以至于……）切分为两部分。前半句理解为 "很少有作家有足够的头脑或文学天赋（literary gift）来坚持从事新闻写作"，其中keep their own end up是个习语，意为 "做好自己分内的事情"，在这里可以结合上下文理解为 "坚持从事新闻写作"，因此，选项D与原文对应，即并非所有作家都有能力从事新闻写作；后半句是前半句的结果，理解为 "所以我不禁想把 '新闻写作' 定义为 '无人问津的作家对那些当红作家的轻蔑之词'"，其中a term of contempt意为 "一个轻蔑之词（指前面的journalism）"，applied by writers作后置定语，修饰a term of contempt，意为 "被作家所使用的"，who are not read是定语从句，修饰writers，直译为 "那些不被（读者）阅读的作家"，可理解为 "无人问津的作家"，to writers who are是前面动词applied的补语，即the term（"journalism"）is applied by the writers who are not read to writers who are (read)，意为 "无人问津的作家对那些当红作家的轻蔑之词"。原文并未提及作家有义务实现新闻工作目标，故A项无中生有。原文末句提到新闻写作被定义为 "轻蔑之词"，并不是说作家成为记者是卑鄙的，故B项也无中生有。原文末句引号内还提到"我不禁想把'新闻写作'定义为……"，并没有提及作家会禁不住从事新闻业，C选项属于主观臆断。

参考译文 20世纪初期至第二次世界大战前夕，英国的报刊评论包罗万象，与现在也是截然不同的。那时，新闻用纸十分便宜，而时尚的艺术评论被当成刊登它的出版物的装饰。在那个遥远的年代，各大报纸的评论家们对所报道的事件进行详尽的评述是理所当然的事情。他们所从事的是严肃的工作，即使像萧伯纳和欧内斯特·纽曼那样从不夸耀自己学问的评论家们，人们也相信他们知道自己在做什么。这些人相信新闻写作是一种职业使命，并为自己的文章能在日报上刊登而感到自豪。"很少有作者有足够的头脑或者文学天赋来坚持从事新闻写作。"纽曼写道，"所以我不禁想把'新闻写作'定义为'那些无人问津的作家对当红作家的轻蔑之词'"。

例 2 George Annas, chair of the health law department at Boston University, maintains that, as long as a doctor prescribes a drug for a legitimate medical purpose, the doctor has done nothing illegal even if the patient uses the drug to hasten death.

(2002年翻译)

　　Which of the following statements is true according to the text?

　　[A] Doctors will be held guilty if they risk their patients' death.

　　[B] Modern medicine has assisted terminally ill patients in painless recovery.

　　[C] The Court ruled that high-dosage pain-relieving medication can be prescribed.

　　[D] A doctor's medication is no longer justified by his intentions.

解析 该题中的D项为强干扰项，解题关键在于理解以上这句话。该句主干为George Annas maintains...，意为"乔治·安娜斯坚持认为……"，that...to hasten death为宾语从句。在宾语从句中，主干为the doctor has done nothing illegal，意为"医生没有做任何非法的事情"；as long as... medical purpose为条件状语从句，意为"只要医生开药（prescribe a drug）是出于合理的（legitimate）医疗目的"；even if...to hasten death为让步状语从句，意为"即使病人服用该药加速了死亡（to hasten death）"。D项的意思是"医生的用药不再（no longer）以他的意图为依据"，刚好与原文内容相反，故排除。A项"如果医生让病人冒死亡的风险，那么医生就有罪"也与原文内容相反，故排除。B项"现代医学已经帮助病人无痛康复"说法过于绝对，显然也排除。C项"法院裁定可以开大剂量的止痛药"与原文意思相符，故为正确答案。

参考译文 波士顿大学健康法律系主任乔治·安娜斯坚持认为，只要医生开药是出于合理的医疗目的，那么即使病人服用该药加速了死亡，医生的行为也没有违法。

三、状语从句在写作中的应用

状语从句也是写作中的常用句型，和状语一样可以起到各种修饰的作用，增强论证的逻辑性，扩展句子的长度。下面我们来学习如何将状语以及状语从句正确地应用到写作中。

① 用于作文开头

在作文开头使用状语，尤其是with独立主格结构表伴随，是非常经典的开头写法。

1 With society developing rapidly 随着社会的快速发展

2 With economy growing 随着经济的增长

3 With the living standard improving 随着生活水平的提高

4 With all the analyses considered 把所有的分析考虑在内

5 With globalization/industrialization/commercialization/urbanization speeding up/accelerating
随着全球化/工业化/商业化/城市化进程的加快

6 With people's living pace/rhythm quickening 随着人们生活节奏的加快

② 插入语

在陈述观点时，使用状语作插入语可以起到附加解释、说明、表达说话者的态度和看法等作用。插入语应放在be动词后、行为动词前，位于助动词和行为动词之间。

1 The girl is, as a matter of fact, beautiful. 事实上，这个女孩很漂亮。

2 The policy, directly or indirectly, influences us. 政策直接或间接地影响着我们。

3 Information technology can, in one way or another, change our life. 信息技术可以以这样或那样的方式改变我们的生活。

③ 写从句

时间、地点、原因、目的、结果、条件、让步、方式、比较等状语从句在写作中的灵活使用都可以让句子变长，使行文逻辑更加严密。下面我们来看几个例子：

1 As a consequence, pollution becomes so grave that quite a few measures should be taken to relieve the current situation.（结果状语从句）
结果，污染变得如此严重，以至于我们应该采取多种措施来缓解目前的状况。

2 Pursuing stars blindly will waste a lot of time although they may work hard or be really handsome.（让步状语从句）
盲目追星会浪费很多时间，尽管那些明星可能很努力或很帅气。

3 The more quickly authorities take measures, the more effectively the issue will be resolved.
（比较状语从句）

当局越快采取措施，这个问题就会得到越有效的解决。

　　下面我们通过以下几个例句来看看如何用添加状语以及状语从句的方式来扩写或翻译句子，使其成为写作佳句。

例1 Information technology changes our life.

扩写 With society developing rapidly, there is no doubt in saying that information technology can, directly or indirectly, bring a great influence on our life due to the fact that information technology improves the efficiency of our work and study.

参考译文 随着社会的快速发展，毫无疑问，信息技术可以直接或间接地给我们的生活带来巨大影响，因为信息技术提高了我们工作和学习的效率。

例2 Ecological balance plays an indispensable role.

扩写 With industrialization accelerating, it is universally acknowledged that ecological balance, in one way or another, plays an indispensable and essential role in our social development and economic growth in that, without ecological balance, we would never build a harmonious society.

参考译文 随着工业化进程的加快，人们普遍认识到生态平衡以这样或那样的方式在我们的社会发展和经济增长中发挥着不可缺少的重要作用，因为没有生态平衡，就没有和谐社会。

例3 China is great.

扩写 It is universally acknowledged that China is, as a matter of fact, very great owing to the truth that China has a history of more than 5,000 years.

参考译文 事实上，中国的伟大是举世公认的，因为中国有五千多年的历史。

例4 随着社会的发展和城市化的加快，环境污染变得日趋严重，这发人深思且值得进一步分析。

参考译文 With society developing and urbanization accelerating, environmental pollution has been becoming increasingly severe, which is very thought-provoking and deserves a further analysis.

例5 如今，乌托邦已然变得不合时宜，因为我们越来越深刻地察觉到自身所面临的种种威胁。

参考译文 Now utopia has grown unfashionable, as we have gained a deeper appreciation of the range of threats facing us.

一、请选择合适的状语从句引导词填空

1. _____ you get lost without a phone or a compass, and you literally can't find north, a few tricks may help you navigate back to civilization.

   (2019年英语一完形)

   [A] Since　　　　[B] If　　　　[C] Though　　　　[D] Until

2. _____ this practice first started decades ago, it was usually limited to freshmen.

   (2019年英语一阅读)

   [A] When　　　　[B] If　　　　[C] Where　　　　[D] Until

3. It eventually raised living standards and created more jobs _____ it destroyed.

   (2018年英语一阅读)

   [A] since　　　　[B] if　　　　[C] although　　　　[D] than

4. _____ somebody pushes corporate quotas as a way to promote gender equity, remember that such policies are largely self-serving measures.

   (2020年英语一阅读)

   [A] Next　　　　[B] Next time　　　　[C] Whichever　　　　[D] Even

5. _____ a job's starting salary seems too small to satisfy an emerging adult's need for rapid content, the transition from school to work can be less of a setback if the start-up adult is ready for the move.

   (2007年新题型)

   [A] Even if　　　　[B] If　　　　[C] before　　　　[D] as

二、阅读理解

States will be able to force more people to pay sales tax when they make online purchases under a Supreme Court decision Thursday that will leave shoppers with lighter wallets but is a big financial win for states.

(2019年英语一阅读)

The Supreme Court decision Thursday will _____.

[A] lead to business' revolutions with states　　　　[B] put most online business in a dilemma

[C] make more online shoppers pay sales tax　　　　[D] forces some states to cut sales tax

一、请选择合适的状语从句引导词填空

1. **答案** B

   解析 空格所在的这句话的意思是"你迷路了，没带手机或指南针"，后接一个and连接的并列分句，意为"你真的找不着北了，有一些技巧能帮助你回到文明社会"。可见前面提到的情况是一种假设，表示条件关系，用if引导，故选B。

   参考译文 如果你在没有手机或指南针的情况下迷路了，真的找不着北了，那么有一些技巧能帮助你导航，重新回到文明社会。

2. **答案** A

   解析 句子主语是it，谓语是was limited to，宾语是freshmen。根据句意可知，空格处引导时间状语从句，应用when引导，故选A。

   参考译文 当数十年前这项政策刚出台时，通常仅适用于新生。

3. **答案** D

   解析 空格前提到more jobs，说明前后存在比较关系，故选择than引导比较状语从句。

   参考译文 它最终提高了人们的生活水平，创造的就业岗位也比破坏的还要多。

4. **答案** B

   解析 前后句存在时间上的先后关系，所以空格处应为引导时间状语从句的连接词。next time意为"下次"，符合句意。此句的主句是祈使句remember that...，that引导宾语从句。

   参考译文 下次当有人将公司配额作为一种促进性别平等的方式时，请记住，此类政策主要是一些自私自利的措施。

5. **答案** A

   解析 前后句为让步关系，因此用even if引导让步状语从句，即"即便起薪低，也能做好过渡"。

   参考译文 即使一份工作的起薪很低，无法满足刚成年的人对即时满足感的需求，但如果这个准成年人已经准备好行动的话，那么他从学校转入职场就不会那么受挫。

二、阅读理解

答案 C

解析 原文明确指出，在这项决议之下，各州将迫使网购者支付营业税（States will be able to force more people to pay sales tax when they make online purchases），when引导

时间状语从句。法规的影响是双向的，一方面消费者要付更多的税，另一方面各州的收入会增加。根据这些信息，不难判断C选项"让更多网购者支付营业税"为正确选项。online shoppers对应原文中的when they make online purchases。

参考译文 根据最高法庭本周四的一项决议，各州可以强制更多人在网上购物时支付营业税。这一决定让更多消费者的花费增多，但对于各州来说无疑是一笔巨大的财政收入。

📋 总结

截至本课，通过14天的学习，我们已经基本掌握了句子的主干与分支、核心与修饰成分，下面我们来进行一个简单的总结。拆解长难句的底层逻辑是：从长到短，从整体到局部，从宏观回归微观，从面到线再到点。因此，面对任何长难句，我们都能应用以下的终极"三步走"模式：

> 1. 抓谓语，定主干（主干公式）
> 2. 辨从句，分层次（名从公式，定从公式，状从公式）
> 3. 辨修饰，分定状（多重定语公式，状语公式）

"特邀嘉宾"之特殊结构精讲

Day 15

本节课我们来讲解特殊结构。考研英语中常见的特殊结构有强调句、倒装句、虚拟语气、比较结构。

一、强调句

1 强调句的作用

强调句是人们为了表达自己的意愿或情感而使用的一种特殊句式。通过各种方式对句子中的某个成分进行强调，使其成为信息中心。

2 强调句的形式

英语中的强调主要有两种：一是强调谓语动词，需要借助助动词，形式为"do/does/did+动词原形"，可起到加强语气的作用；二是强调非谓语（包括主语、宾语、状语、宾语补足语等）。其基本结构是：It+is/was+被强调的成分+that/who...。它的写法很简单，即把一个普通的句子拆分成两部分，把想强调的部分放到"被强调的成分"处，然后将句子余下的部分放到that后面即可。当被强调的是人时，连接词可用who(m)/that，其他情况用that。例如：

1 I did love you. 我确实爱过你。（强调谓语动词）

2 It was your help that weathered bad times for me. 正是有了你的帮助，我才能渡过困难时期。（强调主语）

3 强调句和主语从句的区别

既然强调句和主语从句都可以写成It is/was...that...的形式，那么该如何区分这两者呢？可以采取删除法：

- 若将It is/was和that同时去掉，还原为一般句式后，句子仍然成立，则该句为强调句，因为强调句中的It没有实义，只起语法作用；

- 若去掉It is/was和that并还原为一般句式后，句子不成立，则为主语从句。此时将that...代替It，则句子成立。

翻译时，强调句的It翻译成"正是，就是"。主语从句需将形式主语还原成真正的主语后翻译或直接顺译。总结如下：

句型	区别	翻译方法
强调句	去掉It is/was和that后句子成立	正是/就是……
主语从句	去掉It is/was和that后句子不成立	将形式主语还原成真正的主语或顺译

4 真题应用

(1) 分析下面句子的结构和成分并翻译：

Science does provide us with the best available guide to the future, and it is critical that our nation and the world base important policies on the best judgments that science can provide.

(2005年阅读)

解析 本句是由and连接的并列句，前一分句的主干为Science...provide us with...guide，其中does对谓语动词provide起强调作用，to the future是名词guide的后置定语。后一分句的主干为it is critical that...，其中it为形式主语，真正的主语是第一个that引导的主语从句，其主干为our nation and the world base important policies on...judgments。第二个that引导的是一个定语从句，修饰限定judgments。表语形容词critical意为"极重要的；关键的"，表示重要性，因此主语从句使用了虚拟语气，从句谓语动词base前省略了should。

参考译文 科学确实给我们提供了通往未来的最佳指南，关键是，我们国家和世界各国在制定重要决策时，都应该以科学能提供的最佳判断为依据。

(2) 用上面所学的知识翻译句子：

这个时代确实给我们提供了机遇、变革和挑战，关键是，我们的国家和个人应该将时间和精力放在时代能带来的变革之上。

(2013年、2018年英语一写作)

参考译文 This era does provide us with chances, changes and challenges, and it is critical that our nation and individuals base time and attention on the revolution that the era can bring about.

二、倒装句

1 倒装句的作用

倒装是一种语法手段，用于表示一定的句子结构或强调某一句子成分。

② 倒装句的结构形式（词序移位）

英语句子的语序一般是固定的：主语在前，谓语在后，为陈述语序。谓语的全部或一部分（如助动词或情态动词）放在主语之前的现象称为倒装。倒装有两种情况：全部倒装和部分倒装。

(1) 全部倒装

全部倒装（或完全倒装）是把句子中的谓语动词全部置于主语前。

a. 时间、地点副词或地点介词前置

将陈述语序的"主语+谓语+状语"变为"状语+谓语+主语"，即"*adv./prep....*+动词+主语"的结构，将谓语完全置于主语之前。例如：

Then came the hour. 时间到了。

There is a girl. 有一个女孩。

Here comes the bus. 公交来了。 （2013年英语一写作）

On the boat sit two tourists enjoying the scenery. 在船上坐着两名欣赏风景的游客。

（2011年英语一写作）

At the fork stand hesitantly a crop of college graduates. 许多大学生犹豫地站在岔路口。

（2013年英语一写作）

Along with the many folks looking to make a permanent home in the United States came those who had no intention to stay, and who would make some money and then go home. 伴随很多打算在美国永久安家的人而来的，还有一些无意定居美国的人，他们赚了钱就会返回故土。

（2013年英语二阅读）

(2) 部分倒装

只把谓语的一部分（多为助动词、系动词或情态动词）置于主语前的句子，称为部分倒装（或不完全倒装）。

a. 一般疑问句

将陈述句改为一般疑问句时，需将系动词、情态动词或助动词放在句首，即位于主语前，而构成部分倒装。例如：

You are beautiful. → Are you beautiful?

I love you. → Do I love you?

I loved you. → Did I love you?

I have loved you. → Have I loved you?

I am loving you → Am I loving you?

I was loving you. → Was I loving you?

I should love you. → Should I love you?

I will love you. → Will I love you?

b. only/never/so...前置（表示程度）

在以"only+副词/介词短语/状语从句"开头的句子中，主谓要倒装，即要将助动词、系动词或情态动词放在主语之前。此外，在以表示否定或半否定意义的词或词组如never、hardly、seldom、by no means、under no circumstances等开头的句子中，以及当"so/such...that..."结构中的so、such连同它所直接修饰的成分共同位于句首表示强调时，主句也要进行部分倒装。例如：

Never will I love you. 我绝不会爱上你。

Only when you love me will I love you. 只有你爱我，我才会爱你。

Never before has television served so much to connect different peoples and nations. 电视从未起过如此大的连接不同民族和国家的作用。 (2005年翻译)

Only when humanity began to get its food in a more productive way was there time for other things. 只有当人类开始更有效率地获取食物时，他们才有时间去做其他事情。 (2009年阅读)

Only when humanity begins to cooperate in a more efficient and effective way will there be a society of peace, progress and prosperity. 只有当人类开始以更有效率的方式合作时，才会有一个和平、进步和繁荣的社会。

c. than或as引导的比较状语从句

than或as引导比较状语从句时，从句语序通常不需倒装，但在正式文体中，若主语较长，有时也可倒装。例如：

College seniors taking part in temporary jobs to gain more competitiveness generally have less burdens of schoolwork than do sophomores and juniors. 跟大二、大三的学生相比，通过做兼职来获得更大竞争力的大四学生，其学业负担通常更轻。 (2013年英语二写作)

d. if虚拟条件句的省略

当虚拟条件句中的if被省略时，要把从句中的were、had或should移到主语之前。例如：

If I were a boy, I think I could understand...→ Were I a boy, I think I could understand... 如果我是男孩，我想我可以理解……

e. as的倒装→让步=尽管

当as表示"虽然，尽管"，引导让步状语从句时，句子需要倒装，as相当于though，可以替换。形式为"形容词/副词/名词（零冠词）+ as +主+谓"。例如：

You are beautiful.→ Beautiful as you are, ...

You stand a little taller. →A little taller as you stand, ...

God is a girl. → Girl as God is, ...

尝试分析以下句子的结构和成分，并翻译：

例 1 Odd as it sounds, cosmic inflation(宇宙膨胀) is a scientifically plausible consequence of some respected ideas in elementary-particle physics(基本粒子物理学).　　　　　(1998年翻译)

解析 as引导让步状语从句，其中形容词odd提前，起强调作用，翻译时应按照汉语表达习惯调整语序；主句为主系表结构：cosmic inflation is a...consequence，其中，介词短语of some respected ideas in elementary-particle physics是consequence的后置定语，翻译时前置；而in elementary particle physics 又可看作是 some respected ideas的后置定语，翻译时前置。

参考译文 宇宙膨胀说虽然听上去奇特，但它是基本粒子物理学中一些公认的观点在科学上看来可信的推论。

例 2 Only gradually was the by-product of the institution noted, and only more gradually still was this effect considered as a directive factor in the conduct of the institution.　　(2009年阅读)

解析 整个句子的结构是and连接的并列句，两个分句都是only位于句首的倒装句，第一个分句的助动词was被提到主语前，谓语部分是被动语态was noted。正常语序是the by-product...was noted only gradually。第二个分句的助动词was被提到主语前，谓语部分是被动语态was considered，正常语序是this effect was considered as a directive factor only more gradually，后面的in the conduct of...是介词短语作后置定语。

参考译文 人们只是逐渐注意到制度的这一副产品，而把这种影响视为实施这项制度的一个指导因素则需要更加漫长的过程。

例 3 Only when you nearly lose the beauty of nature _____ conscious of how much you value it.　　(2011年英语一写作)

[A] are you　　　　[B] you are　　　　[C] that you are　　　　[D] you have been

解析 "Only+状语从句"位于句首，此时主句的主谓要进行部分倒装，将you are conscious of的be动词are提前到主语you之前，故答案为A。

参考译文 只有当你快要丧失自然美时，你才会意识到你有多珍视它。

例 4 At the meeting place of the Yangtze River and the Han River _____, which is one of the six metropolitan cities in China.

(2017年英语一写作)

　　[A] lies Wuhan　　　　[B] Wuhan lies　　　　[C] does lie Wuhan　　[D] does Wuhan lie

解析 地点介词位于句首，需进行完全倒装，形成"*adv./prep.*....+动词+主语"的结构，将谓语完全置于主语之前。将陈述句语序的Wuhan lies at the meeting place...倒装成At the meeting place...lies Wuhan，故答案为A。

参考译文 武汉位于长江和汉江的交汇处，是中国六大大都市之一。

三、虚拟语气

　　虚拟语气表示说话人认为他所说的话是与事实相反的主观设想或愿望，或者是不太可能实现的怀疑和推测。虚拟语气是通过句子中谓语动词的特殊形式来表示的。掌握虚拟语气中所使用的各种谓语动词形式变化是掌握虚拟语气的关键，这也是虚拟语气的难点。虚拟语气一般有以下几种形式：

1 虚拟条件句

条件状语从句中的虚拟语气

虚拟语气在if引导的条件句中的用法	从句	主句
表示与现在的事实相反	If+主语+动词的过去式（be动词用were） 如：If I had time, I would attend the meeting.	主语+would(should/could/might)+动词原形
表示与过去的事实相反	If+主语+had+动词的过去分词 如：If he had hurried, he could have caught the train.	主语+would(should/could/might)+have+动词的过去分词
表示与将来的事实相反	If+主语+动词的过去式（be动词用were） if+主语+were to+动词原形 If+主语+should+动词原形 如：If I were to go abroad, I would go to Ireland.	主语+would(should/could/might)+动词原形

1 If I were a boy, I could understand how it feels to love a girl. 如果我是个男孩，我就能理解爱一个女孩的感觉。（与现在的事实相反）

2 If he had played last season, however, he would have been one of 42. 然而，如果他上个赛季参加了比赛，他可能已经成为这42人中的一员了。（与过去的事实相反）

(2008年阅读)

3 Without confidentiality, the trust would have been impaired and the communication of the patients limited. 如果不保密，信任就会受损，病人之间的交流也会受到限制。（与过去的事实相反）

2 真题应用

例1 Wild Bill Donovan would have loved the Internet.   (2003年阅读)

判断正误：The emergence of the Net has received support from fans like Donovan.

解析 would have done结构表示与过去的事实相反。事实上Donovan过去并不喜欢上网，因此上述表达错误。

例2 If appropriate public policies were in place to help all women and all families, women entering top management would be no more newsworthy.   (2013年英语二阅读)

Women entering top management become headlines due to the lack of _____.

[A] more social justice   [B] massive media attention

[C] suitable public policies   [D] greater "soft pressure"

解析 If引导的条件状语从句中，谓语动词为were，使用了虚拟语气，表示与现在的事实相反，即如果现在有适当的公共政策（appropriate public policies），女性担任高管的事件不再会有新闻价值。由此可知，目前缺乏适当的公共政策，故选择C项。

例3 翻译句子：They fear that it hurts their economies, depriving them of much-needed skilled workers who could have taught at their universities, worked in their hospitals and come up with clever new products for their factories to make.   (2012年英语二翻译)

解析 主句为They fear that...，其中that为宾语从句，depriving...workers是现在分词短语作结果状语。who...to make是定语从句，修饰workers，该定语从句中有三个并列的谓语动词could have taught、worked和come up with。could have done结构表示与过去的事实相反，意为"过去本可以……"。

参考译文 他们担心这有损于本国的经济，导致他们损失大量急需的技术人才，这些人才本来可以在自己国内的大学任教，在国内的医院工作或研发出精巧的新产品供本国工厂生产。

③ 建议性虚拟语气

虚拟语气还可用于表示建议、命令或要求等动词后的宾语从句以及有建议、命令或要求等意义的主语从句中，从句的谓语动词形式是should+动词原形，should可以省略。常见的动词有：insist（坚持），order/command（命令），suggest/advise（建议），move/vote（提议），arrange（安排）。

> 注意：insist后的宾语从句既可以表示虚拟语气，也可以表示陈述语气。若所说事件并未发生，则需要用虚拟语气；若所说事件已然发生，则需要用陈述语气。例如：
>
> I insisted that she had read this book. 我坚称她看过这本书。（陈述）
>
> I insisted that she should read this book. 我坚持要她看这本书。（虚拟）
>
> 由某些表示建议、强调重要性或命令的形容词构成的形式主语句型，从句后面也需要使用虚拟语气。例如：
>
> It is necessary/critical/advisable/imperative that +主语+should do...
>
> It is (high) time that...（从句中的谓语动词要用should do或did或were，表示"是做……的时候了""早该……"）

翻译以下句子：

例 1 He ordered that federal funds (should) not be used for such an experiment. (1999年阅读)

参考译文 他下令禁止使用联邦基金做这样的实验。

例 2 有必要采取有效的措施以改善环境恶化的形势。 (2011年英语一写作)

参考译文 It is critical that efficient and effective measures (should) be taken to better the situation of environmental deterioration.

④ as if或as though引导的状语从句

as if或as though引导的状语从句表示与事实相反或不可能实现的事情时，要用虚拟语气。从句谓语动词用一般过去时表示与现在的事实相反，用过去完成时表示与过去的事实相反，意思是"仿佛，似乎"。例如：

There is a running boy making his final spurt to the destination, as if he was embracing the hope of his achievement and victory. 有一个奔跑的男孩正向终点做最后的冲刺，仿若怀揣着对成就和胜利的希望。

(2004年写作)

四、比较结构

比较结构是英语中较复杂的一种语法现象，用来表达人或事物属性或特征的不同程度。比较结构经常出现在翻译、阅读考点句中。在遇到包含比较结构的长难句时，需识别其形式，避免造成语义上的误解。除了常见的形容词与副词同级比较、比较级与最高级外，有些结构看起来像比较结构，甚至与形容词比较级一模一样，但它们在特定语境中并无比较意义，而是更强调肯定或否定的意义，或者说是在比较的基础上表示选择关系。常见的这类结构有：

> A no more...than B：A和B一样不······
>
> A no less...than B：A和B一样······
>
> ...not so much A as B：与其说是A，不如说是B

例 1 Sandberg would be no more newsworthy than any other highly capable person living in a more just society.

参考译文 桑德伯格将和其他生活在一个更加公平的社会中的精英一样，没什么新闻价值。

例 2 Language is a part of our body and no less complicated than it.

参考译文 语言是我们身体的一部分，和身体一样复杂。

例 3 I am not so much a good mother as a good teacher.

参考译文 与其说我是一个好妈妈，不如说我是一个好老师。

 课后练习

一、分析下列强调句、倒装句和比较结构，并翻译

1. I believe it is precisely this permanent coexistence of metaphysical message through physical means that is the strength of music.

(2014年英语一翻译)

2. Especially significant was his view of freedom, which, for him, was associated with the rights and responsibilities of the individual.

(2014年英语一翻译)

3. Only if the jobless arrive at the jobcentre with a CV, register for online job search, and start looking for work will they be eligible for benefit.

(2014年英语一阅读)

4. Perhaps willfully, it may be easier to think about such lengthy timescales than about the more immediate future.

(2013年英语一阅读)

二、按虚拟语气的要求将动词的正确形式填入空格中

1. Most researchers _____ (accept) such a prize if they were offered one.

(2014年英语一阅读)

2. If circumstances always determined the life and prospects of people, then humanity _____ (not progress).

(2011年英语一翻译)

3. European ministers instantly demanded that the International Accounting Standards Board _____ (do) likewise.

(2010年英语一阅读)

4. This year, it was proposed that the system _____ (be changed).

(2013年英语一阅读)

5. "If we _____ (be) really bold, we might even begin to think of high-calorie fast food in the same way as cigarettes..." he said.

(2011年英语一阅读)

✏ 参考答案

一、分析下列强调句、倒装句和比较结构，并翻译

1. 解析 believe后是省略了引导词that的宾语从句。从句中it is...that...构成强调句，去掉后整个句子仍完整。this permanent coexistence是主语，介词短语of metaphysical message through physical means是主语的后置定语。is the strength of music为系表结构。

   参考译文 我认为这样说是很准确的：通过物理方法令形而上学之讯息达到永久共存便是音乐的力量所在。

2. 解析 本句是倒装句，表语significant位于句首，起强调表语的作用，引起全部倒装。正常的语序是His view of freedom was especially significant。翻译的时候可以采用倒装顺序，也可采用正常语序，译为"尤为重要的是他对于自由的看法"或者"他对于自由的看法尤为重要"。his view of freedom后为which引导的非限制性定语从句，修饰freedom，关系代词which在定语从句中作主语。

   参考译文 尤为重要的是他对自由的看法，在他看来，自由关系到个人的权利和责任。

3. 解析 "Only+if引导的条件状语从句"位于句首，引起部分倒装，主句they will be eligible for benefit中助动词will被提前到主语they之前。

参考译文 失业者只有到就业中心递交简历，在求职网上注册并开始寻找工作之后，才有资格获得救济金。

4. 解析 此句中，it为形式主语，真正的主语是to think about such lengthy timescales。比较结构more...than...并列to think about such lengthy timescales和(to think) about the more immediate future，表示前者比后者更容易。

参考译文 或许有人固执地认为，考虑如此漫长的时间跨度要比思考眼前的未来更简单。

二、按虚拟语气的要求将动词的正确形式填入空格中

1. 答案 would accept

   解析 if引导虚拟条件句，对现在的情况进行假设，从句谓语动词were offered用了一般过去时，因此主句谓语动词用would+do的形式。

   参考译文 如果授予研究人员这样的奖，大多数人将会接受。

2. 答案 would never have progressed

   解析 从句和主句动作发生时间不一致时，动词的形式要根据它所表示的时间来调整。if引导虚拟条件句，对现在的情况进行假设。从句谓语动词用了一般过去时，而主句假设过去，因此谓语动词应用would have done的形式。

   参考译文 如果环境总是能决定人们的生活和前景，那人类就永远不会进步。

3. 答案 (should) do

   解析 表示"要求"的谓语动词demanded后接宾语从句，从句需进行虚拟。因此，即便主句使用了一般过去时，从句的谓语动词也不受影响，依然使用(should) do的形式。

   参考译文 欧洲各国部长立即要求国际会计标准委员会也采取同样的行动。

4. 答案 (should) be changed

   解析 it为形式主语，that引导主语从句作真正的主语，由于主语从句位于表示"提议"的动词proposed的后面，需进行虚拟，故从句谓语动词用(should) do的形式。

   参考译文 今年有人提议应该对该体制加以改变。

5. 答案 were

   解析 if引导虚拟条件句，对现在的情况进行假设，事实是"我们并不勇敢"，从句谓语动词用一般过去时，因此填were。

   参考译文 如果我们真的足够勇敢，我们甚至可以开始像看待香烟一样看待高热量的快餐食品。

"特邀嘉宾"之特殊结构应用

本节课我们将通过一些改编过的真题练习来巩固一下考研英语中常用到的特殊结构。

一、选择题

例1 Only when you nearly lose the beauty of nature _____ fully conscious of how much you value it.　　　　　　　　　　　　　　　　　　　　(2011年英语一写作)

　　[A] do you become　　　　　　　　[B] then you become

　　[C] that you become　　　　　　　　[D] have you become

解析 "only+状语从句"开头的句子中,主句的主谓需进行部分倒装,即将助动词、系动词或情态动词放在主语之前。本句谓语动词是become,需要借助助动词do,将其提前到主语you之前构成部分倒装,故正确答案为A。

参考译文 只有当你快失去大自然的美丽时,你才会充分意识到有多珍惜它。

例2 Fool _____ I am, I could not have forgotten to return your music CD.　　(2008年写作)

　　[A] as　　　　　　[B] who　　　　　　[C] that　　　　　　[D] like

解析 主语I和系动词am在空格后,且am后无表语,可知表语fool被提至句首,为部分倒装的一种形式。as表示"虽然,尽管",引导让步状语从句时需进行部分倒装,将表语、状语或动词原形提到as前面。当表语为名词时,名词前面用零冠词,故正确答案为A。

参考译文 虽然我很愚蠢,但我也不可能忘记归还你的音乐光盘。

例3 At the meeting place of the Yangtze River and the Jialing River _____, one of the ten largest cities in China.　　　　　　　　　　　　　　　　　(2017年英语一写作)

　　[A] lies Chongqing　　　　　　　　[B] Chongqing lies

　　[C] does lie Chongqing　　　　　　　[D] does Chongqing lie

解析 本句以表示地点的介词短语at the meeting place of...开头,句子使用完全倒装。原陈述句语序为Chongqing lies at the meeting place of...,完全倒装时需要把谓语动词lies置于主语Chongqing之前,故正确答案为A。

参考译文 重庆位于长江和嘉陵江交汇处,是中国十大城市之一。

例 4 So sudden _____ that the enemy had no time to escape.

[A] did the attack　　　　　　[B] the attack did

[C] was the attack　　　　　　[D] the attack was

解析 此句为"so+形容词"前置引起的部分倒装，强调程度。原句陈述语序为The attack was so sudden that the enemy had no time to escape，倒装时将系动词was提前到主语the attack前，故正确答案为C。

参考译文 突袭如此之快以至于敌人毫无时间逃跑。

例 5 Not until we left our home _____ to know how important the family was for us.

(2014年英语一写作)

[A] did we begin　　[B] had we begun　　[C] we began　　[D] we had begun

解析 当not until引导的时间状语从句位于句首时，主句应部分倒装，从句语序不变。主句陈述语序为we began to know how...，倒装时借用助动词did，将其提至主语we之前，改写为did we begin to know how...，故正确答案为A。

参考译文 直到我们离开自己的家以后，我们才开始体会到家庭对我们如此重要。

例 6 If I were in a movie, then it would be about time that I _____ my head in my hands for a cry.

(2001年选择题)

[A] bury　　　　[B] am burying　　　　[C] buried　　　　[D] would bury

解析 此题考查的是虚拟语气，由if I were...可知if引导虚拟条件句，表示对现在的情况进行假设，主句谓语动词使用"would+do"的形式。同时，it is about time that...也是虚拟语气的一种形式，从句中的谓语动词通常使用一般过去时，表示"该做某事"的态度，故正确答案为C。

参考译文 如果我身处电影之中，我早就抱头痛哭了。

二、写作应用

在作文中，适当使用虚拟语气、倒装句可以为我们的文章增添亮点，这里有一些固定的句型结构值得同学们去学习借鉴。

1 虚拟语气

1 It is high time that we should do sth./we did sth. 是该……的时候了。

2 It is imperative/indispensable/necessary/vital/important/advisable that we should do sth./sth. should be done. 我们做……是必要的/……是非常重要的。

3 a. 要不是有你帮我，我就失败了。（对过去的虚拟）

But for your assistance, I would have failed. / I would not have succeeded.

b. 如果没有规章制度，我们就不会在社会发展/经济增长方面取得任何显著进展。

（对将来的虚拟）

Without rules and regulations, we would not make any remarkable progress in the social development/economic growth.

② 倒装句

1 Only in this way can we address the problem. 只有这样，我们才能解决这个问题。

2 Only by doing so can we better/improve the situation.

只有这样做，我们才能改善这种情况。

3 Only in this way can the problem be addressed.

只有这样，问题才能得到解决。

英语一和英语二大作文的第一句可以采用如下倒装结构去描述漫画或图表：

介词短语+谓语动词+主语（+其他修饰语）

例如

1 In front of computers sit many people. 电脑前坐着许多人。

2 On the lake floats a boat. 湖面上漂浮着一条船。

3 In the middle of the picture is a young girl. 图片中间是一个年轻女孩。

4 Demonstrated above is an array of figures disclosing the changes of sth.

以上所展示的一系列数字显示了……的变化。

 课后练习

按括号内所给的提示翻译句子

1. 我们应该注意到由于盲目追求GDP的增长，我们的生活环境和一些自然资源正在遭受破坏。(it is high time that...)

2. 正是因为这种相互扶持，我们才一直生活在幸福中。(it is because of...that...)

3. 如果一个人没有同事或合作伙伴的协助，那么他很难在事业上有所成就。(Hardly can anyone...without...)

4. 学生从未在学习方面得到如此广泛多样的资源。(Never before...)

5. 然而，一些旅游服务并不如本应该有的那样完善。(as...as...)

📝 参考答案

按括号内所给的提示翻译句子

1. It is high time that we realized the fact that our living environment and some natural resources are being destroyed in the blind pursuit of GDP increase.

2. It is because of this mutual support that we are always immersed in happiness.

3. Hardly can anyone achieve success in his career without the assistance of his colleagues or partners.

4. Never before have students had such a wide variety of resources to help them in their studies.

5. Nevertheless, some tourist services are not as developed as they should have been.

Part 02

搞定 核心长难句

　　本部分精选了21个考研英语阅读真题核心长难句，从考场解题的视角，带着同学们还原考场解题情景，看如何通过使用Part 01学到的语法知识，层层剖析、搞定核心长难句，进而搞定真题。

真题重现

◎ 阅读 Text 3

It can be inferred from Paragraph 3 that _____.

[A] shippers will be charged less without a rival railroad

[B] there will soon be only one railroad company nationwide

[C] overcharged shippers are unlikely to appeal for rate relief

[D] a government board ensures fair play in railway business

◎核心词汇

- rival ['raɪvl] *n.* 竞争对手
- nationwide [ˌneɪʃn'waɪd] *adv.* 在全国范围内
- government ['gʌvənmənt] *n.* 政府
- board [bɔːd] *n.* 委员会
- fair play 公平竞争

解题思路

◎ 理解题目

从第三段可以推断出_____。

[A] 在没有其他铁路公司竞争的情况下，托运人将被收取更少的费用

[B] 很快全国就会只有一家铁路公司

[C] 被多收费的托运人不太可能要求费用减免

[D] 政府委员会确保铁路行业的公平竞争

◎ 定位原文

根据题干中的Paragraph 3，我们定位到原文的第三段：

①The vast consolidation within the rail industry means that most shippers are served by only one rail company. ②Railroads typically charge such "captive" shippers 20 to 30 percent more than they do when another railroad is competing for the business. ③Shippers who feel they are being overcharged have the right to appeal to the federal government's Surface Transportation Board for rate relief, but the process is expensive, time-consuming, and will work only in truly extreme cases.

◎核心词汇

- consolidation [kənˌsɒlɪ'deɪʃn] *n.* 合并
- overcharge [ˌəʊvə'tʃɑːdʒ] *vt.* 对……收费过高
- appeal to 呼吁；申诉
- relief [rɪ'liːf] *n.* 减轻；免除
- process ['prəʊses] *n.* 过程
- time-consuming ['taɪm kənsjuːmɪŋ] *adj.* 费时的
- extreme [ɪk'striːm] *adj.* 非常的，极端的

该题为推断题，因此需结合全段来看。该段第一、二句指出铁路行业合并会导致托运人被多收费，接着最后一句讲述了托运人被多收费时可采取的行动以及限制条件。选项C中的rate relief为最后一句中的原词，因此我们暂时先定位到该句。下面我们先来尝试自己拆分和理解该长难句，之后再看老师的图解分析和参考译文。

· 小试牛刀

Shippers who feel they are being overcharged have the right to appeal to the federal

government's Surface Transportation Board for rate relief, but the process is expensive, time-

consuming, and will work only in truly extreme cases.

· 图解分析

难点总览：本句是由but连接的并列句，but前后的两个分句形成转折；前一分句中，who引导定语从句，修饰先行词shippers，其中feel之后为省略引导词that的宾语从句。

第一层：确定主句

Shippers (who feel they are being overcharged) have the right
主语1　　　　　　定语从句　　　　　　谓语1　宾语

(to appeal to the federal government's Surface Transportation Board for rate relief), but
　　　　　　　　　　right的后置定语　　　　　　　　　　　▲

the process is expensive, time-consuming, and will work [only in truly extreme cases].
主语2　系　　　　表语　　　　　▲　谓语2　　　　　状语

第二层：确定从句

who引导定语从句，修饰先行词shippers，who代替先行词在定语从句中作主语。

who feel they are being overcharged
主　谓　　宾语从句

第三层：确定从句

feel后为省略引导词that的宾语从句，从句谓语为现在进行时的被动语态。

| they are being overcharged |
| 主 谓 |

◎ 参考译文

　　铁路行业的大规模合并意味着大多数托运人仅由一家铁路公司提供服务。与当有另一家铁路公司竞争该业务时相比，铁路公司通常向此类"无权选择的"托运人收取的费用多20%~30%。觉得被收费过高的托运人有权上诉联邦政府地面运输委员会以求费用减免，但是这一过程既昂贵又费时，而且只是在真正极端的案件中才有效。

◎ 回归解题

　　本题选C，为推断题。根据原文Railroads typically charge such "captive" shippers 20 to 30 percent more than they do when another railroad is competing for the business.（与当有另一家铁路公司竞争该业务时相比，铁路公司通常向此类"无权选择的"托运人收取的费用多20%~30%。）可知，没有竞争对手的时候，向托运人收取的费用更多，故选项A中的less（更少）与原文相悖，故排除。选项B中的soon（很快）为无中生有，故排除。根据前面的核心句分析可知，虽然被收费过高的托运人可以上诉要求费用减免，但是该过程昂贵且耗时，而且只在真正极端的情况下才有效，因此他们不太可能上诉，故选项C正确。选项D为无中生有，故排除。

考场
总结

　　解题时，尤其要注意转折连词but之后的内容，其往往会引出作者真正想要表达的观点和态度。

真题重现

◎ 阅读 Text 4

To which of the following statements would McWhorter
most likely agree?

[A] Logical thinking is not necessarily related to the way
we talk.

[B] Black English can be more expressive than standard
English.

[C] Non-standard varieties of human language are just as
entertaining.

[D] Of all the varieties, standard English can best convey
complex ideas.

◎ 核心词汇

- logical ['lɒdʒɪkl] *adj.* 逻辑的
- necessarily [ˌnesə'serəli] *adv.* 必然地
- be related to 与……有关
- expressive [ɪk'spresɪv] *adj.* 有表现力的
- entertaining [ˌentə'teɪnɪŋ] *adj.* 有趣的
- convey [kən'veɪ] *vt.* 传达
- complex ['kɒmpleks] *adj.* 复杂的

解题思路

◎ 理解题目

麦克沃特先生最有可能赞同以下哪种说法？

[A] 逻辑思维不一定与我们说话的方式有关。

[B] 黑人英语比标准英语更有表现力。

[C] 人类语言的非标准变体同样有趣。

[D] 在所有变体中，标准英语最能传达复杂的思想。

◎ 定位原文

各选项中的关键词we talk、Black English、Non-
standard、complex ideas都出现在了原文第四段，因
此我们定位到该段：

①Illustrated with an entertaining array of examples from
both high and low culture, the trend that Mr. McWhorter
documents is unmistakable. ②But it is less clear, to take
the question of his subtitle, why we should, like, care. ③As a
linguist, he acknowledges that all varieties of human
language, including non-standard ones like Black English,

◎ 核心词汇

- illustrate ['ɪləstreɪt] *vt.* 阐明
- an array of 一系列；大量
- document ['dɒkjument] *vt.* 证实
- unmistakable [ˌʌnmɪ'steɪkəbl] *adj.* 确定无疑的
- subtitle ['sʌbtaɪtl] *n.* 副标题
- linguist ['lɪŋgwɪst] *n.* 语言学家
- acknowledge [ək'nɒlɪdʒ] *vt.* 承认
- variety [və'raɪəti] *n.* 种类，品种

141

can be powerfully expressive—there exists no language or dialect in the world that cannot convey complex ideas. ④He is not arguing, as many do, that we can no longer think straight because we do not talk proper.

- dialect ['daɪəlekt] *n.* 方言

◎ 定位核心句

　　而且选项B、C、D的关键词都出现在该段第三句中，因此我们先定位至该句。下面我们来具体分析一下该句的句子结构。

· 小试牛刀

As a linguist, he acknowledges that all varieties of human language, including non-standard

ones like Black English, can be powerfully expressive—there exists no language or dialect in

the world that cannot convey complex ideas.

· 图解分析

难点总览：第一个that引导动词acknowledges的宾语从句；第二个that引导定语从句，修饰先行词language or dialect。

第一层：确定主句

[As a linguist], he acknowledges that all varieties of human language, including non-standard
状语　主语1　谓语1　　　　　　　　　　　　　宾语从句
ones like Black English, can be powerfully expressive—
[there] exists no language or dialect [in the world] (that cannot convey complex ideas).
状语　谓语2　　主语2　　　　　状语　　　　　定语从句

第二层：确定从句

第一个that引导动词acknowledges的宾语从句。

that all varieties of human language, including non-standard ones like Black English,
▲　　　　主语　　　　　　　　　　　　插入语
can be powerfully expressive
系动词　　　表语

142

第二个that引导定语从句，修饰先行词language or dialect，that代替先行词在定语从句中作主语。

> that cannot convey complex ideas
> 主语　　谓语　　　　宾语

◎ 参考译文

　　雅俗文化中的一系列有趣的例子说明，麦克沃特先生论证的这种趋势是明确无误的。但就他的副标题"为什么我们应该喜欢或在意"这个问题来说，答案就不太清楚了。作为一名语言学家，他承认人类的各种语言，包括像黑人英语这样的非标准语言，都具有强大的表达力——世界上任何语言或方言都能传达复杂的思想。他并没有像许多人那样，认为由于我们表达不规范，所以我们就不能好好思考。

◎ 回归解题

　　本题选A，为细节题。选项B、C、D均对应刚分析的长难句。虽然其中提及Black English（黑人英语）作为non-standard ones（非标准语言）的代表，但并没有将其与standard English（标准英语）就表现力进行对比，故排除选项B；选项C对应该段中的an entertaining array of examples（许多有趣的例子），原文中的entertaining（有趣的）修饰例子，而非各种语言，故排除选项C。选项D中的best（最）为无中生有，故排除。通过排除法，可确定选项A正确。最后一句对此作了进一步说明，其中as many do中的do为代动词，代表前面提及的动作，即argue，也就是Many argue that we can no longer think straight because we do not talk proper（许多人认为由于我们表达不规范，所以我们不能好好思考），而原文说的是He is not arguing that...（他不这么认为……）。选项A中的Logical thinking（逻辑思维）对应原文中的think straight（好好思考），the way we talk（我们表达的方式）对应talk proper（表达规范）。

考场
总结
　　本题考点主要考查对核心句中that引导的宾语从句（that all varieties of human language, including non-standard ones like Black English, can be powerfully expressive）的理解。

真题重现

◎ 阅读 Text 2

According to Bruce Alberts, science can serve as _____.

[A] a protector

[B] a judge

[C] a critic

[D] a guide

◎核心词汇

- protector [prə'tektə(r)] *n.* 保护者
- judge [dʒʌdʒ] *n.* 法官，裁判
- critic ['krɪtɪk] *n.* 批评者；评论家

解题思路

◎ 理解题目

根据布鲁斯·艾伯茨的说法，科学可以作为_____。

[A] 保护者   [B] 裁判

[C] 批评者   [D] 向导

◎ 定位原文

◎核心词汇

根据题干中的Bruce Alberts，我们定位到原文的第二段：

①There are upsetting parallels today, as scientists in one wave after another try to awaken us to the growing threat of global warming. ②The latest was a panel from the National Academy of Sciences, enlisted by the White House, to tell us that the Earth's atmosphere is definitely warming and that the problem is largely man-made. ③The clear message is that we should get moving to protect ourselves. ④The president of the National Academy, Bruce Alberts, added this key point in the preface to the panel's report: "Science never has all the answers. ⑤But science does provide us with the best available guide to the future, and it is critical that our nation and the world base important policies on the best judgments that science can provide concerning the future consequences of present actions."

- upsetting [ʌp'setɪŋ] *adj.* 令人心烦的
- parallel ['pærəlel] *n.* 类似事件
- awaken [ə'weɪkən] *vt.* 使意识到
- panel ['pænl] *n.* 专家组
- enlist [ɪn'lɪst] *vt.* 召集，招募
- atmosphere ['ætməsfɪə(r)] *n.* 大气层
- preface ['prefəs] *n.* 前言，序言
- available [ə'veɪləbl] *adj.* 可利用的，可获得的
- guide [gaɪd] *n.* 指南
- critical ['krɪtɪkl] *adj.* 重要的，关键的
- judgment ['dʒʌdʒmənt] *n.* 判断
- concerning [kən'sɜːnɪŋ] *prep.* 关于
- consequence ['kɒnsɪkwəns] *n.* 结果，后果

◎ 定位核心句

再进一步定位至该段第四、五句。引号中的内容表达的正是布鲁斯·艾伯茨所发表的观点，其中出现了转折词But，其后的内容往往是作者想要表达的重点，是我们应重点研究的核心句。下面我们先来尝试自己拆分和理解该长难句，之后再看老师的图解分析和参考译文。

· 小试牛刀

But science does provide us with the best available guide to the future, and it is critical that our

nation and the world base important policies on the best judgments that science can provide

concerning the future consequences of present actions.

· 图解分析

难点总览：and连接并列句；后一个分句中，it为形式主语，真正的主语为critical之后that引导的从句，即主语从句，其中judgments之后的that引导定语从句，修饰judgments。

第一层：确定主句

But science does provide us with the best available guide (to the future), and　it　is critical

　　　▲　主语　　　 谓语（provide sb. with sth.结构）　　　 后置定语　　▲ 形主 系　表

that our nation and the world base important policies on the best judgments that science can

主语从句

provide concerning the future consequences of present actions.

第二层：确定从句

第一个that引导主语从句，仅起连接作用。

that　our nation and the world base important policies ＜on the best judgments＞

　▲　　　 主语　　　　　 谓语　　 宾语　　　 宾语补足语

(that science can provide concerning the future consequences of present actions)

定语从句

第三层：确定从句

第二个that引导定语从句，修饰先行词judgments，that代替先行词在定语从句中作宾语，concerning...为后置定语，修饰that，也就是修饰先行词judgments。

> that science can provide (concerning the future consequences of present actions)
> 宾语　主语　　谓语　　　　　　　　　　后置定语

◎ 参考译文

如今也出现了类似的令人不安的情况，一波又一波的科学家试图使我们意识到全球变暖带来的威胁日益严重。最近一个由白宫招募的美国国家科学院的专家组告诉我们：地球的大气层肯定在变暖，而且这个问题主要是人为造成的。他们所传递的信息很明确，即我们应该立即采取行动保护自己。美国国家科学院院长布鲁斯·艾伯茨在小组报告的序言中补充了这一关键点："科学虽然永远无法解答所有问题。但科学确实为我们提供了通往未来的最佳指南，关键是，我们国家和世界各国在制定重要决策时，都应该以科学能够提供的关于人类现在的行为对未来影响的最佳判断为依据。"

◎ 回归解题

本题选D，为细节题。文中布鲁斯·艾伯茨的话在引号中，其中提到science does provide us with the best available guide to the future（科学确实为我们提供了通往未来的最佳指南）。由此可知，科学可以作为guide（向导），故选项D正确。

> **考场总结**
> 本题考查人物观点，可根据题干中的关键信息词Bruce Alberts快速定位关键句，从而找出正确答案。专有名词（如人名、地名、时间或数字等）都可以作为信息词，在进行扫读时找出对应的信息点，可有效缩短答题时间。

真题重现

◎ 阅读 Text 4

Washington's decision to free slaves originated from his _____.

[A] moral considerations

[B] military experience

[C] financial conditions

[D] political stand

◎核心词汇

- moral ['mɒrəl] *adj.* 道德的
- military ['mɪlətri] *adj.* 军事的
- financial [faɪ'nænʃl] *adj.* 财政的，经济的
- political [pə'lɪtɪkl] *adj.* 政治的
- stand [stænd] *n.* 立场

解题思路

◎ 理解题目

华盛顿释放奴隶的决定源于他的_____。

[A] 道德考量　　　　　　　　　　　[B] 军事经历

[C] 财务状况　　　　　　　　　　　[D] 政治立场

◎ 定位原文

根据题干中的free slaves，我们定位到原文的第六段：

①Still, Jefferson freed Hemings's children—though not Hemings herself or his approximately 150 other slaves. ②Washington, who had begun to believe that *all* men were created equal after observing the bravery of the black soldiers during the Revolutionary War, overcame the strong opposition of his relatives to grant his slaves their freedom in his will. ③Only a decade earlier, such an act would have required legislative approval in Virginia.

◎核心词汇

- slave [sleɪv] *n.* 奴隶
- equal ['iːkwəl] *adj.* 相等的，平等的
- observe [əb'zɜːv] *vt.* 观察到
- bravery ['breɪvəri] *n.* 勇敢
- Revolutionary War (美国)独立战争
- opposition [ˌɒpə'zɪʃn] *n.* 反对
- grant [grɑːnt] *vt.* 授予
- legislative ['ledʒɪslətɪv] *adj.* 立法的

◎ 定位核心句

　　题干中的decision to free slaves "释放奴隶的决定"对应该段中的grant his slaves their freedom "赋予他的奴隶自由"，故答案可进一步定位到该段第二句。下面我们先来尝试自己拆分和理解该长难句，之后再看老师的图解分析和参考译文。

· 小试牛刀

Washington, who had begun to believe that *all* men were created equal after observing the

bravery of the black soldiers during the Revolutionary War, overcame the strong opposition of

his relatives to grant his slaves their freedom in his will.

· 图解分析

难点总览：两个逗号之间插入一个由who引导的非限制性定语从句，修饰前面的Washington，定语从句中包含一个由that引导的宾语从句，作believe的宾语，宾语从句中包含一个"介词+动名词"结构：after observing...。

第一层：确定主句

Washington, (who had begun to believe that *all* men were created equal after observing the
　主语　　　　　　　　　　　　　　　　定语从句
bravery of the black soldiers during the Revolutionary War), overcame the strong opposition
　　　　　　　　　　　　　　　　　　　　　　　　　　　　　　谓语　　　　宾语
(of his relatives) [to grant his slaves their freedom] [in his will].
　后置定语　　　　　　　状语　　　　　　　　状语

第二层：确定从句

who引导定语从句，修饰先行词Washington，who代替先行词在定语从句中作主语。

who had begun to believe that *all* men were created equal after observing the bravery
主语　　　谓语　　　　　　　宾语从句
of the black soldiers during the Revolutionary War

第三层：确定从句

that引导动词believe的宾语从句。

that *all* men were created <equal> [after observing the bravery of the black soldiers
▲　主语　　谓语　主语补足语　　　　　　时间状语
during the Revolutionary War]

148

◎ 参考译文

虽然杰斐逊没有让海明斯本人和他另外的大约150名奴隶获得自由，但他还是给了海明斯的孩子们自由。在目睹了黑奴士兵在美国独立战争中的英勇表现之后，华盛顿开始相信人人生而平等，于是他不顾亲属们的强烈反对，立下遗嘱赋予他的所有奴隶自由。而仅在十年前，这样的行为在弗吉尼亚州还需得到立法会的批准。

◎ 回归解题

本题选B，为细节题。定位句指出，华盛顿是在目睹了黑奴士兵在美国独立战争中的英勇表现之后，才开始相信人人生而平等，于是立下遗嘱让其奴隶获得自由。其中的soldiers（士兵）和Revolutionary War（独立战争；革命战争）均指向选项B"军事经历"，故选项B正确。

> **考场总结**
>
> 本题核心句中，who引导的定语从句对华盛顿进行了补充说明，阐述了其决定释放奴隶的原因，其中的时间状语after observing the bravery of the black soldiers说明了目睹黑奴士兵在美国独立战争中的英勇表现是促使华盛顿相信人人生而平等，从而决定释放奴隶的关键性因素。

核心句 05 ▶ 2009年

真题重现

◎ 阅读 Text 3

The author holds in Paragraph 1 that the importance of education in poor countries _____.

[A] is subject to groundless doubts

[B] has fallen victim of bias

[C] is conventionally downgraded

[D] has been overestimated

◎ 核心词汇

- be subject to 易遭受……
- groundless ['graʊndləs] *adj.* 无根据的
- fall victim of 成为……的受害者
- downgrade [ˌdaʊn'greɪd] *vt.* 低估
- overestimate [ˌəʊvər'estɪmeɪt] *vt.* 夸大

解题思路

◎ 理解题目

作者在第一段中指出，教育在贫穷国家的重要性_____。

[A] 受到了毫无根据的质疑   [B] 遭到了歧视

[C] 通常被低估   [D] 被夸大了

◎ 定位原文

根据题干中的Paragraph 1，我们定位到原文的第一段：

①The relationship between formal education and economic growth in poor countries is widely misunderstood by economists and politicians alike. ②Progress in both areas is undoubtedly necessary for the social, political and intellectual development of these and all other societies; however, the conventional view that education should be one of the very highest priorities for promoting rapid economic development in poor countries is wrong. ③We are fortunate that it is, because building new educational systems there and putting enough people through them to improve economic performance would require two or three generations. ④The findings of a research institution have consistently shown that workers in all countries can be trained on the job to achieve radically higher productivity and, as a result, radically higher standards of living.

◎ 核心词汇

- intellectual [ˌɪntə'lektʃuəl] *adj.* 智力的
- conventional [kən'venʃənl] *adj.* 传统的
- priority [praɪ'ɒrəti] *n.* 优先事项
- promote [prə'məʊt] *vt.* 促使，促进
- fortunate ['fɔːtʃənət] *adj.* 幸运的
- radically ['rædɪkli] *adv.* 根本地，彻底地
- productivity [ˌprɒdʌk'tɪvəti] *n.* 生产力

◎ 定位核心句

再根据education in poor countries定位到该段第一句，但该句只是在说贫穷国家中正规教育与经济增长之间的关系被误解了，与教育在贫穷国家的重要性无关，可跳过。最后定位到第二句，因为句中涉及了教育的重要性的信息。注意，该句后一分句中出现了转折词however，因此答案很有可能出自该分句。下面我们先来尝试自己拆分和理解however分句，之后再看老师的图解分析和参考译文。

· 小试牛刀

however, the conventional view that education should be one of the very highest priorities for

promoting rapid economic development in poor countries is wrong.

· 图解分析

难点总览：that引导同位语从句，对view进行解释说明。

第一层：确定主句

[however], <u>the conventional view</u> {that education should be one of the very highest

　　状语　　　　　　　主语　　　　　　　　　　　　　同位语从句

priorities for promoting rapid economic development in poor countries} <u>is</u> <u>wrong</u>.

　　　　　　　　　　　　　　　　　　　　　　　　　　　　　系　表语

第二层：确定从句

that引导同位语从句，解释说明view。

that <u>education</u> <u>should</u> <u>be</u> <u>one of the very highest priorities</u>

▲　　主语　　系动词　　　　　表语

[for promoting rapid economic development in poor countries]

　　　　　　　　目的状语

◎ 参考译文

　　经济学家和政治家普遍误解了贫穷国家中正规教育与经济增长之间的关系。 这两个领域的进步对于这些贫穷国家和所有其他国家的社会、政治和学术发展无疑是必要的；然而，认为教育应该是促进贫穷国家经济快速发展的重中之重的传统观点是错误的。我们很庆幸这种观点是错误的，因为建立新的教育体系并让足够多的人通过接受教育来推动经济发展需要两到三代人才能完成。一家研究机构的各项调查结果一致表明，所有国家的工人都可以接受在职培训，从根本上实现更高的生产力，从而从根本上提高生活水平。

◎ 回归解题

　　本题选D，为细节题。分析定位句可知，认为"教育应该是促进贫穷国家经济快速发展的重中之重"这一传统观点是错误的，也就是说，作者认为教育在贫穷国家的重要性被夸大了，故选项D正确。

考场
总结

　　本题考查同位语从句，定位句主干是简单的主系表结构，主语的中心词view为抽象名词，后面接了that引导的同位语从句对其作解释说明，理清了这一结构后，就能准确理解作者的观点。

真题重现

◎ 阅读 Text 4

From the principles of the US jury system, we learn that
_____.

[A] both literate and illiterate people can serve on juries

[B] defendants are immune from trial by their peers

[C] no age limit should be imposed for jury service

[D] judgment should consider the opinion of the public

◎ 核心词汇

- literate ['lɪtərət] *adj.* 有文化的
- illiterate [ɪ'lɪtərət] *adj.* 文盲的
- defendant [dɪ'fendənt] *n.* 被告
- immune [ɪ'mjuːn] *adj.* 免除的
  be immune from 免于
- impose [ɪm'pəʊz] *vt.* 强加；施加
  impose A on B 将A强加于B
- judgment ['dʒʌdʒmənt] *n.* 裁决，判决

解题思路

◎ 理解题目

从美国陪审团制度的原则中，我们了解到_____。

[A] 有文化的人和文盲都可以担任陪审员

[B] 被告不受同龄人审判

[C] 出任陪审员不应有年龄限制

[D] 裁决应考虑公众意见

◎ 定位原文

根据题干中的US jury system，我们定位到原文的第一段：

①Many Americans regard the jury system as a concrete expression of crucial democratic values, including the principles that all citizens who meet minimal qualifications of age and literacy are equally competent to serve on juries; that jurors should be selected randomly from a representative cross section of the community; that no citizen should be denied the right to serve on a jury on account of race, religion, sex, or national origin; that defendants are entitled to trial by their peers; and that verdicts should represent the conscience of the community and not just the letter of the law. ②The jury is also said to be the best surviving example of direct rather than representative democracy. ③In a direct democracy, citizens take turns governing themselves, rather than electing representatives to govern for them.

◎ 核心词汇

- jury ['dʒʊəri] *n.* 陪审团
- concrete ['kɒŋkriːt] *adj.* 具体的
- crucial ['kruːʃl] *adj.* 至关重要的
- principle ['prɪnsəpl] *n.* 原理，原则
- qualification [ˌkwɒlɪfɪ'keɪʃn] *n.* 资格
- literacy ['lɪtərəsi] *n.* 有文化
- competent ['kɒmpɪtənt] *adj.* 能胜任的，有能力的
- serve on 在……任职
- be entitled to 有……资格
- trial ['traɪəl] *n.* 审判
- peer [pɪə(r)] *n.* 同龄人
- verdict ['vɜːdɪkt] *n.* 判决
- conscience ['kɒnʃəns] *n.* 良心，良知

再进一步定位至该段第一句。下面我们先来尝试自己拆分和理解该长难句，之后再看老师的图解分析和参考译文。

· 小试牛刀

Many Americans regard the jury system as a concrete expression of crucial democratic values,

including the principles that all citizens who meet minimal qualifications of age and literacy are

equally competent to serve on juries; that jurors should be selected randomly from a

representative cross section of the community; that no citizen should be denied the right to serve

on a jury on account of race, religion, sex, or national origin; that defendants are entitled to trial

by their peers; and that verdicts should represent the conscience of the community and not just

the letter of the law.

· 图解分析

难点总览：principles之后为5个由that引导的并列的同位语从句，对principles的内容进一步补充说明。

第一层：确定主句

Many Americans regard the jury system <as a concrete expression of crucial democratic values>,
    主语   谓语   宾语   宾语补足语

(including the principles) {that all citizens who meet minimal qualifications of age and
    后置定语   同位语从句1

literacy are equally competent to serve on juries}; {that jurors should be selected randomly
                                         同位语从句2

from a representative cross section of the community}; {that no citizen should be denied the
                                  同位语从句3

right to serve on a jury on account of race, religion, sex, or national origin}; {that defendants

同位语从句4

are entitled to trial by their peers}; and {that verdicts should represent the conscience of the

▲   同位语从句5

community and not just the letter of the law}.

第二层：确定从句

同位语从句1

that all citizens (who meet minimal qualifications of age and literacy) are [equally]
　▲　　主语　　　　　　　　　　定语从句　　　　　　系动词 状语

competent [to serve on juries]
　表语　　　　状语

同位语从句2

that jurors should be selected [randomly from a representative cross section of the community]
　▲　　主语　　　谓语　　　　　　　　　　　状语

同位语从句3

that no citizen should be denied the right (to serve on a jury on account of race, religion, sex,
　▲　　主语　　　　谓语　　　宾语　　　　　　　right的后置定语

or national origin)

同位语从句4

that defendants are entitled to trial [by their peers]
　▲　　　主语　　　谓语　　宾语　　状语

同位语从句5

that verdicts should represent the conscience of the community and not just the letter of the law
　▲　　主语　　　谓语　　　　　　宾语1　　　　　▲　　　　宾语2

第三层：确定从句

同位语从句1中包含一个由who引导的定语从句，修饰先行词citizens。

> who meet minimal qualifications (of age and literacy)
> 主语 谓语　　　宾语　　　　　　　　后置定语

◎ 参考译文

　　许多美国人将陪审团制度视为重要的民主价值观的具体体现，其包括以下原则：所有满足最低年龄和文化程度要求的公民都有同等资格加入陪审团；陪审员应从有代表性的社会各阶层中随机选出；任何公民都不应因种族、宗教、性别或国籍而被剥夺担任陪审员的权利；被告有权由同龄人进行审判；判决应该代表社会良知，而不仅仅是法律条文。陪审团（制度）也被认为是直接民主而非代议制民主现存的最佳典范。在直接民主中，公民轮流自治，而不是选举出代表代替他们管理。

◎ 回归解题

　　本题选D，为细节题。解题依据为principles后的五个同位语从句。选项[A]中的illiterate（文盲的）和选项C中的no age limit（没有年龄限制）与同位语从句1中的meet minimal qualifications of age and literacy（满足最低年龄和文化程度要求）相悖，故排除选项A和选项C。选项B中的are immune from（免于）与同位语从句4中的are entitled to（有权）相悖，故排除选项B。选项D对应同位语从句5，其中judgment（裁决）与原文中的verdicts（判决）同义，should consider the opinion of the public（应考虑公众的意见）是对原文中should represent the conscience of the community（应该代表社会良知）的同义改写，故选项D正确。

考场
总结
　　本题考查名词性从句中的同位语从句，本题解题关键句中共包含5个由that引导的同位语从句，对principles作解释说明，解题时可以将这几个同位语从句分别拆译，再对应题干和选项选出正确答案。

真题重现

◎ 阅读 Text 3

The underlined phrase "*these* people" in Paragraph 4 refers to the ones who _____.

[A] stay outside the network of social influence

[B] have little contact with the source of influence

[C] are influenced and then influence others

[D] are influenced by the initial influential

◎ 核心词汇

- phrase [freɪz] *n.* 短语
- refer to 指的是
- contact ['kɒntækt] *n.* 接触，联系
- source [sɔːs] *n.* 来源
- initial [ɪ'nɪʃəl] *adj.* 最初的，初始的

解题思路

◎ 理解题目

第四段中带下划线的"这些人"是指那些_____的人。

[A] 待在社会影响力网络之外　　　　　[B] 与影响源很少接触

[C] 受到他人影响又影响他人　　　　　[D] 受最初有影响力的人影响

◎ 定位原文

根据题干中的Paragraph 4，我们定位到原文的第四段：

①The researchers' argument stems from a simple observation about social influence: With the exception of a few celebrities like Oprah Winfrey—whose outsize presence is primarily a function of media, not interpersonal influence—even the most influential members of a population simply don't interact with that many others. ②Yet it is precisely these non-celebrity influentials who, according to the two-step-flow theory, are supposed to drive social epidemics, by influencing their friends and colleagues directly. ③For a social epidemic to occur, however, each person so affected must then influence his or her own acquaintances, who must in turn influence theirs, and so

◎ 核心词汇

- exception [ɪk'sepʃn] *n.* 例外
- celebrity [sə'lebrəti] *n.* 名人
- interpersonal [ˌɪntə'pɜːsənl] *adj.* 人际关系的
- influential [ˌɪnflʊ'enʃəl] *adj.* 有影响力的 *n.* 有影响力的人
- interact with sb. 与某人互动
- epidemic [ˌepɪ'demɪk] *n.* 流行
- occur [ə'kɜː] *vi.* 发生
- affect [ə'fekt] *vt.* 影响
- acquaintance [ə'kweɪntəns] *n.* 熟人
- in turn 反过来；转过来

on; and just how many others pay attention to each of *these* people has little to do with the initial influential. ④If people in the network just two degrees removed from the initial influential prove resistant, for example, the cascade of change won't propagate very far or affect many people.

- pay attention to 注意到
- have little to do with 与……无关
- resistant [rɪ'zɪstənt] *adj.* 有抵抗力的
- the/a cascade of 大量，许多
- propagate ['prɒpəgeɪt] *vt.* 传播

◎ 定位核心句

再根据underlined phrase "*these* people" 进一步定位到该段第三句。下面我们先来尝试自己拆分和理解该长难句，之后再看老师的图解分析和参考译文。

· 小试牛刀

For a social epidemic to occur, however, each person so affected must then influence his or her

own acquaintances, who must in turn influence theirs, and so on; and just how many others pay

attention to each of *these* people has little to do with the initial influential.

· 图解分析

难点总览：本句由and连接两个并列分句，由分号隔开。分句1中，who引导定语从句，修饰先行词acquaintances；分句2中，how many引导主语从句。

第一层：确定主句

[For a social epidemic to occur], [however], <u>each person</u> (so affected) <u>must then influence</u>
　　　状语　　　　　　　　　　状语　　　主语1　　后置定语　　　　谓语1
his or her own acquaintances, (who must in turn influence theirs, and so on); and
　　　宾语1　　　　　　　　　　　　　定语从句　　　　　　　　　▲
just how many others pay attention to each of *these* people has little to do with
　　　　　主语2（主语从句）　　　　　　　　　　　谓语2
the initial influential.
　宾语2

第二层：确定从句

who引导定语从句，修饰先行词acquaintances，who代替先行词在定语从句中作主语。

157

who must in turn influence theirs, and so on		
主语	谓语	宾语

how many引导主语从句。

[just] how many others	pay attention to	each of *these* people
状语	主语	谓语	宾语

◎ 参考译文

　　研究人员的观点源于对社会影响力的简单观察：除了少数像奥普拉·温弗瑞这样的名人——他们的频繁亮相主要是媒体炒作的结果，而非人际关系的影响——即使人群中最有影响力的成员也根本不与那么多其他人互动。然而，根据两级传播理论，正是这些非名人而有影响力的人直接影响了他们的朋友和同事，从而推动了社会流行。然而，要发生社会大流行，每个被如此影响的人都必须影响他或她自己的熟人，而这些熟人又反过来必定会影响他们的熟人，依此类推；到底有多少人会关注这些中间传播者与最初有影响力的人无关。例如，如果传播网络中的人与最初有影响力的人仅相隔两个层级就被证明是有抵抗力的，那么连串变化就不会传播很远或影响很多人。

◎ 回归解题

　　本题选C，为词义题。通过指示代词these（这些）可知，其指代and之前提到的人，即each person so affected must then influence his or her own acquaintances（每个被如此影响的人都必须影响他或她自己的熟人），这里体现两个特点，先要affected（被影响），然后influence（影响）他人，故选项C正确。选项A为无中生有，故排除；根据文中has little to do with the initial influential（与最初有影响力的人无关），可排除选项B和选项D。

考场总结	本题关键是要找出代词these的指代对象，并理清定语从句的修饰意义。

真题重现

◎ 阅读 Text 1

1. Newspaper reviews in England before World War II were characterized by _____.

[A] free themes

[B] casual style

[C] elaborate layout

[D] radical viewpoints

2. Which of the following would Shaw and Newman most probably agree on?

[A] It is writers' duty to fulfill journalistic goals.

[B] It is contemptible for writers to be journalists.

[C] Writers are likely to be tempted into journalism.

[D] Not all writers are capable of journalistic writing.

◎ 核心词汇

- be characterized by 以……为特征
- casual ['kæʒuəl] adj. 随意的
- elaborate [ɪ'læbərət] adj. 精心制作的
- radical ['rædɪkl] adj. 激进的
- fulfill [fʊl'fɪl] vt. 满足
- contemptible [kən'temptəbl] adj. 可鄙的
- be capable of 有……能力

解题思路

◎ 理解题目

1. 二战前英格兰的报刊评论的特点是_____。

[A] 主题自由 　　　　　　[B] 风格随意

[C] 布局精心 　　　　　　[D] 观点激进

2. 肖和纽曼最有可能赞同以下哪项?

[A] 实现新闻目标是作家的职责。

[B] 作家当记者是可鄙的。

[C] 作家很可能被吸引而进入新闻业。

[D] 并非所有作家都具备新闻写作能力。

◎ 定位原文

根据两题题干中的World War II和Shaw and Newman，我们定位到原文的第三段：

①We are even farther removed from the unfocused newspaper reviews published in England between the turn of the 20th century and the eve of World War II, at a time when newsprint was dirt-cheap and stylish arts criticism was considered an ornament to the publications in which it appeared. ②In those far-off days, it was taken for granted that the critics of major papers would write in detail and at length about the events they covered. ③Theirs was a serious business, and even those reviewers who wore their learning lightly, like George Bernard Shaw and Ernest Newman, could be trusted to know what they were about. ④These men believed in journalism as a calling, and were proud to be published in the daily press. ⑤"So few authors have brains enough or literary gift enough to keep their own end up in journalism," Newman wrote, "that I am tempted to define 'journalism' as 'a term of contempt applied by writers who are not read to writers who are'."

◎ 核心词汇

- be far removed from 迥然不同于
- unfocused [ʌn'fəʊkəst] *adj.* 无焦点的
- review [rɪ'vjuː] *n.* 评论
- publish ['pʌblɪʃ] *vt.* 出版
- stylish ['staɪlɪʃ] *adj.* 时尚的
- criticism ['krɪtɪsɪzəm] *n.* 批评，评论
- ornament ['ɔːnəmənt] *n.* 装饰品
- publication [ˌpʌblɪ'keɪʃn] *n.* 出版；出版物
- journalism ['dʒɜːnəlɪzəm] *n.* 新闻写作
- tempt [tempt] *vt.* 诱惑，引诱
- literary ['lɪtərəri] *adj.* 文学的
- gift [gɪft] *n.* 天赋
- keep one's own end up in 有所成就；站稳脚跟
- define [dɪ'faɪn] *vt.* 下定义
- term [tɜːm] *n.* 术语
- contempt [kən'tempt] *n.* 轻视，轻蔑

◎ 定位核心句

第1题可进一步定位到该段首句，该句概括了20世纪初至二战前文艺评论的特点。

第2题可进一步定位到第三段后半部分，第五句引号中的内容表达出了肖和纽曼的主要观点。下面我们先来尝试自己拆分这两个长难句，之后再看老师的图解分析和参考译文。

·小试牛刀

1. We are even farther removed from the unfocused newspaper reviews published in England

between the turn of the 20th century and the eve of World War II, at a time when newsprint was

dirt-cheap and stylish arts criticism was considered an ornament to the publications in which it

appeared.

2. "So few authors have brains enough or literary gift enough to keep their own end up in journalism," Newman wrote, "that I am tempted to define 'journalism' as 'a term of contempt applied by writers who are not read to writers who are'."

· 图解分析

1. 难点总览：when引导定语从句，修饰先行词time；in which引导定语从句，修饰先行词publications。

第一层：确定主句

We are even farther removed from the unfocused newspaper reviews (published in England)
主语　　　　谓语　　　　　　　　宾语　　　　　　　后置定语

[between the turn of the 20th century and the eve of World War II], (at a time)
　　　　　　　时间状语　　　　　　　　　　　　　状语

(when newsprint was dirt-cheap and stylish arts criticism was considered an ornament to the
　　　　　　　　　　　定语从句

publications in which it appeared).

第二层：确定从句

when引导定语从句，修饰先行词time。

[when] newsprint was dirt-cheap and stylish arts criticism was considered
状语　　主语1　系　表语　　▲　　　　主语2　　　　谓语

<an ornament> (to the publications) (in which it appeared)
主语补足语　　　后置定语　　　　定语从句

第三层：确定从句

in which引导定语从句，修饰先行词publications。

[in which] it appeared
状语　主语 谓语

2. 难点总览：so...that...引导结果状语从句，其中两个who引导定语从句，均修饰其各自的先行词writers，第二个定语从句who are之后承前省略了动词read。

第一层：确定主句

"So few authors have brains enough or literary gift enough [to keep their own end up in
　　主语　　　　谓语　　　　　宾语　　　　　　　　　　　　　状语

journalism]," Newman wrote, [that I am tempted to define 'journalism' as 'a term of
　　　　　　　　　　　　插入语　　　　　　　　　　　　　结果状语从句

contempt applied by writers who are not read to writers who are."]

第二层：确定从句

so...that...引导结果状语从句。

that I am tempted to define 'journalism' <as 'a term of contempt> (applied by writers
▲主　　　谓语　　　　宾语　　　　宾语补足语　　　　后置定语

who are not read to writers who are)

第三层：确定从句

第一个who引导定语从句1，修饰先行词writers，who代替先行词在定语从句中作主语。

who are not read
主语　谓语

第二个who引导定语从句2，修饰先行词writers，who代替先行词在定语从句中作主语，系动词are后承前省略了动词read。

who are (read)
主语　谓语

◎ 参考译文

　　20世纪初期至第二次世界大战前夕，英国的报刊评论包罗万象，与现在也是截然不同的；当时新闻用纸非常便宜，而且人们认为时新的文艺评论是刊登它的出版物的点缀物。在那个遥远的年代，人们理所当然地认为，主流报纸的评论家们会详细地描述他们所报道的事件。他们的工作是严肃的，即使是像乔治·伯纳德·肖和欧内斯特·纽曼那样低调的评论家，人们也相信他们知道自己在做什么。这些人相信新闻写作是一种使命，并为能够在日报上发表文章而感到自豪。"很少有作家有足够的头脑或文学天赋来坚持从事新闻写作，"纽曼写道，"所以我不禁想把'新闻写作'定义为无人问津的作家对当红作家的'轻蔑之词'。"

◎ 回归解题

1. 本题选A，为细节题。题干问及Newspaper reviews（报刊评论）的特点，原文中仅用一个词修饰unfocused（重点不突出的，不聚焦的），意思就是"主题不鲜明"，即"主题自由"，故选项A正确。

2. 本题选D，为细节题。选项A为无中生有，故排除；选项B对应最后一句中的contempt（蔑视，轻视），但原文中说的是无人问津的作家轻视当红作家，而非肖和纽曼的观点，故排除；选项C对应最后一句中的I am tempted to define（我不禁想定义……），其中I指Newman，而非writers（作家），故选项C错误。选项D对应最后一句So few authors have brains enough or literary gift enough to keep their own end up in journalism（很少有作家有足够的头脑或文学天赋来坚持从事新闻写作），也就是说，并非所有作家都有能力从事新闻写作，故选项D正确。

考场
总结　　第1题较为简单，第2题比较难，考查了两个套用的so...that...引导的结果状语从句。

核心句 09 ▶ 2010年英语一

真题重现

◎ 阅读 Text 2

The word "about-face" (Line 2, Para. 3) most probably means _____.

[A] loss of good will

[B] increase of hostility

[C] change of attitude

[D] enhancement of dignity

◎核心词汇

- will [wɪl] *n.* 意愿
- hostility [hɒˈstɪləti] *n.* 敌意
- attitude [ˈætɪtjuːd] *n.* 态度
- enhancement [ɪnˈhɑːnsmənt] *n.* 提升
- dignity [ˈdɪgnəti] *n.* 尊严

解题思路

◎ 理解题目

第三段第二行的单词"about-face"最可能的意思是_____。

[A] 善意的缺失

[B] 敌意的增加

[C] 态度的转变

[D] 尊严的提升

◎ 定位原文

根据题干中的"about-face"(Line 2, Para. 3),我们定位到原文的第三段:

①Curbs on business-method claims would be a dramatic about-face, because it was the Federal Circuit itself that introduced such patents with its 1998 decision in the so-called State Street Bank case, approving a patent on a way of pooling mutual-fund assets. ②That ruling produced an explosion in business-method patent filings, initially by emerging Internet companies trying to stake out exclusive rights to specific types of online transactions. ③Later, more established companies raced to add such patents to their files, if only as a defensive move against rivals that might beat them to the punch. ④In 2005, IBM noted in a court filing that it had been issued more than 300 business-method patents, despite the fact that it questioned the legal basis for granting them. ⑤Similarly, some Wall Street investment firms armed themselves with patents for financial products, even as they took positions in court cases opposing the practice.

◎ 核心词汇

- curb [kɜːb] *n.* 控制,抑制
- claim [kleɪm] *n.* (专利)申请
- dramatic [drəˈmætɪk] *adj.* 戏剧性的
- pool [puːl] *vt.* 集合(资金或资源)
- asset [ˈæset] *n.* 资产
- ruling [ˈruːlɪŋ] *n.* 裁决
- explosion [ɪkˈspləʊʒn] *n.* 激增
- initially [ɪˈnɪʃəli] *adv.* 起初
- emerging [ɪˈmɜːdʒɪŋ] *adj.* 新兴的
- stake out 明确表明(观点或立场)
- exclusive [ɪkˈskluːsɪv] *adj.* 专有的
- defensive [dɪˈfensɪv] *adj.* 防御的
- rival [ˈraɪvl] *n.* 竞争对手
- beat sb. to the punch 先发制人
- oppose [əˈpəʊz] *vt.* 反对

◎ 定位核心句

再进一步定位到该段首句。下面我们先来尝试自己拆分该长难句,之后再看老师的图解分析和参考译文。

Curbs on business-method claims would be a dramatic about-face, because it was the Federal

Circuit itself that introduced such patents with its 1998 decision in the so-called State Street

Bank case, approving a patent on a way of pooling mutual-fund assets.

· 图解分析

难点总览：because引导原因状语从句，从句为强调句句型：it was...that...；其中approving...为现在分词短语作伴随状语。

第一层：确定主句

Curbs (on business-method claims) would be a dramatic about-face, [because it was the

主语　　　后置定语　　　　　　系动词　　　表语　　　　原因状语从句

Federal Circuit itself that introduced such patents with its 1998 decision in the so-called State Street Bank case, approving a patent on a way of pooling mutual-fund assets].

第二层：确定从句

because引导原因状语从句。

because it was the Federal Circuit {itself} that introduced such patents

▲　　　　主语　　　同位语　　谓语　　宾语

[with its 1998 decision] (in the so-called State Street Bank case), [approving a patent on a

状语　　　　　　　后置定语　　　　　　伴随状语

way of pooling mutual-fund assets]

◎ 参考译文

对商业方法专利申请的限制将会是一个戏剧性的转变，因为正是联邦巡回法院本身在其1998年对所谓的"州街银行案"做出的判决中引入了此类专利，同意对一种筹集共同基金资产的方法授予专利。该裁决导致商业方法专利申请激增，最初是新兴的互联网公司试图对特定类型的在线交易明确表示专有权。后来，更成熟的公司竞相将此类专利添加到他们的档案中，以期作为防止竞争对手抢占先机的防御性措施。2005年，IBM公司在一份法庭文件中指出，尽管它质疑授予这些专利的法律依据，但它已经获得了300

多项商业方法专利。类似地，华尔街的一些投资公司也利用金融产品专利来武装自己，即使他们在法庭上反对这种做法。

◎ 回归解题

本题选C，为词义题。根据because之前的curbs（限制）和because引导的原因状语从句中的introduced（引入）可知，Federal Circuit（联邦巡回法院）的行为前后相悖，态度发生了巨大转变，故选项C正确。

考场
总结

本题考查原因状语从句和强调句，because引导的原因状语从句是一个强调句句型，强调的是主语the Federal Circuit，去掉it was和that可还原成：the Federal Circuit itself introduced such patents with its 1998 decision in the case。

核心句 (10) ▸ 2011年英语二

真题重现

◎ 阅读 Text 3

Which of the following can be inferred from Paragraph 3 about the Bauhaus?

[A] It was founded by Ludwig Mies van der Rohe.

[B] Its designing concept was affected by World War II.

[C] Most American architects used to be associated with it.

[D] It had a great influence upon American architecture.

◎ 核心词汇

- found [faʊnd] *vt.* 创立，创建
- concept ['kɒnsept] *n.* 理念
- be associated with 与……有关系
- architecture ['ɑːkɪtektʃə(r)] *n.* 建筑

解题思路

◎ 理解题目

关于包豪斯，我们可以从第三段中推断出以下哪项？

[A] 它由路德维希·密斯·凡德罗创立。

[B] 其设计理念受到二战的影响。

[C] 大多数美国建筑师曾与它有关。

[D] 它对美国建筑产生了巨大影响。

根据题干中的Paragraph 3，我们定位到原文的第三段：

①Economic condition was only a stimulus for the trend toward efficient living. ②The phrase "less is more" was actually first popularized by a German, the architect Ludwig Mies van der Rohe, who like other people associated with the Bauhaus, a school of design, emigrated to the United States before World War II and took up posts at American architecture schools. ③These designers came to exert enormous influence on the course of American architecture, but none more so than Mies.

- stimulus ['stɪmjələs] *n.* 促进因素
- efficient [ɪ'fɪʃnt] *adj.* 高效的
- popularize ['pɒpjələraɪz] *vt.* 使……流行
- architect ['ɑːkɪtekt] *n.* 建筑师
- associate [ə'səʊʃɪeɪt] *vt.* 把……联系在一起
- emigrate ['emɪɡreɪt] *vi.* 移民(出境)
- take up 从事
- post [pəʊst] *n.* 职位

◎ 定位核心句

再根据Bauhaus进一步定位到该段第二句。该句有48个单词，不仅长而且成分复杂。下面我们先来尝试自己拆分和理解该长难句，之后再看老师的图解分析和参考译文。

· 小试牛刀

The phrase "less is more" was actually first popularized by a German, the architect Ludwig Mies

van der Rohe, who like other people associated with the Bauhaus, a school of design, emigrated

to the United States before World War II and took up posts at American architecture schools.

· 图解分析

难点总览：who引导定语从句，修饰前面的人。

第一层：确定主句

The phrase {"less is more"} was actually first popularized [by a German],
主语　　phrase的同位语　　　　　　谓语　　　　　　状语
{the architect Ludwig Mies van der Rohe}, (who like other people associated with the Bauhaus,
　　　　a German的同位语　　　　　　　　　　　　　　定语从句
a school of design, emigrated to the United States before World War II and took up posts at American architecture schools).

第二层：确定从句

who引导定语从句，修饰先行词Ludwig Mies van der Rohe，who代替先行词在定语从句中作主语。

who	[like other people (associated with the Bauhaus, {a school of design})],		emigrated
主语	状语　　　　　　people的后置定语　　　　　Bauhaus的同位语		谓语1

[to the United States] [before World War II] and took up posts [at American architecture schools]

状语　　　　　时间状语　　　▲　谓语2 宾语　　　　　　地点状语

◎ 参考译文

　　经济状况只是高效生活趋势的一个刺激因素。"少即是多"这个说法其实最早是由德国建筑师路德维希·密斯·凡德罗推广出来的，像其他与包豪斯设计学院有关的建筑设计师一样，他于二战前移居美国并在美国多所建筑学校任职。这些设计师们对美国建筑的发展历程产生了巨大的影响，但其中影响最大的还要数密斯。

◎ 回归解题

　　本题选D，为推断题。选项A中的founded（创立）为无中生有，故排除；选项B中的World War II与密斯有关，但原文并没有提及其与包豪斯的关系，故排除；选项C中的most（大多数）为无中生有，原文仅提及other people（其他人），而没有评价"多少"，故排除。根据最后一句中的These designers came to exert enormous influence on the course of American architecture（这些设计师们对美国建筑的发展历程产生了巨大的影响），而核心句提及这些人均与包豪斯有关，故可以推断出，包豪斯对美国建筑产生了巨大影响，故选项D正确。

考场
总结

　　本题核心句包含多个复杂的语法成分，如同位语、定语从句、后置定语、状语等。解题关键是找到核心句的主干The phrase "less is more" was actually first popularized by a German，并理清定语从句与其先行词之间的修饰关系。通过"主干公式"可将句子化繁为简，再结合上下文，从而选出正确答案。

真题重现

◎ 阅读 Text 3

Consumers may create "earned" media when they are _____.

[A] obsessed with online shopping at certain Web sites

[B] inspired by product-promoting e-mails sent to them

[C] eager to help their friends promote quality products

[D] enthusiastic about recommending their favorite products

◎ 核心词汇

- obsess [əb'ses] *vt.* 使着迷
- inspire [ɪn'spaɪə(r)] *vt.* 激发，激励
- promote [prə'məʊt] *vt.* 推广，推销
- quality ['kwɒləti] *adj.* 优质的
- enthusiastic [ɪnˌθjuːzi'æstɪk] *adj.* 热心的，热情的
- recommend [ˌrekə'mend] *vt.* 推荐

解题思路

◎ 理解题目

当消费者_____时可能会创造"赢得"媒体。

[A] 沉迷于在某些网站上网购   [B] 受到发送给他们的产品推销邮件的启发

[C] 想要帮他们的朋友推广优质产品   [D] 热心推荐他们最喜欢的产品

◎ 定位原文

根据题干的中"earned" media，我们定位到原文的第一段：

①The rough guide to marketing success used to be that you got what you paid for. ②No longer. ③While traditional "paid" media—such as television commercials and print advertisements—still play a major role, companies today can exploit many alternative forms of media. ④Consumers passionate about a product may create "earned" media by willingly promoting it to friends, and a company may leverage "owned" media by sending e-mail alerts about products and sales to customers registered with its Web site. ⑤The way consumers now approach the process of making purchase decisions means that marketing's impact stems from a broad range of factors beyond conventional paid media.

◎ 核心词汇

- rough [rʌf] *adj.* 粗略的
- commercial [kə'mɜːʃl] *n.* 商业广告
- exploit [ɪk'splɔɪt] *vt.* 利用
- alternative [ɔːl'tɜːnətɪv] *adj.* 可供替代的
- passionate ['pæʃənət] *adj.* 热情的
- leverage ['liːvərɪdʒ] *vt.* 充分利用
- alert [ə'lɜːt] *n.* 提醒
- register ['redʒɪstə(r)] *vt.* 注册；登记
- impact ['ɪmpækt] *n.* 影响
- stem from 源于
- conventional [kən'venʃnl] *adj.* 传统的

再进一步定位至该段倒数第二句。下面我们先来尝试自己拆分和理解该长难句，之后再看老师的图解分析和参考译文。

· 小试牛刀

Consumers passionate about a product may create "earned" media by willingly promoting it to

friends, and a company may leverage "owned" media by sending e-mail alerts about products

and sales to customers registered with its Web site.

· 图解分析

难点总览：and连接并列句，两个分句均包含介词短语by...，在句中作方式状语。

Consumers (passionate about a product) may create "earned" media
主语1　　　Consumers的后置定语　　谓语1　　　宾语1

[by willingly promoting it to friends], and a company may leverage "owned" media
　　方式状语1　　　　　▲　　主语2　　　谓语2　　　　宾语2

[by sending e-mail alerts about products and sales to customers registered with its Web site].
　　　　　　　　　　　方式状语2

重要补充：

方式状语by sending...为介宾结构，而sending A to B为双宾语结构。

[by sending e-mail alerts (about products and sales) to customers (registered with its Web site)].
　　　直接宾语　　　alerts的后置定语　　　间接宾语　　customers的后置定语

◎ 参考译文

　　过去，营销成功的大致准则是"一分钱，一分货"。但现在不再这样了。虽然传统的"付费"媒体——如电视广告和平面广告——仍然发挥着重要作用，但如今公司还可以利用许多其他的媒体形式。酷爱某种产品的消费者可能会自愿向朋友推荐该产品，从而创造"赢得"媒体，而公司可能会通过向在其网站上注册的客户发送关于产品和销售信息的电子邮件提醒来充分利用"自有"媒体。如今消费者对于作出购买决策这一过程的处理方式表明，营销的影响力源于传统付费媒体之外的广泛因素。

本题选D，为细节题。定位句指出，"酷爱某种产品的消费者可能会自愿向朋友推荐该产品，从而创造'赢得'媒体"，换句话说，消费者主动向他人推荐自己喜欢的产品时，可能会创造"赢得"媒体，故选项D正确。选项A中的online shopping（网购）为无中生有，故排除；选项B对应的是"owned" media，而非"earned" media，故排除；选项C中的help their friends promote（帮他们的朋友推广）为无中生有，故排除。

考场总结

earned media、owned media和paid media

经常会听到earned media、owned media和paid media这三个词，earned media是"赢得媒体"，即用户的口碑；owned media是"自有媒体"，即企业自有的网站、微信或微博等；而paid media是"付费媒体"，即付费购买的传播渠道，比如CCTV新闻联播前的报时广告和网站搜索广告等。本题核心句考查方式状语by willingly promoting it to friends，修饰create "earned media"这一动作。

核心句 ⑫ ▶ 2012年英语二

真题重现

◎ 阅读 Text 3

Those who are against gene patents believe that _____.

[A] genetic tests are not reliable

[B] only man-made products are patentable

[C] patents on genes depend much on innovation

[D] courts should restrict access to genetic tests

◎核心词汇

- patent ['pætnt] *n.* 专利
- reliable [rɪ'laɪəbl] *adj.* 可靠的
- depend on 取决于，依赖于
- innovation [ˌɪnə'veɪʃn] *n.* 创新
- restrict [rɪ'strɪkt] *vt.* 限制

解题思路

◎ 理解题目

反对基因专利的人认为_____。

[A] 基因检测不可靠

[B] 只有人造产品才可获得专利

[C] 基因专利很大程度上依赖于创新

[D] 法院应限制使用基因检测

◎ 定位原文

根据题干中的against gene patents，我们定位到原文的第三段：

①But as companies continue their attempts at personalized medicine, the courts will remain rather busy. ②The Myriad case itself is probably not over. ③Critics make three main arguments against gene patents: a gene is a product of nature, so it may not be patented; gene patents suppress innovation rather than reward it; and patents' monopolies restrict access to genetic tests such as Myriad's. ④A growing number seem to agree. ⑤Last year a federal task-force urged reform for patents related to genetic tests. ⑥In October the Department of Justice filed a brief in the Myriad case, arguing that an isolated DNA molecule "is no less a product of nature...than are cotton fibres that have been separated from cotton seeds."

◎ 定位核心句

再进一步定位到该段第三句。下面我们先来尝试自己拆分和理解该长难句，之后再看老师的图解分析和参考译文。

· 小试牛刀

Critics make three main arguments against gene patents: a gene is a product of nature, so it may

not be patented; gene patents suppress innovation rather than reward it; and patents' monopolies

restrict access to genetic tests such as Myriad's.

· 图解分析

难点总览：冒号之后用分号分隔三句话，对arguments进行解释说明。

第一层：确定主句

> Critics make three main arguments (against gene patents):
>
> 主语 谓语 宾语 后置定语
>
> a gene is a product of nature, so it may not be patented; gene patents suppress innovation rather
>
> than reward it; and patents' monopolies restrict access to genetic tests such as Myriad's.
>
> 对arguments进行解释说明

第二层：确定起解释说明作用的三个分句

分句1

> a gene is a product of nature, [so it may not be patented]
>
> 主语 系 表语 结果状语从句

分句2

> gene patents suppress innovation rather than reward it
>
> 主语 谓语1 宾语1 ▲ 谓语2 宾语2

分句3

> patents' monopolies restrict access (to genetic tests such as Myriad's)
>
> 主语 谓语 宾语 access的后置定语

◎ 参考译文

　　但随着许多公司继续尝试个性化医疗，法院仍然将相当忙碌。Myriad案本身可能并未完结。批评者主要提出了三个反对基因专利的理由：基因是自然的产物，因此不可获得专利；基因专利抑制创新，而非鼓励创新；专利垄断限制了基因检测的使用，如对于Myriad公司基因检测的使用。越来越多的人似乎同意这种观点。去年，一个联邦专项工作组敦促对基因检测方面的专利进行改革。在10月，司法部发布了一则关于Myriad案的简报，认为分离的DNA分子"与从棉籽中分离出来的棉纤维一样，都是自然的产物……"。

◎ 回归解题

　　本题选B，为细节题。题干中的Those who are against gene patents（反对基因专利的人）对应原文中的critics（批评者），题干中的believe（认为）对应原文中的make...

arguments（提出……理由），故正确答案与冒号后的三个理由有关。选项A中的not reliable（不可靠）为无中生有，故排除。选项B对应第一个理由：a gene is a product of nature, so it may not be patented（基因是自然的产物，因此不可获得专利），也就是说，只有人造产品才可获得专利，故选项B正确；选项C对应第二个理由：gene patents suppress innovation（基因专利抑制创新），而非依赖创新，故排除选项C；选项D对应第三个理由，原文提及patents' monopolies（专利垄断）而非courts（法院）会restrict access to genetic tests（限制基因检测的使用），这属于弊端，说明作者是提倡使用基因检测的，故排除选项D。

考场
总结

　　本题关键是理解冒号后的三个理由，第一个理由中的结果状语从句so it may not be patented说明了不可获得专利的情况，反过来也说明了可获得专利的情况；考点属于正话反说。

核心句 ⑬ ▶ 2012年英语二

真题重现

◎ 阅读 Text 4

The research of Till Von Wachter suggests that in the recession graduates from elite universities tend to _____.

[A] lag behind the others due to decreased opportunities

[B] catch up quickly with experienced employees

[C] see their life chances as dimmed as the others'

[D] recover more quickly than the others

◎核心词汇

- recession [rɪ'seʃn] *n.* 倒退，衰退
- elite [eɪ'li:t] *adj.* 精英的
- lag behind 落后于
- dim [dɪm] *vt.* 使变暗淡
- recover [rɪ'kʌvə(r)] *v.* 恢复

解题思路

◎ 理解题目

蒂尔·冯·瓦赫特的研究表明，在经济衰退中的名牌大学毕业生往往_____。

[A] 由于机会减少而落后于其他人　　　　[B] 很快就赶上了经验丰富的员工

[C] 和其他人一样认为人生机会渺茫　　　[D] 比其他人更快恢复

根据题干中的The research of Till Von Wachter，我们定位到原文的第四段：

①Income inequality usually falls during a recession, but it has not shrunk in this one. ②Indeed, this period of economic weakness may reinforce class divides, and decrease opportunities to cross them—especially for young people. ③The research of Till Von Wachter, the economist at Columbia University, suggests that not all people graduating into a recession see their life chances dimmed: those with degrees from elite universities catch up fairly quickly to where they otherwise would have been if they had graduated in better times; it is the masses beneath them that are left behind.

◎ 核心词汇

- inequality [ˌɪnɪˈkwɒləti] *n.* 不平等
- shrink [ʃrɪŋk] *v.* 缩小
- reinforce [ˌriːɪnˈfɔːs] *vt.* 加强
- divide [dɪˈvaɪd] *n.* 差异
- degree [dɪˈɡriː] *n.* 学位
- fairly [ˈfeəli] *adv.* 相当地
- leave...behind 把……抛在后面

◎ 定位核心句

再根据题干中的in the recession和graduates进一步定位到该段第三句。该句较长，共有59个单词。下面我们先来尝试自己拆分和理解该长难句，之后再看老师的图解分析和参考译文。

· 小试牛刀

The research of Till Von Wachter, the economist at Columbia University, suggests that not all

people graduating into a recession see their life chances dimmed: those with degrees from elite

universities catch up fairly quickly to where they otherwise would have been if they had

graduated in better times; it is the masses beneath them that are left behind.

· 图解分析

难点总览：第一个that引导动词suggests的宾语从句，冒号后是对该宾语从句的补充说明，包含两个并列分句。其中，where引导介词to的宾语从句，if引导条件状语从句，为虚拟语气句式，主句和从句均为对过去行为的虚拟。分号后的分句为it is...that...强调句句型。

第一层：确定主句

The research of Till Von Wachter, {the economist at Columbia University}, suggests
主语　　　　　　　　　Till Von Wachter的同位语　　　谓语

that not all people graduating into a recession see their life chances dimmed:
宾语从句

those with degrees from elite universities catch up fairly quickly to where they otherwise would
对宾语从句的补充说明

have been if they had graduated in better times; it is the masses beneath them that are left behind.

第二层：确定从句

第一个that引导动词suggests的宾语从句。

that not all people (graduating into a recession) see their life chances <dimmed>
▲　　主语　　　　　　后置定语　　　　　谓语　　　宾语　　宾语补足语

第三层：确定起补充说明作用的两个分句

分句1，包含where引导的宾语从句和if引导的条件状语从句。

those (with degrees from elite universities) catch up fairly quickly to
主语　　　　　后置定语　　　　　　　　谓语

where they otherwise would have been if they had graduated in better times
宾语从句

分句2，为强调句句型。

it is the masses (beneath them) that are left behind
主语　　　后置定语　　　谓语

第四层：确定从句

where引导介词to的宾语从句，where在从句中作表语。

where they [otherwise] would have been [if they had graduated in better times]
表语 主语　状语　　　系动词　　　　　　条件状语从句

176

第五层：确定从句

if引导条件状语从句，使用了虚拟语气。

> if <u>they</u> <u>had graduated</u> [in better times]
> ▲ 主语   谓语   时间状语

◎ 参考译文

　　收入不平等通常在经济衰退期间缩小，但在这次经济危机中并没有缩小。事实上，这段经济疲软时期可能会加剧阶级鸿沟，并减少跨越阶级鸿沟的机会——尤其是对年轻人而言。哥伦比亚大学的经济学家蒂尔·冯·瓦赫特的研究表明，不是所有毕业就遇到衰退时期的人都认为人生机会渺茫：那些毕业于名牌大学的人很快就会到达其在繁荣时期毕业时本该达到的位置，落后的是那些不如他们的普通大众。

◎ 回归解题

　　本题选D，为细节题。选项A中的lag behind对应原文中的are left behind，该短语所在句it is the masses beneath them that are left behind是一个强调句句型，还原后是：the masses beneath them are left behind.，其中them指代前面的those with degrees from elite universities，即题干中的graduates from elite universities（名牌大学毕业生）。故该句翻译成：在名牌大学水准之下的大众们被抛在后面。所以，名牌大学毕业生没有因为机会减少而落后，故排除选项A。选项B原文未提及，排除不选。原文提到名牌大学毕业生不会同其他人一样，排除选项C。正确答案为选项D，名牌大学毕业生会更快从经济衰退中恢复过来，达到更高的成就。

考场
总结
　　本题考查宾语从句以及冒号后起补充说明作用的并列句。注意，冒号后的内容往往是解题的重要信息，在解题时要尤其注意。

真题重现

◎ 阅读 Text 3

According to the first paragraph, economic downturns would _____.

[A] ease the competition of man vs. machine

[B] highlight machines' threat to human jobs

[C] provoke a painful technological revolution

[D] outmode our current economic structure

◎ 核心词汇

- ease [i:z] v. 缓解
- competition [ˌkɒmpəˈtɪʃn] n. 竞争
- highlight [ˈhaɪlaɪt] vt. 突出；强调
- threat [θret] n. 威胁
- provoke [prəˈvəʊk] vt. 激起；引起
- outmode [ˌaʊtˈməʊd] vt. 使……过时；淘汰
- structure [ˈstrʌktʃə(r)] n. 结构

解题思路

◎ 理解题目

根据第一段，经济衰退将_____。

[A] 缓和人与机器的竞争

[B] 突显机器对人类工作的威胁

[C] 引发一场艰难的技术革命

[D] 淘汰我们目前的经济结构

◎ 定位原文

根据题干中的 first paragraph，我们定位到原文的第一段：

①The concept of *man versus machine* is at least as old as the industrial revolution, but this phenomenon tends to be most acutely felt during economic downturns and fragile recoveries. ②And yet, it would be a mistake to think we are right now simply experiencing the painful side of a boom and bust cycle. ③Certain jobs have gone away for good, outmoded by machines. ④Since technology has such an insatiable appetite for eating up human jobs, this phenomenon will continue to restructure our economy in ways we cannot immediately foresee.

◎ 核心词汇

- concept [ˈkɒnsept] n. 概念
- versus [ˈvɜːsəs] prep. ……对……
- at least 至少
- industrial [ɪnˈdʌstriəl] adj. 工业的
- revolution [ˌrevəˈluːʃn] n. 革命
- phenomenon [fəˈnɒmɪnən] n. 现象
- acutely [əˈkjuːtli] adv. 强烈地
- economic [ˌiːkəˈnɒmɪk] adj. 经济的
- downturn [ˈdaʊntɜːn] n. 低迷时期
- fragile [ˈfrædʒaɪl] adj. 脆弱的
- recovery [rɪˈkʌvəri] n. 恢复，复苏
- insatiable [ɪnˈseɪʃəbl] adj. 贪得无厌的
- appetite [ˈæpɪtaɪt] n. 胃口；欲望
- foresee [fɔːˈsiː] vt. 预见

再根据economic downturns进一步定位到该段首句。下面我们先来尝试自己拆分和理解该长难句，之后再看老师的图解分析和参考译文。

· 小试牛刀

The concept of *man versus machine* is at least as old as the industrial revolution, but this

phenomenon tends to be most acutely felt during economic downturns and fragile recoveries.

· 图解分析

难点总览：but连接并列句。

The concept of *man versus machine* is at least as old as the industrial revolution,
　　　　　主语1　　　　　　　系动词　　　　　　　表语

but this phenomenon tends to be most acutely felt
▲　　　主语2　　　　　　　谓语

[during economic downturns and fragile recoveries].
　　　　　　　　时间状语

◎ 参考译文

"人机竞争"的概念至少与工业革命一样古老，但在经济衰退和惨淡的复苏期间，这种现象往往最为强烈地被察觉到。然而，如果认为我们现在只是在经历经济繁荣和萧条周期所带来的痛苦的一面，那就大错特错了。某些工作已经永远消失了，被机器淘汰了。由于科技总是贪得无厌地吞噬着人们的工作，这种现象将继续以我们无法立即预见的方式重构我们的经济。

◎ 回归解题

本题选B，为细节题。定位句指出，在经济衰退和惨淡复苏期间，这种现象往往最为强烈地被察觉到，其中this phenomenon（这种现象）指的是but之前提及的*man versus machine*（人机竞争），也就是说机器对人类造成了威胁，故选项B正确，其中highlight（突显）对应原文中的tends to be most acutely felt，machines' threat to human jobs对应原文中的*man versus machine*。选项A中的ease（缓和）与原文中的most acutely felt相悖，故排除；选项C中的provoke（引发）为无中生有，故排除；选项D中的outmode源于该段第三句，但文中说的是Certain jobs...outmoded by machines（机器淘汰了某些工作），而非经济衰退淘汰经济结构，故排除。

考场总结　本题考查对定位句中but之后的内容的理解，同时需要明确this phenomenon的指代对象。

核心句 (15) ▸ 2015年英语一

真题重现

◎ 阅读 Text 1

Which of the following is shown to be odd, according to Paragraph 4?

[A] Aristocrats' excessive reliance on inherited wealth.

[B] The role of the nobility in modern democracies.

[C] The simple lifestyle of the aristocratic families.

[D] The nobility's adherence to their privileges.

◎ 核心词汇
- odd [ɒd] *adj.* 奇怪的
- aristocrat ['ærɪstəkræt] *n.* 贵族
- reliance [rɪ'laɪəns] *n.* 依赖
- nobility [nəʊ'bɪləti] *n.* 贵族
- adherence [əd'hɪərəns] *n.* 坚持

解题思路

◎ 理解题目

根据第四段，下列哪项是奇怪的？

[A] 贵族对继承财富的过度依赖。

[B] 贵族在现代民主国家中的作用。

[C] 贵族家庭的简朴生活方式。

[D] 贵族对特权的坚持。

◎ 定位原文

根据题干中的Paragraph 4，我们定位到原文的第四段：

①Even so, kings and queens undoubtedly have a downside. ②Symbolic of national unity as they claim to be, their very history—and sometimes the way they behave today—embodies outdated and indefensible

◎ 核心词汇
- undoubtedly [ʌn'daʊtɪdli] *adv.* 无疑
- downside ['daʊnsaɪd] *n.* 不利方面
- symbolic [sɪm'bɒlɪk] *adj.* 象征性的
- outdated [ˌaʊt'deɪtɪd] *adj.* 过时的
- indefensible [ˌɪndɪ'fensəbl] *adj.* 站不住脚的

privileges and inequalities. ③At a time when Thomas Piketty and other economists are warning of rising inequality and the increasing power of inherited wealth, it is bizarre that wealthy aristocratic families should still be the symbolic heart of modern democratic states.

- privilege ['prɪvəlɪdʒ] *n.* 特权
- inequality [ˌɪnɪ'kwɒləti] *n.* 不平等
- inherit [ɪn'herɪt] *v.* 继承
- bizarre [bɪ'zɑː(r)] *adj.* 奇怪的
- aristocratic [ˌærɪstə'krætɪk] *adj.* 贵族的
- democratic [ˌdemə'krætɪk] *adj.* 民主的

◎ 定位核心句

再根据odd进一步定位到该段最后一句，odd意为"奇怪的，古怪的"，与该句中的bizarre同义。下面我们先来尝试自己拆分和理解该长难句，之后再看老师的图解分析和参考译文。

· 小试牛刀

At a time when Thomas Piketty and other economists are warning of rising inequality and the

increasing power of inherited wealth, it is bizarre that wealthy aristocratic families should still

be the symbolic heart of modern democratic states.

· 图解分析

难点总览：when引导定语从句，修饰先行词time；it为形式主语，that引导主语从句作真正的主语，注意其中的should意为"竟然"。

第一层：确定主句

[At a time] (when Thomas Piketty and other economists are warning of rising inequality
时间状语　　　　　　　　　　　定语从句
and the increasing power of inherited wealth), it　is bizarre that wealthy aristocratic families
　　　　　　　　　　　　　　　　　　形主 系 表语　　　　主语从句
should still be the symbolic heart of modern democratic states.

第二层：确定从句

when引导定语从句，修饰先行词time。

第三层：确定从句

that引导主语从句，在主句中作真正的主语。

◎ 参考译文

即便如此，国王和王后无疑也有其不利的一面。虽然他们自称是国家统一的象征，但他们独一无二的历史——以及他们如今某些时候的行为方式——体现了过时而站不住脚的特权和不平等。在托马斯·皮凯蒂和其他经济学家提醒（人们）注意不平等的加剧和因继承财富而不断扩大的权力时，富有的贵族家庭竟仍然是现代民主国家的核心象征，这是很奇怪的。

◎ 回归解题

本题选B，为细节题。选项A中的excessive reliance on（过度依赖于）为无中生有，故排除。选项B是对定位句中主语从句的概括，其中nobility（贵族）对应原文中的wealthy aristocratic families（富有的贵族家庭）；modern democracies（现代民主）对应modern democratic states（现代民主国家）；role（作用）对应the symbolic heart（核心象征），故选项B正确。选项C中的simple lifestyle（简朴生活方式）为无中生有，故排除。选项D中的privileges（特权）出现在第四段第二句中，但"对特权的坚持"这一表述为无中生有，故排除。

考场
总结

　　本题考查对it作形式主语、that引导的主语从句作真正的主语这一特殊句式的理解。当主语从句较长时，为避免头重脚轻，往往用it作形式主语，而将真正的主语——主语从句放在后面。常见的句式有：

　　1) It + be + *n.* + that引导的主语从句

　　2) It + be + *adj.* + that引导的主语从句

　　3) It + be + known/said/believed/reported等 + that引导的主语从句

真题重现

◎ 阅读 Text 2

The authors of the research article are optimistic because _____.

[A] the problem is solvable

[B] their approach is costless

[C] the recruiting rate has increased

[D] their findings appeal to students

◎ 核心词汇

- solvable ['sɒlvəbl] *adj.* 可以解决的
- recruit [rɪ'kruːt] *v.* 招收
- appeal to 吸引

解题思路

◎ 理解题目

该研究文章的作者很乐观，因为_____。

[A] 问题是可以解决的

[B] 他们的方法是无成本的

[C] 招生率提高了

[D] 他们的发现对学生有吸引力

◎ 定位原文

根据题干中的The authors...are optimistic，我们定位到原文的第二段：

But the article is actually quite optimistic, as it outlines a potential solution to this problem, suggesting that an approach (which involves a one-hour, next-to-no-cost program) can close 63 percent of the achievement gap (measured by such factors as grades) between first-generation and other students.

◎ 核心词汇

- optimistic [ˌɒptɪ'mɪstɪk] *adj.* 乐观的
- outline ['aʊtlaɪn] *vt.* 概述
- potential [pə'tenʃl] *adj.* 潜在的，可能的
- approach [ə'prəʊtʃ] *n.* 方法
- involve [ɪn'vɒlv] *vt.* 涉及，包括
- solution [sə'luːʃn] *n.* 解决方案
- gap [gæp] *n.* 差距

◎ 定位核心句

该段仅有一句，共45个单词。下面我们先来尝试自己拆分和理解该长难句，之后再看老师的图解分析和参考译文。

But the article is actually quite optimistic, as it outlines a potential solution to this problem,

suggesting that an approach (which involves a one-hour, next-to-no-cost program) can close 63

percent of the achievement gap (measured by such factors as grades) between first-generation

and other students.

· 图解分析

难点总览：as引导原因状语从句，其中suggesting...为现在分词短语作伴随状语；that引导动词suggesting的宾语从句；which引导定语从句，修饰先行词approach。

第一层：确定主句

> But the article is actually quite optimistic, [as it outlines a potential solution to this problem,
> ▲　　主语　系　　　表语　　　　　　　　　　　原因状语从句
> suggesting that an approach (which involves a one-hour, next-to-no-cost program) can
> close 63 percent of the achievement gap (measured by such factors as grades) between first-
> generation and other students].

第二层：确定从句

as引导原因状语从句。

> as it outlines a potential solution (to this problem), [suggesting that an approach (which
> ▲主　谓语　　　宾语　　　　后置定语　　　　　　　伴随状语
> involves a one-hour, next-to-no-cost program) can close 63 percent of the achievement gap
> (measured by such factors as grades) between first-generation and other students]

第三层：确定从句

that引导动词suggesting的宾语从句。

> that an approach (which involves a one-hour, next-to-no-cost program) can close
> ▲　　主语　　　　　　定语从句　　　　　　　　谓语

63 percent of the achievement gap (measured by such factors as grades)
　　　　　　　　宾语　　　　　　　　　　　　gap的后置定语
(between first-generation and other students)
　　　　　　grades的后置定语

第四层：确定从句

which引导定语从句，修饰先行词approach，which代替先行词在定语从句中作主语。

which involves a one-hour, next-to-no-cost program
主语　谓语　　　　宾语

◎ 参考译文

　　但这篇文章实际上是相当乐观的，因为它概述了这个问题的潜在解决方案，表明有一种方法（包括一个近乎免费的一小时计划）可以将"初代"大学生和其他学生之间的成就差距（以成绩等因素衡量）缩小63%。

◎ 回归解题

　　本题选A，为细节题。题干中的because（因为）对应原文中的as，都表示原因，故推测答案源自as之后的内容，由it outlines a potential solution to this problem（它概述了这个问题的潜在解决方案）可知，这篇文章认为这个问题是可以解决的，故选项A正确，其中solvable（可解决的）对应原文中的potential solution（潜在的解决方案）。选项B中的costless（无成本）与原文中next-to-no-cost（近乎无成本）不完全对等，故排除；选项C和选项D为无中生有，故排除。

考场
总结

　　本题关键是要抓住as引导的原因状语从句as it outlines a potential solution to this problem...，并找出从句的主干，正确选项the problem is solvable是对主干中a potential solution to this problem的同义改写。

真题重现

◎ 阅读 Text 1

According to the first paragraph, what would happen in France?

[A] New runways would be constructed.

[B] Physical beauty would be redefined.

[C] Websites about dieting would thrive.

[D] The fashion industry would decline.

◎ 核心词汇

- runway ['rʌnweɪ] n. T形台
- construct [kən'strʌkt] vt. 建造
- redefine [,riːdɪ'faɪn] vt. 重新定义
- website ['websaɪt] n. 网站
- thrive [θraɪv] vi. 繁荣
- decline [dɪ'klaɪn] vi. 衰退

解题思路

◎ 理解题目

根据第一段，法国将发生什么？

[A] 将建造新的T台。

[B] 将重新定义形体美。

[C] 关于节食的网站将会蓬勃发展。

[D] 时尚业将衰落。

◎ 定位原文

根据题干中的first paragraph，我们定位到原文的第一段：

①France, which prides itself as the global innovator of fashion, has decided its fashion industry has lost an absolute right to define physical beauty for women. ②Its lawmakers gave preliminary approval last week to a law that would make it a crime to employ ultra-thin models on runways. ③The parliament also agreed to ban websites that "incite excessive thinness" by promoting extreme dieting.

◎ 核心词汇

- pride oneself as... 以……为傲
- innovator ['ɪnəveɪtə(r)] n. 创新者
- industry ['ɪndəstri] n. 行业
- absolute ['æbsəluːt] adj. 绝对的
- define [dɪ'faɪn] vt. 给……下定义
- preliminary [prɪ'lɪmɪnəri] adj. 初步的
- employ [ɪm'plɔɪ] vt. 利用
- incite [ɪn'saɪt] vt. 煽动
- excessive [ɪk'sesɪv] adj. 过度的

◎ 定位核心句

　　再根据France进一步定位到该段首句。该句有26个单词，长度适中。下面我们先来尝试自己拆分和理解该长难句，之后再看老师的图解分析和参考译文。

· 小试牛刀

France, which prides itself as the global innovator of fashion, has decided its fashion industry

has lost an absolute right to define physical beauty for women.

· 图解分析

难点总览：两个逗号之间插入一个which引导的非限制性定语从句，修饰先行词France；谓语动词has decided之后为省略引导词that的宾语从句。

第一层：确定主句

France, (which prides itself as the global innovator of fashion),	has decided
主语　　　　　　　定语从句	谓语
its fashion industry has lost an absolute right to define physical beauty for women.	
宾语从句	

第二层：确定从句

which引导非限制性定语从句，修饰先行词France，which代替先行词在定语从句中作主语。

which	prides	itself	<as the global innovator of fashion>
主语	谓语	宾语	宾语补足语

has decided后为省略引导词that的宾语从句。

its fashion industry	has lost	an absolute right	(to define physical beauty for women)
主语	谓语	宾语	right的后置定语

◎ 参考译文

　　以全球时尚创新者自居的法国已经判定，其时尚业已失去定义女士形体美的绝对权利。其立法机关上周初步通过了一项法律，该法律规定雇佣超瘦模特走T台为犯罪行为。议会还赞同取缔那些通过宣扬极端节食来"煽动过度瘦身"的网站。

◎ 回归解题

　　本题选B，为推断题。核心句的主干为France has decided its fashion industry has lost an absolute right to define physical beauty for women.（法国已经判定其时尚业已失去定义

女士形体美的绝对权利。）后两句进一步说明法国时尚界以前定义的女性超瘦形体美的标准如今将被改变，这与选项B对应，故选项B正确。选项A中的runway（T台）在文中有提及，但constructed（建造）为无中生有，故排除；选项C中的Websites about dieting（关于节食的网站）在文中有提及，但thrive（蓬勃发展）为无中生有，故排除；选项D中的fashion industry（时尚业）在文中有提及，但decline（衰落）为无中生有，故排除。

> **考场总结**
>
> 本题核心句包含定语从句、宾语从句、后置定语、宾语补足语等，解题的关键在于找出核心句主干并识别出不定式短语作后置定语，即to define physical beauty for women作right的后置定语。

核心句 ⑱ ▸ 2016年英语二

真题重现

◎ 阅读 Text 4

Both young and old agree that _____.

[A] good-paying jobs are less available

[B] the old made more life achievements

[C] housing loans today are easy to obtain

[D] getting established is harder for the young

◎ 核心词汇

- available [əˈveɪləbl] *adj.* 可获得的
- achievement [əˈtʃiːvmənt] *n.* 成就
- loan [ləʊn] *n.* (借出的) 贷款
- establish [ɪˈstæblɪʃ] *vt.* 建立

解题思路

◎ 理解题目

年轻人和老年人都赞同_____。

[A] 高薪工作更难找了

[B] 老年人取得了更多人生成就

[C] 如今住房贷款很容易获得

[D] 年轻人更难站稳脚跟

◎ 定位原文

根据题干中的Both young and old agree，我们定位到原文的第五段：

◎ 核心词汇

①Young and old converge on one key point: Overwhelming majorities of both groups said they believe it is harder for young people today to get started in life than it was for earlier generations. ②While younger people are somewhat more optimistic than their elders about the prospects for those starting out today, big majorities in both groups believe those "just getting started in life" face a tougher climb than earlier generations in reaching such signpost achievements as securing a good-paying job, starting a family, managing debt, and finding affordable housing.

- converge on 就……达成一致
- overwhelming [ˌəʊvə'welmɪŋ] adj. （数量）巨大的
- majority [mə'dʒɒrəti] n. 大多数
- generation [ˌdʒenə'reɪʃn] n. 代
- optimistic [ˌɒptɪ'mɪstɪk] adj. 乐观的
- prospect ['prɒspekt] n. 前景
- tough [tʌf] adj. 艰难的
- signpost ['saɪnpəʊst] n. 路标
- secure [sɪ'kjʊə(r)] vt. 获得
- affordable [ə'fɔːdəbl] adj. 负担得起的

◎ 定位核心句

题干中的agree对应原文中的converge on "就……达成一致"和believe "认为"，因此可再进一步定位到该段首句。下面我们先来尝试自己拆分和理解该长难句，之后再看老师的图解分析和参考译文。

· 小试牛刀

Young and old converge on one key point: Overwhelming majorities of both groups said they

believe it is harder for young people today to get started in life than it was for earlier

generations.

· 图解分析

难点总览：冒号前的句子为主句，冒号后的句子是对one key point的补充说明。在冒号后的句子中，said之后为省略引导词that的宾语从句；believe之后也为省略引导词that的宾语从句；than引导比较状语从句。

第一层：确定主句

Young and old	converge on	one key point:
主语1	谓语1	宾语

Overwhelming majorities of both groups said they believe it is harder for young people

	主语2	谓语2	宾语从句

today to get started in life than it was for earlier generations.

第二层：确定从句

said后为省略引导词that的宾语从句。

> <u>they</u> <u>believe</u> it is harder for young people today to get started in life than it was for earlier
> 主语 谓语 　　　　　　　　　　　　　　宾语从句
> generations

第三层：确定从句

believe后为省略引导词that的宾语从句。

> <u>it</u> 　<u>is</u> 　<u>harder</u> [for young people today] <u>to get started in life</u>
> 形主 系 表 　　　　　状语 　　　　　　真正的主语
> [than it was for earlier generations]
> 　　　比较状语从句

第四层：确定从句

than引导比较状语从句，且从句中的真正主语因和than前比较的部分的主语to get started in life一致，因此省略掉了。

> than <u>it</u> <u>was</u> [for earlier generations]
> ▲ 主 系 　　　状语

◎ 参考译文

　　年轻人和老年人在一个关键点上达成了共识：这两个群体中的绝大多数人都表示，他们认为现在年轻人的人生起步要比前几代人更难。虽然年轻人比他们的长辈更看好如今刚起步的人的前景，但双方绝大多数人都认为，与前几代人相比，那些"人生刚刚起步"的人在实现诸如获得高薪工作、成家、管理债务和找到经济适用房等标志性成就上面临着更艰难的攀登之路。

◎ 回归解题

　　本题选D，为细节题。由定位句中believe后的宾语从句it is harder for young people today to get started in life than it was for earlier generations可知，现在年轻人的人生起步要比前几代人更难，选项D与原文意思一致，故选项D正确。选项A中的good-paying jobs、

选项B中的achievements和选项C中的housing loans均来自最后并列的内容，但都与题干无关，故均排除。

考场
总结　　本题关键是找到定位句中两个省略引导词that的宾语从句，并识别出it作形式主语、不定式作真正的主语这一特殊句型。

核心句 19 ▶ 2016年英语二

真题重现

◎ 阅读 Text 2

It can be learned from Paragraph 3 that unintentional harm-doers will not be prosecuted if they _____.

[A] agree to pay a sum for compensation

[B] volunteer to set up an equally big habitat

[C] offer to support the WAFWA monitoring job

[D] promise to raise funds for USFWS operations

◎核心词汇

• compensation [ˌkɒmpenˈseɪʃn] n. 赔偿金

• volunteer [ˌvɒlənˈtɪə(r)] v. 自愿做 (某事)

• set up 建立

• monitor [ˈmɒnɪtə(r)] vt. 监视

• promise [ˈprɒmɪs] v. 承诺

解题思路

◎ 理解题目

从第三段可以得知，如果无意伤害的人_____，他们就不会被起诉。

[A] 同意支付一笔赔偿金　　　　　　　　　[B] 自愿建立一个同样大的栖息地

[C] 提供支持 WAFWA 监控工作　　　　　　[D] 承诺为 USFWS 运营筹集资金

◎ 定位原文

根据题干中的Paragraph 3，我们定位到原文的第三段：

①Under the plan, for example, the agency said it would not prosecute landowners or businesses that unintentionally

◎核心词汇

• agency [ˈeɪdʒənsi] n. 机构

• prosecute [ˈprɒsɪkjuːt] v. 起诉

• unintentionally [ˌʌnɪnˈtenʃənəli] adv. 非故意地

191

kill, harm, or disturb the bird, as long as they had signed a range-wide management plan to restore prairie chicken habitat. ②Negotiated by USFWS and the states, the plan requires individuals and businesses that damage habitat as part of their operations to pay into a fund to replace every acre destroyed with 2 new acres of suitable habitat. ③The fund will also be used to compensate landowners who set aside habitat. ④USFWS also set an interim goal of restoring prairie chicken populations to an annual average of 67,000 birds over the next 10 years. ⑤And it gives the Western Association of Fish and Wildlife Agencies (WAFWA), a coalition of state agencies, the job of monitoring progress. ⑥Overall, the idea is to let "states remain in the driver's seat for managing the species," Ashe said.

- as long as 只要
- sign [saɪn] v. 签字，签署
- negotiate [nɪˈɡəʊʃieɪt] vt. 协商
- damage [ˈdæmɪdʒ] vt. 损害，伤害
- operation [ˌɒpəˈreɪʃn] n. 运营
- destroy [dɪˈstrɔɪ] vt. 破坏
- suitable [ˈsuːtəbl] adj. 适当的
- compensate [ˈkɒmpenseɪt] vt. 赔偿，补偿
- set aside 预留
- interim [ˈɪntərɪm] adj. 中期的
- coalition [ˌkəʊəˈlɪʃn] n. 联盟

◎ 定位核心句

　　再根据题干中的unintentional harm-doers will not be prosecuted进一步定位至该段首句。下面我们先来尝试自己拆分和理解该长难句，之后再看老师的图解分析和参考译文。

· 小试牛刀

Under the plan, for example, the agency said it would not prosecute landowners or businesses

that unintentionally kill, harm, or disturb the bird, as long as they had signed a range-wide

management plan to restore prairie chicken habitat.

· 图解分析

难点总览：said后为省略引导词that的宾语从句；businesses后的that引导定语从句，修饰先行词landowners or businesses；as long as引导条件状语从句。

第一层：确定主句

[Under the plan], for example, the agency said it would not prosecute landowners or
　　　状语　　　　　　插入语　　　　主语　谓语　　　　　宾语从句

businesses that unintentionally kill, harm, or disturb the bird, as long as they had signed

a range-wide management plan to restore prairie chicken habitat.

第二层：确定从句

省略引导词that的宾语从句，作said的宾语。

　it　would not prosecute landowners or businesses
主语　　谓语　　　　　　　宾语

(that unintentionally kill, harm, or disturb the bird, as long as they had signed a range-wide

management plan to restore prairie chicken habitat)
　　　　　　　　　　　定语从句

第三层：确定从句

that引导定语从句，修饰先行词landowners or businesses，that代替先行词在定语从句中
作主语。

that unintentionally kill, harm, or disturb the bird, [as long as they had signed a range-wide
主语　　　　　　　谓语　　　　　　宾语　　　　　条件状语从句

range-wide management plan to restore prairie chicken habitat]

第四层：确定从句

as long as引导条件状语从句。

as long as they had signed a range-wide management plan (to restore prairie chicken habitat)
　▲　主语　谓语　　　　　宾语　　　　　　　　　plan的后置定语

◎ 参考译文

　　例如，根据该计划，该机构表示，只要土地所有者或企业签署过重建草原鸡栖息地
的一系列涉及面广泛的管理计划，它就不会起诉他们无意杀死、伤害或扰乱该鸟类。经
过USFWS和各州协商，该计划要求在其运营过程中破坏栖息地的个人和企业向一项基金

支付费用，用2英亩新的合适的栖息地替换被破坏的1英亩。该基金还将用于补偿那些留出了栖息地的土地所有者。USFWS还设定了一个中期目标，即在未来10年内将草原鸡的数量恢复到年均67,000只。它还将监控进展这一任务交给了鱼类及野生动植物管理局西部联盟（由州立机构组成的联盟）。总体而言，其目的是让"各州继续在管理物种方面发挥主导作用。"阿什说。

◎ 回归解题

　　本题选A，为细节题。题干中的if（如果）对应原文定位句中的as long as（只要）。该条件句提及，"只要土地所有者或企业签署过重建草原鸡栖息地的一系列涉及面广泛的管理计划，它（该机构）就不会起诉……"，然而并没有直接对应的选项。文章后续内容对该管理计划进一步展开描述。根据下文The fund will also be used to compensate landowners who set aside habitat，可知"该基金还将用于补偿那些留出了栖息地的土地所有者"，其中also表明上文也是谈论"赔偿"的事情，故选项A正确。选项B中的equally big（同样大）与原文不符，原文中说的是replace every acre destroyed with 2 new acres of suitable habitat（用2英亩新的合适栖息地替换被破坏的1英亩），可知毁1赔2，而非等同大小，故排除；选项C中的WAFWA对应该段倒数第二句，其中it指上句中的USFWS，而非导致破坏的人，故排除选项C；选项D中的USFWS operations与原文中的their operations（他们的运营）不符，原文中的their指代的对象是导致破坏的个人和企业，故排除选项D。

考场
总结

　　本题主要考查对as long as引导的条件状语从句的理解，说明无意破坏栖息地的人免受起诉的条件。

真题重现

◎ 阅读 Text 2

What was the original purpose of grade forgiveness?

[A] To help freshmen adapt to college learning.

[B] To maintain colleges' graduation rates.

[C] To prepare graduates for a challenging future.

[D] To increase universities' income from tuition.

◎ 核心词汇

- freshman ['freʃmən] *n.*（大学）一年级新生
- adapt to 适应
- maintain [meɪn'teɪn] *vt.* 保持，维持
- tuition [tju'ɪʃn] *n.* 学费

解题思路

◎ 理解题目

成绩宽容的初衷是什么？

[A] 帮助大一新生适应大学学习。 [B] 维持大学的毕业率。

[C] 使毕业生为充满挑战的未来做好准备。 [D] 增加大学的学费收入。

◎ 定位原文

根据题干中的original purpose和grade forgiveness，我们定位到原文的第三段：

①The use of this little-known practice has accelerated in recent years, as colleges continue to do their utmost to keep students in school (and paying tuition) and improve their graduation rates. ②When this practice first started decades ago, it was usually limited to freshmen, to give them a second chance to take a class in their first year if they struggled in their transition to college-level courses. ③But now most colleges, save for many selective campuses, allow all undergraduates, and even graduate students, to get their low grades forgiven.

◎ 核心词汇

- practice ['præktɪs] *n.* 通常的做法，惯例
- accelerate [ək'seləreɪt] *v.*（使）加快，促进
- do one's utmost to do sth. 尽最大努力做某事
- graduation rate 毕业率
- struggle ['strʌgl] *vi.* 挣扎，奋斗，努力
- transition [træn'zɪʃn] *n.* 过渡，转变
- save for 除……之外
- selective campus 名牌大学

　　再进一步定位到该段第二句。该句有36个单词，是个长难句。下面我们先来尝试自己拆分和理解该句，之后再看老师的图解分析和参考译文。

· 小试牛刀

When this practice first started decades ago, it was usually limited to freshmen, to give them a

second chance to take a class in their first year if they struggled in their transition to college-

level courses.

· 图解分析

难点总览：本句中包含when引导的时间状语从句和if引导的条件状语从句，该条件句使用了虚拟语气。

第一层：确定主句

[When this practice first started decades ago], it was usually limited to freshmen,
　　　　　时间状语从句　　　　　　　　主语　　谓语　　　　　宾语

[to give them a second chance to take a class in their first year]
　　　　　　　　　目的状语

[if they struggled in their transition to college-level courses].
　　　　　条件状语从句

第二层：确定从句

when引导时间状语从句。

When this practice [first] started [decades ago]
　▲　　主语　　状语 谓语　　时间状语

if引导条件状语从句。

if they struggled [in their transition (to college-level courses)]
▲ 主语 谓语　　　状语　　　transition的后置定语

196

◎ 参考译文

近年来，随着各大高校一直尽最大努力让学生留在学校（并支付学费），提高毕业率，这种鲜为人知的做法越来越普遍。几十年前这种做法刚实行时，通常仅限于大一新生，如果在向大学水平的课程过渡的过程中遇到困难，他们在第一学年有重修课程的机会。但现在，除了许多名牌大学外，大多数大学都对所有本科生（甚至研究生）考试得低分持宽容态度。

◎ 回归解题

本题选A，为细节题。根据题干关键词original purpose和grade forgiveness可定位到第三段第二句，其中original对应该句中的first，grade forgiveness对应句中的this practice。由第二句可知，"成绩宽容"这一做法最初仅限于大一新生，初衷是帮助他们顺利过渡到大学课程的学习，原文transition to college-level courses（过渡到大学水平的课程）对应A项中的adapt to college learning（适应大学学习），因此A项表述正确，故本题选A。B项针对第三段第一句中的graduation rates设置干扰，即近年来高校采用成绩宽容做法的目的变成了"提高毕业率"，但这不是"成绩宽容"的初衷，故排除。文中并未提及C项相关信息，故排除。D项针对第三段第一句中的tuition设置干扰，该句指出"各大高校一直尽最大努力让学生留在学校（并支付学费）"，由此可推断出成绩宽容的做法会增加大学的学费收入，但其并非大学实行这一做法的初衷（original purpose），该项属于答非所问，故排除。

考场
总结

本题核心句包含时间状语从句和if引导的虚拟条件句等，解题的关键在理解if条件句使用的虚拟语气，即if they struggled in their transition to college-level courses。

真题重现

◎ 阅读 Text 3

According to Paragraph 1, art-science collaborations have

_____.

[A] caught the attention of critics

[B] received favorable responses

[C] promoted academic publishing

[D] sparked heated public disputes

◎ 核心词汇

- collaboration [kə,læbə'reɪʃn] n. 合作，协作
- critic ['krɪtɪk] n. 评论家；批评者
- favorable ['feɪvərəbl] adj. 有利的；赞成的
- spark [spɑːk] vt. 引发，触发
- dispute [dɪ'spjuːt] n. 争论，辩论，纠纷

解题思路

◎ 理解题目

根据第一段可知，艺术与科学的合作已经_____。

[A] 引起了评论家的注意   [B] 得到了积极的响应

[C] 促进了学术出版   [D] 引发了激烈的公共争议

◎ 定位原文

根据题干中的Paragraph 1，我们定位到原文的第一段：

①Enlightening, challenging, stimulating, fun. ②These were some of the words that *Nature* readers used to describe their experience of art-science collaborations in a series of articles on partnerships between artists and researchers. ③Nearly 40% of the roughly 350 people who responded to an accompanying poll said, they had collaborated with artists; and almost all said they would consider doing so in future.

◎ 核心词汇

- enlightening [ɪn'laɪtnɪŋ] adj. 启迪的，使人获得启发的
- stimulating ['stɪmjuleɪtɪŋ] adj. 激励人的；振奋人心的
- respond [rɪ'spɒnd] v. 回答，回应；作出反应
- accompanying [ə'kʌmpəniɪŋ] adj. 陪伴的；附随的
- poll [pəʊl] n. 民意调查，民意测验

◎ 定位核心句

再根据art-science collaborations和分析进一步定位到该段第三句。该句有30个单

词，长度适中。下面我们先来尝试自己拆分和理解该长难句，之后再看老师的图解分析和参考译文。

· 小试牛刀

Nearly 40% of the roughly 350 people who responded to an accompanying poll said,

they had collaborated with artists; and almost all said they would consider doing so in future.

· 图解分析

难点总览：本句包含两个由分号隔开的并列分句，第一个分句中包含定语从句和宾语从句，第二个分句中包含宾语从句。

第一层：确定主句

分句1，包含who引导的定语从句和省略引导词that的宾语从句。

Nearly 40% of the roughly 350 people (who responded to an accompanying poll)
     主语   定语从句

said, they had collaborated with artists;
谓语   宾语从句

分句2，包含省略引导词that的宾语从句。

and almost all said they would consider doing so in future.
▲ 主语 谓语   宾语从句

第二层：确定从句

who引导限制性定语从句，修饰先行词people。

who responded to an accompanying poll
主语 谓语   宾语

宾语从句1

they had collaborated with artists
主语   谓语 宾语

宾语从句2

> they would consider doing so [in future]
> 主语　　谓语　　　　　宾语　　时间状语

◎ 参考译文

富于启发、颇具挑战、振奋人心、饶有乐趣。在一系列以艺术家与科研人员的合作关系为主题的文章中，《自然》杂志的读者用了这样一些词汇来描述其对于艺术与科学合作的感受。在大约350个接受随文所附问卷调查的人中，近40%的人表示，他们曾与艺术家合作过；而且几乎所有人都表示他们今后会考虑与艺术家合作。

◎ 回归解题

本题选B，为细节题。由题干信息Paragraph 1、art-science collaborations可定位至首段（②句art-science collaborations、③句collaborated）。全段介绍了《自然》杂志随附问卷的调查结果：大约350名读者接受了调查，他们用"富于启发、颇具挑战、振奋人心、饶有乐趣"等词来描述自己对于艺术与科学合作的感受，其中近40%的人说自己与艺术家合作过，而且几乎所有人都表示今后会考虑与艺术家合作。由此可见，艺术与科学的合作已经得到了积极响应与一致认可，故B项正确。

考场
总结

本题核心句包含一个定语从句和两个宾语从句，解题的关键在于找出两个并列分句，并识别出宾语从句中的内容。

Part 03

语法 与 长难句 大闯关

　　该部分包含100道语法和长难句综合练习题，按每5题为1关，分为20关，建议同学们在学习完Part 01、Part 02后每天做1个闯关训练，从易到难，复习检测所学语法知识点，实操拆解长难句，进一步强化巩固学习成果。

本部分每关都包含重温语法和小试牛刀两个任务。同学们需要先完成重温语法的5道小题，复习自测对应的语法知识点（建议作题时先遮盖右侧"核心词汇"所给重点词汇提示，尽量尝试独立完成）；再进入小试牛刀核对答案，在重温语法的基础上，带着对句子核心语法点的掌握，自己尝试去拆解并翻译句子，最后再扫码对照解析查漏补缺。

 Round 01 ▾

扫码看解析

· 重温语法

本关考点：非谓语动词 　　　　　　　　　　　　　　　　　　　核心词汇

1. _____ whom you are addressing, the problems will be different. (2002年阅读) [A] To depend on 　　[B] Depending on [C] Depended on 　　[D] Having depended on	• depend on 取决于 • address [əˈdres] vt. 对……谈话
2. Certain jobs have gone away for good, _____ by machines. (2014年英语二阅读) [A] to outmode 　　[B] outmoding [C] outmoded 　　[D] having outmoded	• go away 消失 • for good 永远 • outmode [ˌaʊtˈməʊd] vt. 使……过时；淘汰
3. _____ with their American counterparts, Japanese newspapers are much more stable. (2011年英语二阅读) [A] To compare 　　[B] Comparing [C] Compared 　　[D] Having Compared	• compare A with B 将A与B进行比较 • counterpart [ˈkaʊntəpɑːt] n. 对应的人或事物 • stable [ˈsteɪbl] adj. 稳定的
4. Issues _____ from automation need to be tackled. (2018年英语一阅读) [A] to arise 　　[B] arising [C] arisen 　　[D] being arisen	• issue [ˈɪʃuː] n. 问题 • arise [əˈraɪz] vi. 由……引起 • automation [ˌɔːtəˈmeɪʃn] n. 自动化 • tackle [ˈtækl] vt. 解决；处理
5. Women are still suffering much stress _____ by men. (2008年阅读) [A] to cause 　　[B] causing [C] caused 　　[D] having caused	• suffer [ˈsʌfə(r)] v. 遭受 • stress [stres] n. 压力 • cause [kɔːz] vt. 引起

· 小试牛刀

尝试拆分句子，标注句子成分，并翻译。

1. Depending on whom you are addressing, the problems will be different.

2. Certain jobs have gone away for good, outmoded by machines.

3. Compared with their American counterparts, Japanese newspapers are much more stable.

4. Issues arising from automation need to be tackled.

5. Women are still suffering much stress caused by men.

 Round 02 ▾

· 重温语法

本关考点：非谓语动词；定语从句；同位语从句	核心词汇
1. The data _____ so far are out of date. (2006年阅读) [A] to collect　　　　[B] collecting [C] collected　　　　[D] having collected	• data ['deɪtə] *n.* 数据 • collect [kə'lekt] *vt.* 收集 • so far 到目前为止 • out of date 过时
2. Some art dealers were awaiting better chances _____. (2010年英语二阅读) [A] to come　　　　[B] coming [C] come　　　　[D] having come	• dealer ['diːlə(r)] *n.* 经销商，商人 • await [ə'weɪt] *vt.* 等候

3. This is a skill _____ will help them all throughout life. (2020年英语二完形)

[A] who   [B] where

[C] what   [D] that

- skill [skɪl] *n.* 技能；技巧
- throughout [θruːˈaʊt] *prep.* 贯穿

4. Most fisheries are well below that, _____ is a bad way to do business. (2006年阅读)

[A] who   [B] that

[C] which   [D] whose

- fishery [ˈfɪʃəri] *n.* 渔场
- below [bɪˈləʊ] *prep.* 在……下面

5. There's no doubt _____ our peer groups exert enormous influence on our behavior. (2012年英语一阅读)

[A] whether   [B] that

[C] what   [D] why

- peer [pɪə(r)] *n.* 同龄人
- exert [ɪɡˈzɜːt] *vt.* 施加
- enormous [ɪˈnɔːməs] *adj.* 巨大的
- behavior [bɪˈheɪvjə(r)] *n.* 行为

·小试牛刀

尝试拆分句子，标注句子成分，并翻译。

1. The data collected so far are out of date.

2. Some art dealers were awaiting better chances to come.

3. This is a skill that will help them all throughout life.

4. Most fisheries are well below that, which is a bad way to do business.

5. There's no doubt that our peer groups exert enormous influence on our behavior.

· 重温语法

本关考点：同位语从句；谓语动词的时态和语态；强调句	核心词汇
1. There is plenty of evidence _____ the quality of the teachers is the most important variable. (2012年英语一阅读) [A] whether [B] that [C] what [D] why	• plenty ['plenti] *n.* 大量(~ of) • evidence ['evɪdəns] *n.* 证据 • variable ['veərɪəbl] *n.* 变量
2. It did know he _____ a problem. (2006年新题型) [A] has [B] have [C] had [D] having	• problem ['prɒbləm] *n.* 问题
3. I _____ do this since I was four. (2013年英语二翻译) [A] had been able to [B] am able to [C] was able to [D] have been able to	• since [sɪns] *conj.* 自从
4. By 1854 slavery _____ everywhere except Spain's 17 colonies. (2007年完形) [A] had been abolished [B] has been abolished [C] was abolished [D] would be abolished	• slavery ['sleɪvəri] *n.* 奴隶制 • abolish [ə'bɒlɪʃ] *vt.* 废除 • colony ['kɒləni] *n.* 殖民地
5. Science _____ provide us with the best available guide to the future, and it is critical that our nation and the world base important policies on the best judgments that science can provide. (2005年阅读) [A] / [B] do [C] does [D] did	• provide [prə'vaɪd] *vt.* 提供 • available [ə'veɪləbl] *adj.* 可获得的 • guide [gaɪd] *n.* 指南 • critical ['krɪtɪkl] *adj.* 重要的，关键的 • policy ['pɒləsi] *n.* 政策 • judgment ['dʒʌdʒmənt] *n.* 判断

· 小试牛刀

尝试拆分句子，标注句子成分，并翻译。

1. There is plenty of evidence that the quality of the teachers is the most important variable.

2. It did know he had a problem.

3. I have been able to do this since I was four.

4. By 1854 slavery had been abolished everywhere except Spain's 17 colonies.

5. Science does provide us with the best available guide to the future, and it is critical that our nation and the world base important policies on the best judgments that science can provide.

📋 Round ④ ▾

· **重温语法**

本关考点：部分倒装；虚拟语气；谓语动词的时态和语态	核心词汇
1. Never before _____ television served so much to connect different peoples and nations. (2005年翻译) [A] /　　　　　　　　　　[B] have [C] had　　　　　　　　　[D] has	• connect [kə'nekt] vt. 连接；联系 • people ['piːpl] n. 民族
2. Only when humanity began to get its food in a more productive way _____ there time for other things. (2009年阅读) [A] is　　　　　　　　　　[B] was [C] are　　　　　　　　　[D] were	• humanity [hjuˈmænəti] n. 人类 • productive [prəˈdʌktɪv] adj. 有生产力的

3. If appropriate public policies _____ in place to help all women—whether CEOs or their children's caregivers—and all families, women entering top management would be no more newsworthy.

(2013年英语二阅读)

- appropriate [əˈprəʊpriət] *adj.* 适当的
- newsworthy [ˈnjuːzwɜːði] *adj.* 有报道价值的

[A] is   [B] was

[C] are   [D] were

4. It is critical that our nation and the world _____ base important policies on the best judgments that science can provide.   (2005年阅读)

- critical [ˈkrɪtɪkl] *adj.* 重要的，关键的
- judgment [ˈdʒʌdʒmənt] *n.* 判断

[A] would   [B] /

[C] could   [D] might

5. Overwhelming majorities of both groups said they believe it is harder for young people today to get started in life than it _____ for earlier generations.

(2016年英语二阅读)

- overwhelming [ˌəʊvəˈwelmɪŋ] *adj.* 压倒性的
- majority [məˈdʒɒrəti] *n.* 大多数
- generation [ˌdʒenəˈreɪʃn] *n.* 代

[A] is   [B] are

[C] was   [D] were

· 小试牛刀

尝试拆分句子，标注句子成分并翻译。

1. Never before has television served so much to connect different peoples and nations.

2. Only when humanity began to get its food in a more productive way was there time for other things.

3. If appropriate public policies were in place to help all women—whether CEOs or their

   children's caregivers—and all families, women entering top management would be no more

   newsworthy.

   ----

4. It is critical that our nation and the world base important policies on the best judgments

   that science can provide.

   ----

5. Overwhelming majorities of both groups said they believe it is harder for young people

   today to get started in life than it was for earlier generations.

· 重温语法

本关考点：非谓语动词；定语从句；强调句；形容词作后置定语；同位语从句

	核心词汇

1. During the 2016 presidential campaign, nearly a quarter of web content _____ by Twitter users in the politically critical state of Michigan was fake news, according to the University of Oxford. (2018年英语一阅读)

   [A] was shared   [B] shared

   [C] sharing   [D] had shared

- presidential [ˌprezɪ'denʃl] *adj.* 总统的
- campaign [kæm'peɪn] *n.* 竞选
- quarter ['kwɔːtə(r)] *n.* 四分之一
- content ['kɒntent] *n.* 内容
- fake [feɪk] *adj.* 假的

2. He asserted, also, that his power to follow a long and purely abstract train of thought was very limited, _____ he felt certain that he never could have succeeded with mathematics. (2008年翻译)

   [A] for which reason   [B] for that reason

   [C] for what reason   [D] for whose reason

- assert [ə'sɜːt] *vt.* 声称；断言
- purely ['pjʊəli] *adv.* 纯净地；纯粹地
- abstract ['æbstrækt] *adj.* 抽象的
- mathematics [ˌmæθə'mætɪks] *n.* 数学(=math)

3. Yet it is precisely these non-celebrity influentials _____, according to the two-step-flow theory, are supposed to drive social epidemics, by influencing their friends and colleagues directly. (2010年英语一阅读)

   [A] which   [B] what

   [C] whose   [D] who

- precisely [prɪ'saɪsli] *adv.* 正是
- celebrity [sə'lebrəti] *n.* 名人
- influential [ˌɪnflu'enʃəl] *n.* 有影响力的人
- epidemic [ˌepɪ'demɪk] *n.* 流行
- colleague ['kɒliːɡ] *n.* 同事

4. Sternberg notes that traditional tests best assess analytical and verbal skills but fail to measure creativity and practical knowledge, components _____ also critical to problem solving and life success. (2007年阅读)

   [A] is   [B] /

   [C] are   [D] were

- note [nəʊt] *vt.* 指出
- assess [ə'ses] *vt.* 评估
- analytical [ˌænə'lɪtɪkl] *adj.* 分析的
- verbal ['vɜːbl] *adj.* 语言的
- fail to do 没能够……
- creativity [ˌkriːeɪ'tɪvəti] *n.* 创造力
- practical ['præktɪkl] *adj.* 实践的
- component [kəm'pəʊnənt] *n.* 组成部分

5. The policy follows similar efforts from other journals, after widespread concern _____ basic mistakes in data analysis are contributing to the irreproducibility of many published research findings.　(2015年英语一阅读)

[A] which [B] that

[C] what [D] whose

- journal ['dʒɜːnl] *n.* 期刊，杂志
- concern [kən'sɜːn] *n.* 关心，担忧
- analysis [ə'næləsɪs] *n.* 分析

· 小试牛刀

尝试拆分句子，标注句子成分，并翻译。

1. During the 2016 presidential campaign, nearly a quarter of web content shared by Twitter users in the politically critical state of Michigan was fake news, according to the University of Oxford.

2. He asserted, also, that his power to follow a long and purely abstract train of thought was very limited, for which reason he felt certain that he never could have succeeded with mathematics.

3. Yet it is precisely these non-celebrity influentials who, according to the two-step-flow theory, are supposed to drive social epidemics, by influencing their friends and colleagues directly.

4. Sternberg notes that traditional tests best assess analytical and verbal skills but fail to measure creativity and practical knowledge, components also critical to problem solving and life success.

_____

_____

5. The policy follows similar efforts from other journals, after widespread concern that basic mistakes in data analysis are contributing to the irreproducibility of many published research findings.

_____

_____

Round (06) ▾

· 重温语法

本关考点：非谓语动词；定语从句	核心词汇
1. _____ caregiver assessments and the children's self-observations, she rated each child's overall sympathy level and his or her tendency to feel negative emotions after moral transgressions. (2019年英语二阅读) [A] Used [B] Using [C] To use [D] Being used	• assessment [əˈsesmənt] n. 评价 • observation [ˌɒbzəˈveɪʃn] n. 观察 • sympathy [ˈsɪmpəθi] n. 同情(~for) • tendency [ˈtendənsi] n. 趋势，倾向 • emotion [ɪˈməʊʃn] n. 情绪，情感 • moral [ˈmɒrəl] adj. 道德的 • transgression [trænzˈgreʃn] n. 违反
2. Today, we live in a world _____ GPS systems, digital maps, and other navigation apps are available on our smartphones. (2019年英语一阅读) [A] when [B] where [C] how [D] why	• navigation [ˌnævɪˈgeɪʃn] n. 导航

3. The casino issued to him, as a good customer, a "Fun Card", _____ when used in the casino earns points for meals and drinks, and enables the casino to track the user's gambling activities. (2006年新题型)

[A] /   [B] that

[C] which   [D] what

- issue ['ɪʃuː] *vt.* 发布，发行
- earn [ɜːn] *vt.* 获得
- track [træk] *v.* 追踪
- gamble ['gæmbl] *v.* 赌博

4. The food industry will be alarmed that such senior doctors back such radical moves, especially the call to use some of the tough tactics _____ have been deployed against smoking over the last decade. (2011年英语二新题型)

[A] what   [B] /

[C] that   [D] who

- industry ['ɪndəstri] *n.* 行业，产业
- alarmed [ə'lɑːmd] *adj.* 恐慌的
- senior ['siːnɪə(r)] *adj.* 高级的；资深的
- back [bæk] *vt.* 支持
- radical ['rædɪkl] *adj.* 激进的
- tough [tʌf] *adj.* 强硬的
- tactic ['tæktɪk] *n.* 策略
- deploy [dɪ'plɔɪ] *vt.* 利用

5. With the use of eye-tracking technology, Julia Minson of the Harvard Kennedy School of Government concluded that eye contact can signal very different kinds of messages, _____ on the situation. (2020年英语一新题型)

[A] depends   [B] depended

[C] depending   [D] to depend

- technology [tek'nɒlədʒi] *n.* 技术
- conclude [kən'kluːd] *v.* 总结
- contact ['kɒntækt] *n.* 接触
- signal ['sɪgnəl] *v.* 发信号
- situation [ˌsɪtʃu'eɪʃn] *n.* 情形

· 小试牛刀

尝试拆分句子，标注句子成分，并翻译。

1. Using caregiver assessments and the children's self-observations, she rated each child's overall sympathy level and his or her tendency to feel negative emotions after moral transgressions.

2. Today, we live in a world where GPS systems, digital maps, and other navigation apps are

available on our smartphones.

3. The casino issued to him, as a good customer, a "Fun Card", which when used in the casino

earns points for meals and drinks, and enables the casino to track the user's gambling activities.

4. The food industry will be alarmed that such senior doctors back such radical moves,

especially the call to use some of the tough tactics that have been deployed against smoking

over the last decade.

5. With the use of eye-tracking technology, Julia Minson of the Harvard Kennedy School

of Government concluded that eye contact can signal very different kinds of messages,

depending on the situation.

· 重温语法

本关考点：定语从句；并列结构；同位语从句	核心词汇

1. This is now a question for Gloria Mackenzie, an 84-year-old widow _____ recently emerged from her small, tin-roofed house in Florida to collect the biggest undivided lottery jackpot in history. (2014年英语二阅读)

   [A] who   [B] which

   [C] what   [D] /

- widow ['wɪdəʊ] *n.* 寡妇
- emerge [ɪ'mɜːdʒ] *vi.* 浮现，出现
- lottery ['lɒtəri] *n.* 彩票
- jackpot ['dʒækpɒt] *n.* 头奖

2. When younger kids learn computer science, they learn that it's not just a confusing, endless string of letters and numbers—_____ a tool to build apps, or create artwork, or test hypotheses. (2016年英语二阅读)

   [A] and   [B] or

   [C] but   [D] /

- endless ['endləs] *adj.* 无尽的
- string [strɪŋ] *n.* 绳；串
- hypothesis [haɪ'pɒθəsiːs] *n.* 假设；假说（复数 hypotheses）

3. As a result, they have lost the parachute _____ they once had in times of financial setback—a back-up earner (usually Mom) who could go into the workforce if the primary earner got laid off or fell sick.

   (2007年阅读)

   [A] who   [B] whose

   [C] what   [D] /

- parachute ['pærəʃuːt] *n.* 降落伞
- financial [faɪ'nænʃl] *adj.* 金融的，财务的
- workforce ['wɜːkfɔːs] *n.* 劳动力
- primary ['praɪməri] *adj.* 主要的
- lay off 解雇

4. On June 7 Google pledged not to "design or deploy AI" _____ would cause "overall harm," or to develop AI-directed weapons or use AI for surveillance that would violate international norms. (2019年英语一阅读)

   [A] that   [B] who

   [C] what   [D] where

- pledge [pledʒ] *vt.* 承诺
- deploy [dɪ'plɔɪ] *v.* 部署
- weapon ['wepən] *n.* 武器
- surveillance [sɜː'veɪləns] *n.* 监视
- violate ['vaɪəleɪt] *vt.* 侵犯；违反
- norm [nɔːm] *n.* 规范，标准

5. Furthermore, the highest CEO salaries are paid to outside candidates, not to the cozy insider picks, another sign _____ high CEO pay is not some kind of depredation at the expense of the rest of the company.

- candidate ['kændɪdeɪt] *n.* 候选人
- cozy ['kəʊzi] *adj.* 关系密切的
- depredation [,deprə'deɪʃn] *n.* 掠夺
- at the expense of 以⋯⋯为代价

(2020年英语二阅读)

[A] which   [B] what

[C] who   [D] that

· 小试牛刀

尝试拆分句子，标注句子成分，并翻译。

1. This is now a question for Gloria Mackenzie, an 84-year-old widow who recently emerged

   from her small, tin-roofed house in Florida to collect the biggest undivided lottery jackpot in

   history.

   ----

2. When younger kids learn computer science, they learn that it's not just a confusing, endless

   string of letters and numbers—but a tool to build apps, or create artwork, or test

   hypotheses.

   ----

3. As a result, they have lost the parachute they once had in times of financial setback—a back-up earner (usually Mom) who could go into the workforce if the primary earner got laid off or fell sick.

---

4. On June 7 Google pledged not to "design or deploy AI" that would cause "overall harm," or to develop AI-directed weapons or use AI for surveillance that would violate international norms.

---

5. Furthermore, the highest CEO salaries are paid to outside candidates, not to the cozy insider picks, another sign that high CEO pay is not some kind of depredation at the expense of the rest of the company.

·重温语法

本关考点：定语从句；同位语从句；非谓语动词；动词不定式复合结构；宾语从句

核心词汇

1. His primary task is not to ~~think~~ about the moral code _____ governs his activity, any more than a businessman is expected to dedicate his energies to an exploration of rules of conduct in business. (2006年翻译)

   [A] who   [B] which

   [C] where   [D] when

- code [kəʊd] *n.* 准则
- govern ['gʌvn] *vt.* 支配
- dedicate ['dedɪkeɪt] *vt.* 致力于
  dedicate A to B 将A致力于B
- exploration [,eksplə'reɪʃn] *n.* 探索

2. The idea _____ the journalist must understand the law more profoundly than an ordinary citizen rests on an understanding of the established conventions and special responsibilities of the news media. (2007年翻译)

   [A] that   [B] which

   [C] what   [D] where

- journalist ['dʒɜːnəlɪst] *n.* 记者
- profoundly [prə'faʊndli] *adv.* 深刻地
- rest on 基于
- convention [kən'venʃn] *n.* 惯例
- responsibility [rɪ,spɒnsə'bɪləti] *n.* 责任

3. This success, coupled with later research _____ that memory itself is not genetically determined, led Ericsson to conclude that the act of memorizing is more of a cognitive exercise than an intuitive one.

   (2007年阅读)

   [A] showed   [B] shown

   [C] to show   [D] showing

- couple ['kʌpl] *vt.* 连同
- genetically [dʒə'netɪkli] *adv.* 遗传地
- determine [dɪ'tɜːmɪn] *vt.* 决定
- memorize ['meməraɪz] *vt.* 记忆
- cognitive ['kɒgnətɪv] *adj.* 认知的
- intuitive [ɪn'tjuːɪtɪv] *adj.* 直觉的

4. There are fundamental public health problems, like dirty hands instead of a soap habit, that remain killers only because we can't figure out _____ to change people's habits. (2010年英语二阅读)

   [A] what   [B] who

   [C] which   [D] how

- fundamental [,fʌndə'mentl] *adj.* 基本的，基础的
- instead of 代替
- remain [rɪ'meɪn] *link v.* 仍然是
- figure out 弄清楚；整明白

5. In the West, before mass communication and literacy, the most powerful mass medium was the church, which reminded worshippers that their souls were in danger and _____ they would someday be meat for worms.

(2006年阅读)

[A] which   [B] that

[C] what   [D] who

- literacy ['lɪtərəsi] *n.* 识字
- medium ['miːdɪəm] *n.* 媒体（复数 media）
  mass medium 大众媒体
- remind [rɪ'maɪnd] *vt.* 提醒
  remind sb. of sth. 提醒某人某事
  remind sb. that... 提醒某人……
- worshipper ['wɜːʃɪpə(r)] *n.* 信徒
- soul [səʊl] *n.* 心灵；灵魂
- worm [wɜːm] *n.* 蠕虫

· 小试牛刀

尝试拆分句子，标注句子成分，并翻译。

1. His primary task is not to think about the moral code which governs his activity, any more than a businessman is expected to dedicate his energies to an exploration of rules of conduct in business.

2. The idea that the journalist must understand the law more profoundly than an ordinary citizen rests on an understanding of the established conventions and special responsibilities of the news media.

3. This success, coupled with later research showing that memory itself is not genetically

   determined, led Ericsson to conclude that the act of memorizing is more of a cognitive

   exercise than an intuitive one.

4. There are fundamental public health problems, like dirty hands instead of a soap habit, that

   remain killers only because we can't figure out how to change people's habits.

5. In the West, before mass communication and literacy, the most powerful mass medium was

   the church, which reminded worshippers that their souls were in danger and that they would

   someday be meat for worms.

· 重温语法

本关考点：非谓语动词；动名词的复合结构；定语从句	核心词汇
1. A 2014 survey _____ in Australia, Britain, and the United States by the University of Wisconsin-Madison found that young people's reliance on social media led to greater political engagement. (2018年英语一阅读) [A] conducts [B] conducted [C] conducting [D] to conduct	• reliance [rɪˈlaɪəns] *n.* 依赖，信赖 • social media 社交媒体 • political [pəˈlɪtɪkl] *adj.* 政治的 • engagement [ɪnˈɡeɪdʒmənt] *n.* 参与
2. The challenge the computer mounts to television thus bears little similarity to one format _____ by another in the manner of record players being replaced by CD players. (2012年英语一新题型) [A] replacing [B] replaced [C] to replace [D] being replaced	• challenge [ˈtʃælɪndʒ] *n.* 挑战 • format [ˈfɔːmæt] *n.* 格式 • in the manner of 以……的方式

3. If one received a grape without _____ provide her token in exchange at all, the other either tossed her own token at the researcher or out of the chamber, or refused to accept the slice of cucumber. (2005年阅读)
 	
[A] had to   [B] has to
[C] to have to   [D] having to
	• token [ˈtəʊkən] *n.* 代币
	• exchange [ɪksˈtʃeɪndʒ] *n.* 交换
	    in exchange 作为交换
	• toss [tɒs] *vt.* 扔；投
	    toss A at B 把A掷向B
	• chamber [ˈtʃeɪmbə(r)] *n.* 房间
	• slice [slaɪs] *n.* 薄片

4. The anthropological concept of "culture," like the concept of "set" in mathematics, is an abstract concept _____ makes possible immense amounts of concrete research and understanding. (2003年翻译) [A] what [B] which [C] who [D] whose	• anthropological [ˌænθrəpəˈlɒdʒɪkl] *adj.* 人类学的 • concept [ˈkɒnsept] *n.* 概念 • immense [ɪˈmens] *adj.* 巨大的 • concrete [ˈkɒnkriːt] *adj.* 具体的

5. When the United States entered just such a glowing period after the end of the Second World War, it had a market eight times larger than any competitor, _____ its industries unparalleled economies of scale.

(2000年阅读)

[A] gave   [B] give

[C] gives   [D] giving

- glow [gləʊ] *vi.* 发光
- competitor [kəm'petɪtə(r)] *n.* 竞争者
- scale [skeɪl] *n.* 规模

· 小试牛刀

尝试拆分句子，标注句子成分，并翻译。

1. A 2014 survey conducted in Australia, Britain, and the United States by the University of Wisconsin-Madison found that young people's reliance on social media led to greater political engagement.

2. The challenge the computer mounts to television thus bears little similarity to one format being replaced by another in the manner of record players being replaced by CD players.

3. If one received a grape without having to provide her token in exchange at all, the other either tossed her own token at the researcher or out of the chamber, or refused to accept the slice of cucumber.

4. The anthropological concept of "culture," like the concept of "set" in mathematics, is an abstract concept which makes possible immense amounts of concrete research and understanding.

5. When the United States entered just such a glowing period after the end of the Second World War, it had a market eight times larger than any competitor, giving its industries unparalleled economies of scale.

 **Round 10** ▾

· 重温语法

本关考点：非谓语动词；谓语动词的时态和语态；宾语从句；原因状语从句

1. They should exhibit strong interest and respect for whatever currently interests their fledging adult while _____ a partner in exploring options for the future.

(2007年新题型)

[A] become   [B] becomes

[C] becoming   [D] became

核心词汇

- exhibit [ɪgˈzɪbɪt] *vt.* 展现
- partner [ˈpɑːtnə(r)] *n.* 伙伴
- explore [ɪkˈsplɔː(r)] *vt.* 探索
- option [ˈɒpʃn] *n.* 选择，选项

2. Airborne technologies, such as different types of radar and photographic equipment _____ by airplanes or spacecraft, allow archaeologists to learn about what lies beneath the ground without digging.

(2014年英语一新题型)

[A] carries

[B] carried

[C] carrying

[D] to carry

- airborne ['eəbɔːn] adj. 机载的
- radar ['reɪdɑː(r)] n. 雷达
- photographic [ˌfəʊtə'græfɪk] adj. 照相的；摄影的
- archaeologist [ˌɑːki'ɒlədʒɪst] n. 考古学家
- beneath [bɪ'niːθ] prep. 在……之下
- dig [dɪg] v. 挖掘

3. Studies of both animals and humans have shown that sex hormones somehow affect the stress response, causing females under stress to produce more of the trigger chemicals than _____ males under the same conditions.

(2008年阅读)

[A] does

[B] did

[C] do

[D] doing

- hormone ['hɔːməʊn] n. 荷尔蒙；激素
- somehow ['sʌmhaʊ] adv. 以某种方式
- affect [ə'fekt] vt. 影响
- response [rɪ'spɒns] n. 回应
- trigger ['trɪgə(r)] n. 起因，诱因
- chemical ['kemɪkl] n. 化学物质，化学品
- condition [kən'dɪʃn] n. [pl.]条件，环境

4. It tells the fashion industry _____ it must take responsibility for the signal it sends women, especially teenage girls, about the social tape-measure they must use to determine their individual worth.

(2016年英语一阅读)

[A] what

[B] who

[C] which

[D] that

- take responsibility for 为……负责
- signal ['sɪgnəl] n. 信号
- individual [ˌɪndɪ'vɪdʒuəl] adj. 个人的

5. Darwinism seems to offer justification, _____ if all humans share common origins, it seems reasonable to suppose that cultural diversity could also be traced to more constrained beginnings.

(2012年英语一翻译)

[A] although

[B] for

[C] when

[D] where

- justification [ˌdʒʌstɪfɪ'keɪʃn] n. 正当理由
- common ['kɒmən] adj. 共同的
- origin ['ɒrɪdʒɪn] n. 起源，源头
- reasonable ['riːznəbl] adj. 合理的
- diversity [daɪ'vɜːsəti] n. 多样性
- trace [treɪs] vt. 追踪
- constrained [kən'streɪnd] adj. 有限的

尝试拆分句子，标注句子成分，并翻译。

1. They should exhibit strong interest and respect for whatever currently interests their fledging adult while becoming a partner in exploring options for the future.

2. Airborne technologies, such as different types of radar and photographic equipment carried by airplanes or spacecraft, allow archaeologists to learn about what lies beneath the ground without digging.

3. Studies of both animals and humans have shown that sex hormones somehow affect the stress response, causing females under stress to produce more of the trigger chemicals than do males under the same conditions.

4. It tells the fashion industry that it must take responsibility for the signal it sends women, especially teenage girls, about the social tape-measure they must use to determine their individual worth.

5. Darwinism seems to offer justification, for if all humans share common origins, it seems reasonable to suppose that cultural diversity could also be traced to more constrained beginnings.

⌐ Round ⑪ ▾

· 重温语法

本关考点：表语从句；同位语从句；结果状语从句；让步状语从句；定语从句	核心词汇
1. One more reason not to lose sleep over the rise in oil prices is _____, unlike the rises in the 1970s, it has not occurred against the background of general commodity-price inflation and global excess demand. (2002年阅读)	• occur [əˈkɜː(r)] *vi.* 发生 • against [əˈgenst] *prep.* 以⋯⋯为背景 • background [ˈbækgraʊnd] *n.* 背景 • inflation [ɪnˈfleɪʃn] *n.* 膨胀；通货膨胀 • excess [ɪkˈses] *n.* 过度 • demand [dɪˈmɑːnd] *n.* 要求，需求

[A] what   [B] which

[C] who   [D] that

2. They should start by discarding California's lame argument _____ exploring the contents of a smartphone is similar to going through a suspect's purse.

(2015年英语一阅读)

- discard [dɪ'skaːd] *vt.* 丢弃
- lame [leɪm] *adj.* 蹩脚的
- argument ['aːgjumənt] *n.* 论点
- be similar to 与…相似
- suspect [sə'spekt] *n.* 嫌疑犯
- purse [pɜːs] *n.* 钱包

[A] that   [B] which

[C] what   [D] who

3. Knowing the results of Epley's study, it makes sense that many people hate photographs of themselves so viscerally _____ they don't even recognize the person in the picture as themselves. (2014年英语二阅读)

- make sense 有道理，讲得通
- viscerally ['vɪsərəli] *adv.* 发自内心地
- recognize ['rekəgnaɪz] *vt.* 承认

[A] which   [B] that

[C] who   [D] why

4. _____ families don't sit down to eat together as frequently as before, millions of Britons will nonetheless have got a share this weekend of one of the nation's great traditions: the Sunday roast. (2020年英语一完形)

- frequently ['friːkwəntli] *adv.* 频繁地；经常地
- nonetheless [ˌnʌnðə'les] *adv.* 虽然如此
- tradition [trə'dɪʃn] *n.* 传统
- roast [rəʊst] *n.* 烤肉

[A] Because   [B] Even if

[C] As if   [D] If

5. Television is one of the means by _____ these feelings are created and conveyed. (2005年翻译)

- convey [kən'veɪ] *vt.* 传送，传达

[A] that   [B] which

[C] what   [D] whom

尝试拆分句子，标注句子成分，并翻译。

1. One more reason not to lose sleep over the rise in oil prices is that, unlike the rises in the

   1970s, it has not occurred against the background of general commodity-price inflation and

   global excess demand.

2. They should start by discarding California's lame argument that exploring the contents of a

   smartphone is similar to going through a suspect's purse.

3. Knowing the results of Epley's study, it makes sense that many people hate photographs

   of themselves so viscerally that they don't even recognize the person in the picture as

   themselves.

4. Even if families don't sit down to eat together as frequently as before, millions of Britons will nonetheless have got a share this weekend of one of the nation's great traditions: the Sunday roast.

5. Television is one of the means by which these feelings are created and conveyed.

🖹 Round ⑫ ▾

· 重温语法

本关考点：宾语从句；定语从句；固定搭配	核心词汇
1. They should read _____ he had to say about drugs. (2005年新题型) 　[A] that 　　　　[B] when 　[C] how 　　　　[D] what	• drug [drʌg] *n.* 毒品
2. Many in the medical community acknowledge that the assisted-suicide debate has been fueled in part by the despair of patients for _____ modern medicine has prolonged the physical agony of dying. (2002年阅读) 　[A] which 　　　　[B] what 　[C] that 　　　　[D] whom	• medical ['medɪkl] *adj.* 医学的 • community [kə'mjuːnəti] *n.* 团体；界 • acknowledge [ək'nɒlɪdʒ] *vt.* 承认 • in part 部分地 • despair [dɪ'speə(r)] *n.* 绝望 • prolong [prə'lɒŋ] *vt.* 延长 • agony ['ægəni] *n.* 痛苦

3. Rather than just focusing on GDP, over 40 different sets of criteria from health, education and civil society engagement have been measured to get a more rounded assessment of _____ countries are performing.

(2017年英语一阅读)

- rather than 而不是
- focus on 聚焦于
- criterion [kraɪ'tɪərɪən] *n.* 标准（复数 criteria）

[A] when   [B] where

[C] how   [D] why

4. Somewhere from the 19th century onward, more artists began seeing happiness as meaningless, phony or, worst of all, boring, as we went from Wordsworth's *daffodils* _____ Baudelaire's *flowers of evil*.

(2006年阅读)

- onward ['ɒnwəd] *adv.* 向前
- evil ['iːvl] *n.* 邪恶

[A] on   [B] at

[C] in   [D] to

5. Unlike their absolutist counterparts in the Gulf and Asia, most royal families have survived because they allow voters _____ the difficult search for a non-controversial but respected public figure.

(2015年英语一阅读)

- counterpart ['kaʊntəpɑːt] *n.* 对应物
- controversial [ˌkɒntrə'vɜːʃl] *adj.* 有争议的
- public figure 公众人物

[A] avoiding   [B] to avoid

[C] avoided   [D] avoids

· 小试牛刀

尝试拆分句子，标注句子成分，并翻译。

1. They should read what he had to say about drugs.

2. Many in the medical community acknowledge that the assisted-suicide debate has been

fueled in part by the despair of patients for whom modern medicine has prolonged the

physical agony of dying.

3. Rather than just focusing on GDP, over 40 different sets of criteria from health, education

and civil society engagement have been measured to get a more rounded assessment of how

countries are performing.

4. Somewhere from the 19th century onward, more artists began seeing happiness as

meaningless, phony or, worst of all, boring, as we went from Wordsworth's *daffodils* to

Baudelaire's *flowers of evil*.

5. Unlike their absolutist counterparts in the Gulf and Asia, most royal families have survived because they allow voters to avoid the difficult search for a non-controversial but respected public figure.

📖 Round ⑬ ▾

· 重温语法

本关考点：宾语从句；非谓语动词；部分倒装；谓语动词的时态和语态	核心词汇
1. Now Japan has largely fulfilled its economic needs, and young people don't know _____ they should go next. (2000年阅读) [A] when　　　　[B] how [C] why　　　　[D] where	• fulfill [fʊlˈfɪl] vt. 满足
2. The basic compact _____ representative government assumes that public officials will hear from their constituents and act on their concerns. (2017年英语一阅读) [A] to be underlain　　[B] underlies [C] underlying　　　　[D] underlain	• compact [ˈkɒmpækt] n. 契约 • representative [ˌreprɪˈzentətɪv] adj. 有代表性的 • constituent [kənˈstɪtʃuənt] n. 选民
3. Only if the jobless arrive at the jobcentre with a CV, register for online job search, and start looking for work _____ they be eligible for benefit—and then they should report weekly rather than fortnightly. (2014年英语一阅读) [A] do　　　　[B] have [C] will　　　　[D] /	• eligible [ˈelɪdʒəbl] adj. 有资格的 • fortnightly [ˈfɔːtnaɪtli] adv. 两周一次地

4. The company, a major energy supplier in New England, _____ justified outrage in Vermont last week when it announced it was reneging on a longstanding commitment to abide by the state's strict nuclear regulations. (2012年英语一阅读)

- outrage ['aʊtreɪdʒ] *n.* 暴怒
- announce [ə'naʊns] *vt.* 宣布
- renege on 背弃
- commitment [kə'mɪtmənt] *n.* 许诺
- abide by 遵守
- strict [strɪkt] *adj.* 严厉的，严格的
- regulation [ˌregjʊ'leɪʃn] *n.* 规则

[A] had provoked   [B] provoke

[C] provokes   [D] provoked

5. The findings of a research institution _____ consistently shown that workers in all countries can be trained on the job to achieve radically higher productivity and, as a result, radically higher standards of living.

(2009年阅读)

- institution [ˌɪnstɪ'tjuːʃn] *n.* 机构
- consistently [kən'sɪstəntli] *adv.* 一致地
- productivity [ˌprɒdʌk'tɪvəti] *n.* 生产力
- standard of living 生活水平

[A] have   [B] has

[C] is   [D] are

· 小试牛刀

尝试拆分句子，标注句子成分，并翻译。

1. Now Japan has largely fulfilled its economic needs, and young people don't know where they should go next.

2. The basic compact underlying representative government assumes that public officials will hear from their constituents and act on their concerns.

3. Only if the jobless arrive at the jobcentre with a CV, register for online job search, and start looking for work will they be eligible for benefit—and then they should report weekly rather than fortnightly.

4. The company, a major energy supplier in New England, provoked justified outrage in Vermont last week when it announced it was reneging on a longstanding commitment to abide by the state's strict nuclear regulations.

5. The findings of a research institution have consistently shown that workers in all countries can be trained on the job to achieve radically higher productivity and, as a result, radically higher standards of living.

·重温语法

本关考点：部分倒装；祈使句；并列结构；定语从句	核心词汇

1. Nor _____ any evidence that those who self-enhanced the most were doing so to make up for profound insecurities. *(2014年英语二阅读)*

   [A] there was   [B] there were

   [C] was there   [D] were there

   - make up for 弥补

2. Next time somebody pushes corporate quotas as a way to promote gender equity, _____ that such policies are largely self-serving measures that make their sponsors feel good but do little to help average women. *(2020年英语一阅读)*

   [A] remember   [B] to remember

   [C] remembering   [D] remembered

   - equity ['ekwəti] *n.* 公平
   - self-serving [ˌself 'sɜːvɪŋ] *adj.* 自私自利的
   - sponsor ['spɒnsə(r)] *n.* 赞助者

3. Realistic optimists are those who make the best of things that happen, _____ not those who believe everything happens for the best. *(2014年英语二翻译)*

   [A] and   [B] or

   [C] nor   [D] but

   - realistic [ˌrɪə'lɪstɪk] *adj.* 现实的
   - optimist ['ɒptɪmɪst] *n.* 乐观主义者
   - make the best of 充分利用

4. It identifies the undertreatment of pain and the aggressive use of "ineffectual and forced medical procedures _____ may prolong and even dishonor the period of dying" as the twin problems of end-of-life care. *(2002年阅读)*

   [A] what   [B] who

   [C] that   [D] how

   - identify [aɪ'dentɪfaɪ] *vt.* 确定，识别
   - ineffectual [ˌɪnɪ'fektʃuəl] *adj.* 无效的
   - procedure [prə'siːdʒə(r)] *n.* 程序
   - dishonor [dɪs'ɒnə(r)] *vt.* 侮辱；玷辱

5. Priestly explains how the deep blue color of the assistant's sweater descended over the years from fashion shows to department stores and to the bargain bin _____ the poor girl doubtless found her garment. *(2013年英语一阅读)*

   [A] in what   [B] in that

   [C] in which   [D] in whom

   - descend [dɪ'send] *v.* 下降
   - fashion show 时装秀
   - department store 百货商店
   - garment ['ɡɑːmənt] *n.* 衣服，服装

尝试拆分句子，标注句子成分，并翻译。

1. Nor was there any evidence that those who self-enhanced the most were doing so to make up for profound insecurities.

2. Next time somebody pushes corporate quotas as a way to promote gender equity, remember that such policies are largely self-serving measures that make their sponsors feel good but do little to help average women.

3. Realistic optimists are those who make the best of things that happen, but not those who believe everything happens for the best.

4. It identifies the undertreatment of pain and the aggressive use of "ineffectual and forced medical procedures that may prolong and even dishonor the period of dying" as the twin problems of end-of-life care.

5. Priestly explains how the deep blue color of the assistant's sweater descended over the

years from fashion shows to department stores and to the bargain bin in which the poor girl

doubtless found her garment.

F. Round ⑮ ▾

· 重温语法

本关考点：条件状语从句；独立主格结构；定语从句；谓语动词的时态和语态；非谓语动词	核心词汇
1. Even if a job's starting salary seems too small to satisfy an emerging adult's need for rapid content, the transition from school to work can be less of a setback _____ the start-up adult is ready for the move. (2007年新题型) [A] though　　[B] if [C] before　　[D] as	• even if 即使 • satisfy ['sætɪsfaɪ] *vt.* 满足 • content ['kɒntent] *n.* 满足 • transition [træn'zɪʃn] *n.* 过渡 • be ready for 为……做好准备
2. For much of the past year, President Bush campaigned to move Social Security to a saving-account model, with retirees _____ much or all of their guaranteed payments for payments depending on investment returns.　　　　(2007年阅读) [A] trade　　　[B] traded [C] trading　　[D] have traded	• campaign [kæm'peɪn] *v.* 发起活动；参与竞选 • model ['mɒdl] *n.* 模式 • trade A for B 用A换B • guarantee [ˌɡærən'tiː] *vt.* 确保，保证 • investment [ɪn'vestmənt] *n.* 投资

3. States will be able to force more people to pay sales tax when they make online purchases under a Supreme Court decision Thursday _____ will leave shoppers with lighter wallets but is a big financial win for states.

(2019年英语一阅读)

[A] /   [B] that

[C] what   [D] who

- force sb. to do sth. 强迫某人做某事
- purchase ['pɜːtʃəs] n. 购买；购买物

4. Bob Liodice, the chief executive of the Association of National Advertisers, says consumers _____ worse off if the industry cannot collect information about their preferences.   (2013年英语一阅读)

[A] are   [B] were

[C] will be   [D] would be

- chief executive 首席执行官
- worse off 糟糕；情况不佳
- preference ['prefrəns] n. 偏爱

5. He has also criticized the celebrity chef Jamie Oliver's high-profile attempt _____ school lunches in England as an example of how "lecturing" people was not the best way to change their behavior. (2011年英语二新题型)

[A] improving   [B] to improve

[C] improved   [D] improves

- criticize ['krɪtɪsaɪz] vt. 批评
- chef [ʃef] n. 厨师
- high-profile [ˌhaɪ'prəʊfaɪl] adj. 高调的
- attempt [ə'tempt] n. 尝试

· 小试牛刀

尝试拆分句子，标注句子成分，并翻译。

1. Even if a job's starting salary seems too small to satisfy an emerging adult's need for rapid content, the transition from school to work can be less of a setback if the start-up adult is ready for the move.

2. For much of the past year, President Bush campaigned to move Social Security to a saving-account model, with retirees trading much or all of their guaranteed payments for payments depending on investment returns.

3. States will be able to force more people to pay sales tax when they make online purchases under a Supreme Court decision Thursday that will leave shoppers with lighter wallets but is a big financial win for states.

4. Bob Liodice, the chief executive of the Association of National Advertisers, says consumers will be worse off if the industry cannot collect information about their preferences.

5. He has also criticized the celebrity chef Jamie Oliver's high-profile attempt to improve school lunches in England as an example of how "lecturing" people was not the best way to change their behavior.

· 重温语法

本关考点：谓语动词；定语从句；固定搭配；非谓语动词；定语从句	核心词汇

1. Most of the women she interviewed—but only a few of the men—_____ lack of communication as the reason for their divorces.　-　　　　(2010年英语二阅读)

   [A] gave   [B] giving

   [C] given   [D] to give

- interview ['ɪntəvjuː] vt. 采访
- communication [kə,mjuːnɪ'keɪʃn] n. 交流，沟通
- divorce [dɪ'vɔːs] n. 离婚

2. The family's increasing poverty forced Dickens out of school at age 12 to work in Warren's Blacking Warehouse, a shoe-polish factory, _____ the other working boys mocked him as "the young gentleman".

   (2017年英语一新题型)

   [A] when   [B] where

   [C] how   [D] why

- poverty ['pɒvəti] n. 贫穷
- polish ['pɒlɪʃ] n. 抛光；擦亮
- mock [mɒk] v. 嘲笑

3. The commission ignores that for several decades America's colleges and universities have produced graduates who don't know the content and character of liberal education and are thus _____ its benefits.

   (2014年英语一阅读)

   [A] depriving   [B] deprived

   [C] depriving of   [D] deprived of

- commission [kə'mɪʃn] n. 委员会
- ignore [ɪg'nɔː] vt. 忽视
- character ['kærəktə(r)] n. 特点
- liberal education 文科教育；人文教育
- be deprived of 被剥夺……

4. To win over these young workers, manufacturers have to clear another major hurdle: parents, who lived through the worst U.S. economic downturn since the Great Depression, _____ them to avoid the factory.

   (2017年英语二新题型)

   [A] told   [B] telling

   [C] to tell   [D] being told

- manufacturer [,mænju'fæktʃərə(r)] n. 制造商
- hurdle ['hɜːdl] n. 障碍
- economic [,iːkə'nɒmɪk] adj. 经济的
- downturn ['daʊntɜːn] n. 低迷时期
- Great Depression 经济大萧条

5. If robots are to reach the next stage of laborsaving utility, they will have to operate with less human supervision and be able to make at least a few decisions for themselves—goals _____ pose a real challenge.

(2002年阅读)

- stage [steɪdʒ] *n.* 阶段
- utility [juːˈtɪləti] *n.* 使用
- operate [ˈɒpəreɪt] *v.* 操作；运作
- supervision [ˌsuːpəˈvɪʒn] *n.* 监督
- make decisions 做决定
- pose a challenge 产生挑战

[A] what   [B] /

[C] that   [D] who

· **小试牛刀**

尝试拆分句子，标注句子成分，并翻译。

1. Most of the women she interviewed—but only a few of the men—gave lack of

communication as the reason for their divorces.

2. The family's increasing poverty forced Dickens out of school at age 12 to work in Warren's

Blacking Warehouse, a shoe-polish factory, where the other working boys mocked him as "the

young gentleman".

3. The commission ignores that for several decades America's colleges and universities have

produced graduates who don't know the content and character of liberal education and are

thus deprived of its benefits.

4. To win over these young workers, manufacturers have to clear another major hurdle: parents, who lived through the worst U.S. economic downturn since the Great Depression, telling them to avoid the factory.

5. If robots are to reach the next stage of laborsaving utility, they will have to operate with less human supervision and be able to make at least a few decisions for themselves—goals that pose a real challenge.

· 重温语法

本关考点：同位语；定语从句；非谓语动词；结果状语从句；并列句

核心词汇

1. California has asked the justices to refrain from a sweeping ruling, particularly _____ upsets the old assumptions that authorities may search through the possessions of suspects at the time of their arrest.

(2015年英语一阅读)

[A] one   [B] that

[C] one that   [D] that one

- justice ['dʒʌstɪs] *n.* 法官
- refrain from 避免
- particularly [pə'tɪkjələli] *adv.* 特别，尤其
- assumption [ə'sʌmpʃn] *n.* 假设
- authority [ɔː'θɒrəti] *n.* 权威；当局
- possession [pə'zeʃn] *n.* 拥有物；财产

2. For many people, before Obamacare the only way _____ insurance was through a job that provided health insurance. (2015年英语二阅读)

[A] to get   [B] getting

[C] gotten   [D] got

- insurance [ɪnˈʃʊərəns] *n.* 保险

3. It's just that they're dealing with so many more things _____ they become worn out from it more visibly and sooner. (2008年阅读)

[A] which   [B] what

[C] that   [D] who

- deal with 处理；处置
- become worn out 变得筋疲力尽
- visibly [ˈvɪzəbli] *adv.* 明显地

4. However, whether such a sense of fairness evolved independently in capuchins and humans, _____ whether it stems from the common ancestor that the species had 35 million years ago, is, as yet, an unanswered question. (2005年阅读)

[A] and   [B] but

[C] or   [D] nor

- a sense of fairness 公平意识
- evolve [ɪˈvɒlv] *v.* 演变；进化
- stem from 源自
- ancestor [ˈænsestə(r)] *n.* 祖先
- as yet (用于否定句)迄今为止

5. When this practice first started decades ago, it was usually limited to freshmen, to give them a second chance _____ a class in their first year if they struggled in their transition to college-level courses. (2019年英语一阅读)

[A] takes   [B] take

[C] to take   [D] taking

- practice [ˈpræktɪs] *n.* 惯例(做法)
- be limited to 限于

·小试牛刀

尝试拆分句子，标注句子成分，并翻译。

1. California has asked the justices to refrain from a sweeping ruling, particularly one that

upsets the old assumptions that authorities may search through the possessions of suspects at

the time of their arrest.

2. For many people, before Obamacare the only way to get insurance was through a job that

provided health insurance.

3. It's just that they're dealing with so many more things that they become worn out from it

more visibly and sooner.

4. However, whether such a sense of fairness evolved independently in capuchins and humans,

or whether it stems from the common ancestor that the species had 35 million years ago, is,

as yet, an unanswered question.

5. When this practice first started decades ago, it was usually limited to freshmen, to give

them a second chance to take a class in their first year if they struggled in their transition to

college-level courses.

· 重温语法

本关考点：宾语从句；强调句；非谓语动词；定语从句	核心词汇
1. Both France and the United States are involved in the organization's work, but France's digital services tax and the American response raise questions about _____ the future holds for the international tax system. (2020年英语一阅读) [A] that [B] where [C] when [D] what	• be involved in 参与 • digital ['dɪdʒɪtl] *adj.* 数字的 • raise [reɪz] *vt.* 引起
2. It was only after I started to write a weekly column about the medical journals, and began to read scientific papers from beginning to end, _____ I realized just how bad much of the medical literature frequently was. (2019年英语一翻译) [A] which [B] that [C] / [D] what	• column ['kɒləm] *n.* 专栏 • literature ['lɪtrətʃə(r)] *n.* 文献
3. Not surprisingly, newly _____ discovery claims and credible discoveries that appear to be important and convincing will always be open to challenge and potential modification or refutation by future researchers. (2012年英语一阅读) [A] publishing [B] published [C] to publish [D] to be published	• credible ['kredəbl] *adj.* 可信的 • modification [ˌmɒdɪfɪ'keɪʃn] *n.* 修改 • refutation [ˌrefju'teɪʃn] *n.* 驳斥
4. He argued that human evolution was characterized by a struggle he called the "survival of the fittest," _____ weaker races and societies must eventually be replaced by stronger, more advanced races and societies. (2009年新题型) [A] in what [B] in that [C] in which [D] in whom	• evolution [ˌiːvə'luːʃn] *n.* 进化；演变 • be characterized by 以……为特征 • struggle ['strʌɡl] *n.* 斗争 • eventually [ɪ'ventʃuəli] *adv.* 最终 • replace [rɪ'pleɪs] *vt.* 取代，代替

5. If we know we will overreact to consumer products or housing options when we see a happy face, we can take a moment before _____. (2013年英语二阅读)

- overreact [ˌəʊvəri'ækt] *vi.* 反应过度
- consumer [kən'sjuːmə(r)] *n.* 消费者
- take a moment 稍等片刻

[A] buy   [B] buying

[C] bought   [D] to buy

·小试牛刀

尝试拆分句子，标注句子成分，并翻译。

1. Both France and the United States are involved in the organization's work, but France's digital services tax and the American response raise questions about what the future holds for the international tax system.

2. It was only after I started to write a weekly column about the medical journals, and began to read scientific papers from beginning to end that I realized just how bad much of the medical literature frequently was.

3. Not surprisingly, newly published discovery claims and credible discoveries that appear to be important and convincing will always be open to challenge and potential modification or refutation by future researchers.

4. He argued that human evolution was characterized by a struggle he called the "survival of the fittest," in which weaker races and societies must eventually be replaced by stronger, more advanced races and societies.

5. If we know we will overreact to consumer products or housing options when we see a happy face, we can take a moment before buying.

🄴 Round ⑲ ▾

· 重温语法

本关考点：非谓语动词；宾语从句；时间状语从句；表语从句；目的状语从句

核心词汇

1. Even demographics are working against the middle class family, as the odds of _____ a weak elderly parent—and all the attendant need for physical and financial assistance—have jumped eightfold in just one generation. (2007年阅读)

   [A] have   [B] having
   [C] to have   [D] had

- demographics [ˌdeməˈɡræfɪks] n. [pl.]人口统计数据
- the odds of … …的可能性
- attendant [əˈtendənt] adj. 随之而来的
- eightfold [ˈeɪtˌfəʊld] adv. 八倍地

2. But brain researchers have discovered _____ we consciously develop new habits, we create parallel paths, and even entirely new brain cells, that can jump our trains of thought onto new, innovative tracks. (2009年阅读)

   [A] that that   [B] when when
   [C] when that   [D] that when

- consciously [ˈkɒnʃəsli] adv. 有意识地
- parallel [ˈpærəlel] adj. 平行的
- entirely [ɪnˈtaɪəli] adv. 完全地
- innovative [ˈɪnəveɪtɪv] adj. 创新的

3. Negotiated by USFWS and the states, the plan requires individuals and businesses that damage habitat as part of their operations to pay into a fund to replace every acre _____ with 2 new acres of suitable habitat.

(2016年英语二阅读)

[A] destroys   [B] destroying

[C] destroyed   [D] to be destroyed

- negotiate [nɪˈɡəʊʃieɪt] vt. 商谈
- require [rɪˈkwaɪə(r)] vt. 需要；要求
- individual [ˌɪndɪˈvɪdʒuəl] n. 个人
- acre [ˈeɪkə(r)] n. 英亩

4. What they found, in attempting to model thought, _____ the human brain's roughly one hundred billion nerve cells are much more talented—and human perception far more complicated—than previously imagined.

(2002年阅读)

[A] that   [B] is that

[C] is   [D] that is

- attempt [əˈtempt] vt. 尝试，试图
- model [ˈmɒdəl] vt. 模拟
- perception [pəˈsepʃn] n. 理解(力)；感知(力)
- complicated [ˈkɒmplɪkeɪtɪd] adj. 复杂的
- previously [ˈpriːvɪəsli] adv. 之前
- imagine [ɪˈmædʒɪn] vt. 想象

5. In December 2010 America's Federal Trade Commission (FTC) proposed adding a "do not track" (DNT) option to internet browsers, _____ users could tell advertisers that they did not want to be followed.

(2013年英语一阅读)

[A] so that   [B] in that

[C] now that   [D] for that

- propose [prəˈpəʊz] vt. 建议
- internet browser 网络浏览器
- advertiser [ˈædvətaɪzə(r)] n. 广告商

· 小试牛刀

尝试拆分句子，标注句子成分，并翻译。

1. Even demographics are working against the middle class family, as the odds of having a

weak elderly parent—and all the attendant need for physical and financial assistance—have

jumped eightfold in just one generation.

2. But brain researchers have discovered that when we consciously develop new habits, we create parallel paths, and even entirely new brain cells, that can jump our trains of thought onto new, innovative tracks.

3. Negotiated by USFWS and the states, the plan requires individuals and businesses that damage habitat as part of their operations to pay into a fund to replace every acre destroyed with 2 new acres of suitable habitat.

4. What they found, in attempting to model thought, is that the human brain's roughly one hundred billion nerve cells are much more talented—and human perception far more complicated—than previously imagined.

5. In December 2010 America's Federal Trade Commission (FTC) proposed adding a "do not track" (DNT) option to internet browsers, so that users could tell advertisers that they did not want to be followed.

· 重温语法

本关考点：主语从句；强调句；谓语动词的时态；定语从句；宾语从句	核心词汇

1. _____ motivated him, we were to understand, was his zeal for "fundamental fairness"—protecting the taxpayer, controlling spending and ensuring that only the most deserving claimants received their benefits.

(2014年英语一阅读)

[A] That   [B] Who

[C] As   [D] What

- motivate ['məʊtɪveɪt] vt. 激发；激励
- zeal [ziːl] n. 热心，热情
- fairness ['feənəs] n. 公平；公正
- claimant ['kleɪmənt] n. 要求者；索赔者

2. It is against that background _____ the information commissioner, Elizabeth Denham, has issued her damning verdict against the Royal Free hospital trust under the NHS, which handed over to DeepMind the records of 1.6 million patients in 2015 on the basis of a vague agreement which took far too little account of the patients' rights and their expectations of privacy.

(2018年英语一阅读)

[A] which   [B] what

[C] that   [D] who

- commissioner [kə'mɪʃənə(r)] n. 委员
- damning ['dæmɪŋ] adj. 可以定罪的
- verdict ['vɜːdɪkt] n. 判决
- hand over 递交
- vague [veɪg] adj. 含糊的
- privacy ['prɪvəsi] n. 隐私

3. More than 60,000 people _____ the PTKs since they first became available without prescriptions last year, according to Doug Fogg, chief operating officer of Identigene, which makes the over-the-counter kits.

(2009年阅读)

[A] purchased   [B] purchase

[C] have purchased   [D] had purchased

- available [ə'veɪləbl] adj. 可获得的
- prescription [prɪ'skrɪpʃn] n. 处方

4. As a description of the next music director of an orchestra _____ has hitherto been led by musicians like Gustav Mahler and Pierre Boulez, that seems likely to have struck at least some *Times* readers as faint praise. (2011年英语一阅读)

[A] what [B] who

[C] that [D] /

- orchestra ['ɔ:kɪstrə] *n.* 管弦乐队
- hitherto [ˌhɪðə'tu:] *adv.* 迄今为止

5. While polls show Britons rate "the countryside" alongside the royal family, Shakespeare and the National Health Service (NHS) as _____ makes them proudest of their country, this has limited political support. (2016年英语一阅读)

[A] that [B] who

[C] what [D] /

- poll [pəʊl] *n.* 民意调查
- rate...as... 评价……为……
- royal ['rɔɪəl] *adj.* 王室的，皇家的
- support [sə'pɔ:t] *n.* 支持

· 小试牛刀

尝试拆分句子，标注句子成分，并翻译。

1. What motivated him, we were to understand, was his zeal for "fundamental fairness"—

protecting the taxpayer, controlling spending and ensuring that only the most deserving

claimants received their benefits.

2. It is against that background that the information commissioner, Elizabeth Denham, has

issued her damning verdict against the Royal Free hospital trust under the NHS, which

handed over to DeepMind the records of 1.6 million patients in 2015 on the basis of a vague

agreement which took far too little account of the patients' rights and their expectations of

privacy.

3. More than 60,000 people have purchased the PTKs since they first became available without prescriptions last year, according to Doug Fogg, chief operating officer of Identigene, which makes the over-the-counter kits.

4. As a description of the next music director of an orchestra that has hitherto been led by musicians like Gustav Mahler and Pierre Boulez, that seems likely to have struck at least some *Times* readers as faint praise.

5. While polls show Britons rate "the countryside" alongside the royal family, Shakespeare and the National Health Service (NHS) as what makes them proudest of their country, this has limited political support.

图书在版编目(CIP)数据

恋练有句：16天搞定考研英语语法和长难句 / 谭剑波编著. -- 2版. -- 北京：群言出版社，2024.3
ISBN 978-7-5193-0928-2

Ⅰ. ①恋… Ⅱ. ①谭… Ⅲ. ①英语－语法－研究生－入学考试－自学参考资料②英语－句法－研究生－入学考试－自学参考资料 Ⅳ. ①H319.35

中国国家版本馆CIP数据核字(2024)第052454号

责任编辑：侯　莹
封面设计：黄　蕊

出版发行：群言出版社
地　　址：北京市东城区东厂胡同北巷1号（100006）
网　　址：www.qypublish.com（官网书城）
电子信箱：dywh@xdf.cn　qunyancbs@126.com
联系电话：010-62418641　65267783　65263836
法律顾问：北京法政安邦律师事务所
经　　销：全国新华书店

印　　刷：河北泓景印刷有限公司
版　　次：2024年3月第2版
印　　次：2024年3月第1次印刷
开　　本：710mm×1000mm　1/16
印　　张：16.75
字　　数：276千字
书　　号：ISBN 978-7-5193-0928-2
定　　价：58.00元